BATMAN

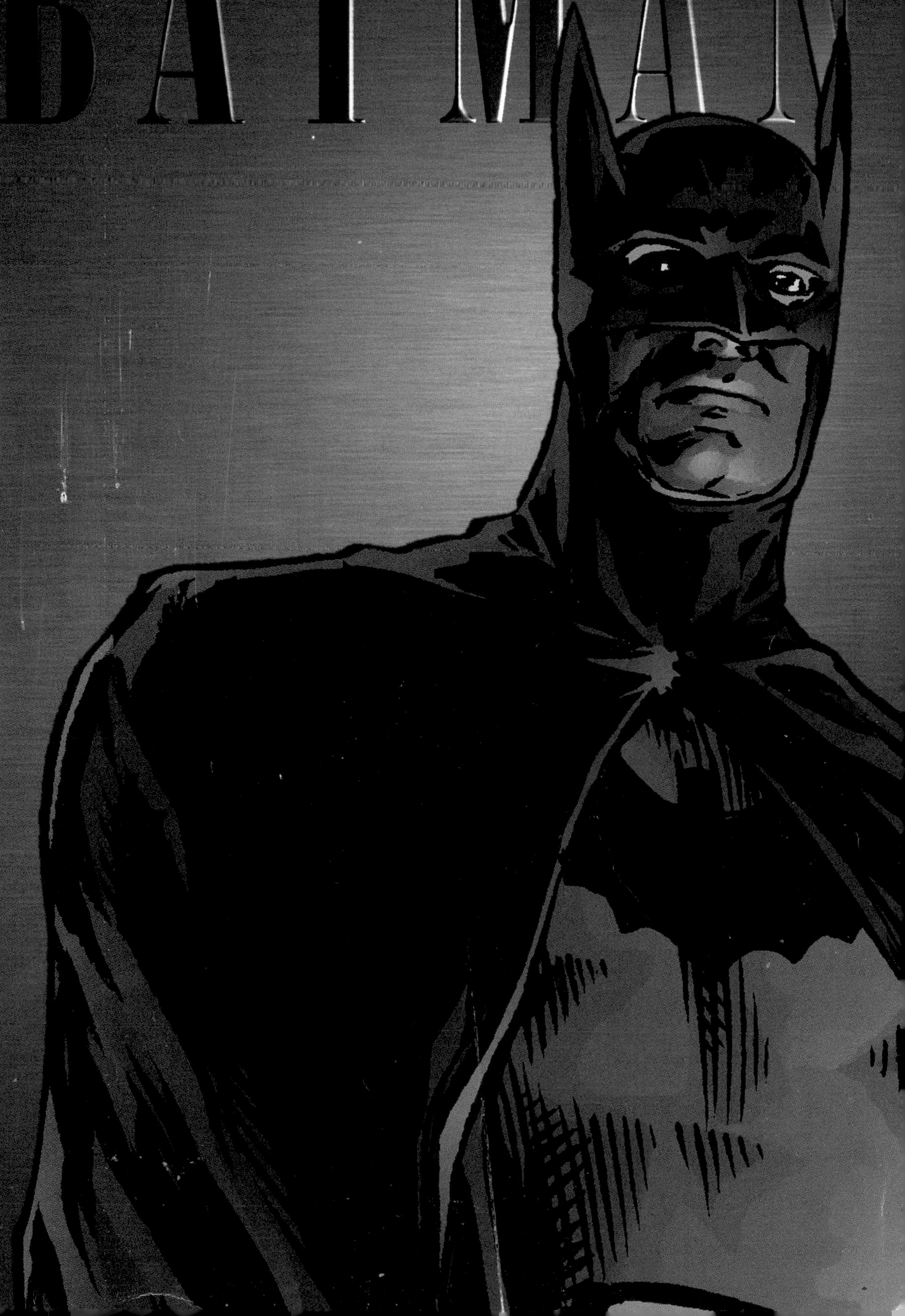

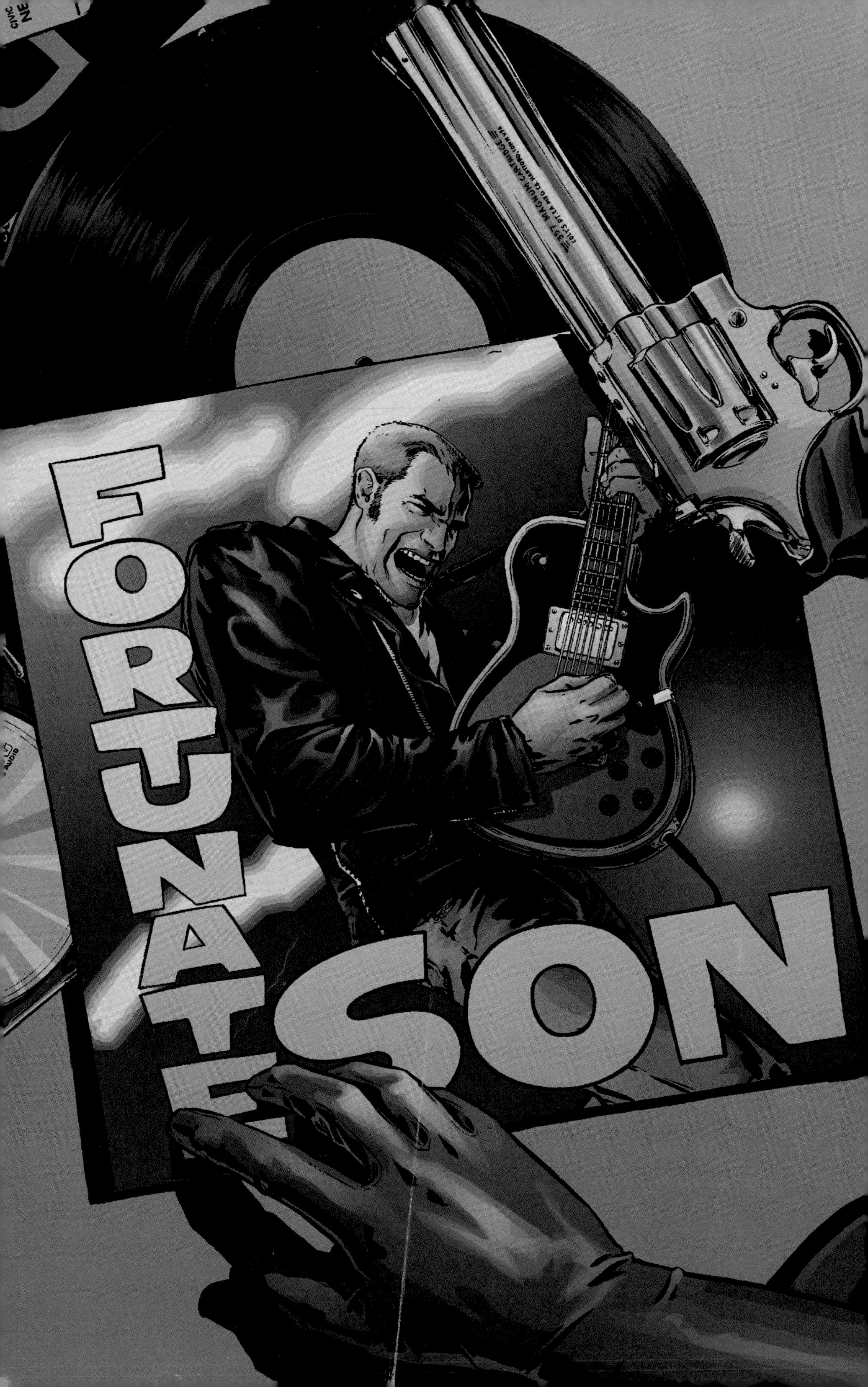
FORTUNATE
SON

BATMAN

fortunate son

WRITER
gerard jones
ARTIST
gene ha

COLORIST
gloria vasquez

SEPARATOR
digital chameleon

LETTERER
willie schubert

BATMAN CREATED BY
bob kane

dc comics JENETTE KAHN PRESIDENT & EDITOR-IN-CHIEF • PAUL LEVITZ EXECUTIVE VICE PRESIDENT & PUBLISHER MIKE CARLIN EXECUTIVE EDITOR • ARCHIE GOODWIN AND JORDAN B. GORFINKEL EDITORS GEORG BREWER DESIGN DIRECTOR • AMIE BROCKWAY ART DIRECTOR • RICHARD BRUNING VP-CREATIVE DIRECTOR • PATRICK CALDON VP-FINANCE & OPERATIONS • DOROTHY CROUCH VP-LICENSED PUBLISHING TERRI CUNNINGHAM VP-MANAGING EDITOR • JOEL EHRLICH SENIOR VP-ADVERTISING & PROMOTIONS ALISON GILL EXECUTIVE DIRECTOR-MANUFACTURING • LILLIAN LASERSON VP & GENERAL COUNSEL JIM LEE EDITORIAL DIRECTOR-WILDSTORM • JOHN NEE VP & GENERAL MANAGER-WILDSTORM BOB WAYNE VP-DIRECT SALES

batman: fortunate son PUBLISHED BY DC COMICS, 1700 BROADWAY, NEW YORK, NY 10019. COPYRIGHT © 1999 DC COMICS. ALL RIGHTS RESERVED. ALL CHARACTERS FEATURED IN THIS ISSUE, THE DISTINCTIVE LIKE-NESSES THEREOF, AND ALL RELATED INDICIA ARE TRADEMARKS OF DC COMICS. THE STORIES, CHARACTERS AND INCIDENTS MENTIONED IN THIS MAGAZINE ARE ENTIRELY FICTIONAL. PRINTED ON RECYCLABLE PAPER. PRINTED IN CANADA.
DC COMICS. A DIVISION OF WARNER BROS.— A TIME WARNER ENTERTAINMENT COMPANY

COVER ART: GENE HA
ADDITIONAL COLOR AND SEPARATIONS (COVERS AND PP 4, 96): MATT HOLLINGSWORTH

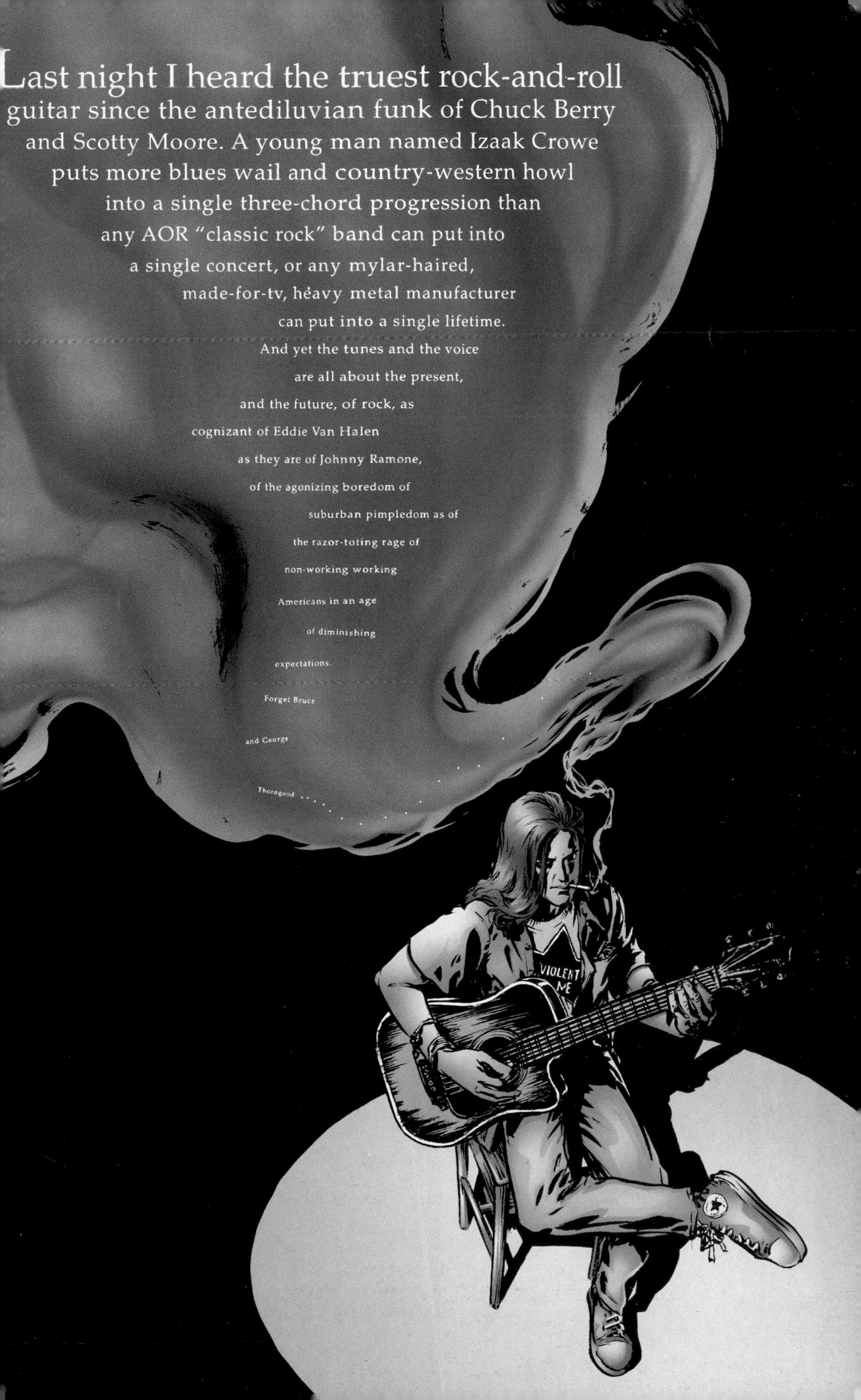
Last night I heard the truest rock-and-roll guitar since the antediluvian funk of Chuck Berry and Scotty Moore. A young man named Izaak Crowe puts more blues wail and country-western howl into a single three-chord progression than any AOR "classic rock" band can put into a single concert, or any mylar-haired, made-for-tv, heavy metal manufacturer can put into a single lifetime.
And yet the tunes and the voice are all about the present, and the future, of rock, as cognizant of Eddie Van Halen as they are of Johnny Ramone, of the agonizing boredom of suburban pimpledom as of the razor-toting rage of non-working working Americans in an age of diminishing expectations.
Forget Bruce and George Thorogood . . . .

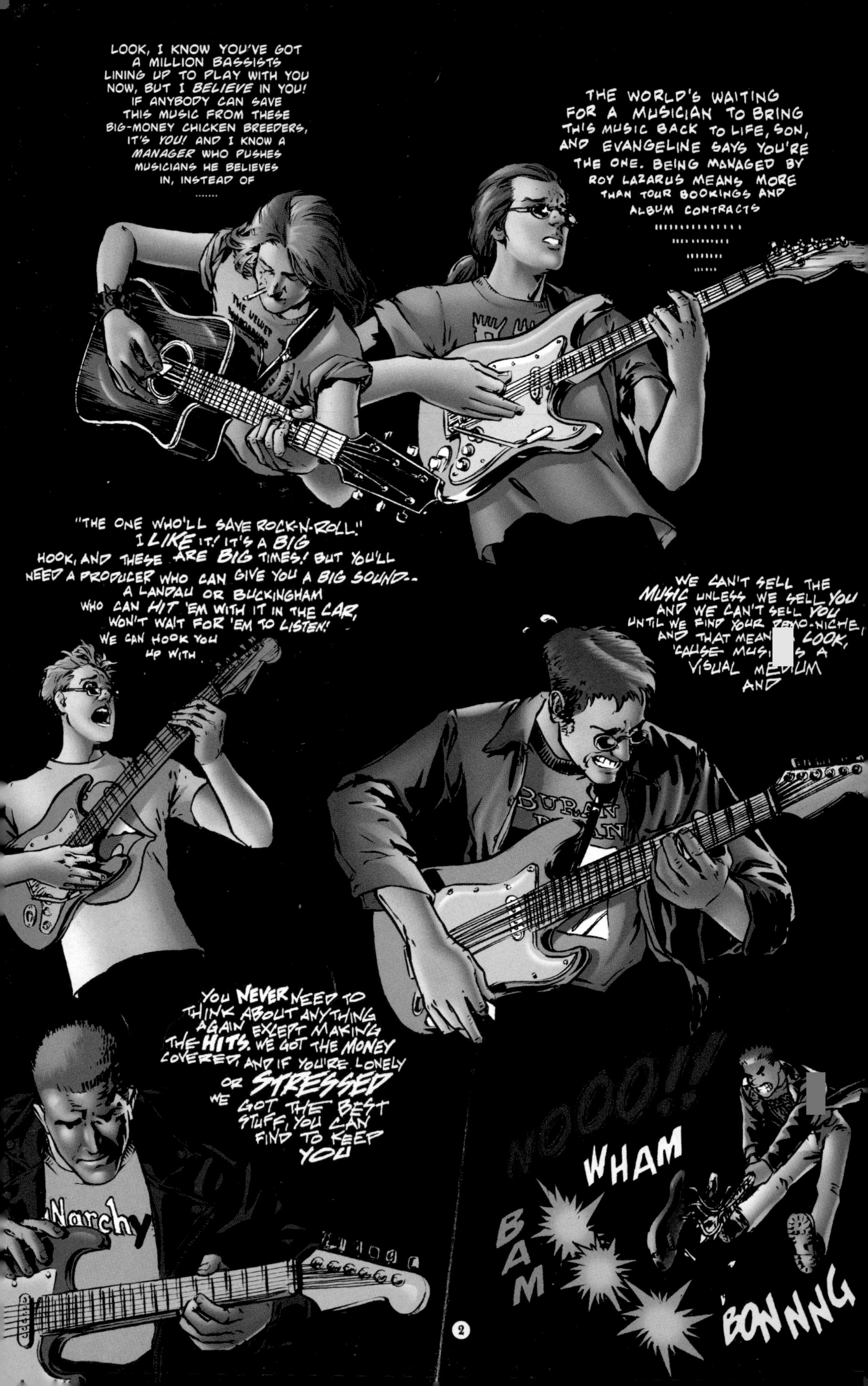
LOOK, I KNOW YOU'VE GOT A MILLION BASSISTS LINING UP TO PLAY WITH YOU NOW, BUT I BELIEVE IN YOU! IF ANYBODY CAN SAVE THIS MUSIC FROM THESE BIG-MONEY CHICKEN BREEDERS, IT'S YOU! AND I KNOW A MANAGER WHO PUSHES MUSICIANS HE BELIEVES IN, INSTEAD OF ......
THE WORLD'S WAITING FOR A MUSICIAN TO BRING THIS MUSIC BACK TO LIFE, SON, AND EVANGELINE SAYS YOU'RE THE ONE. BEING MANAGED BY ROY LAZARUS MEANS MORE THAN TOUR BOOKINGS AND ALBUM CONTRACTS
"THE ONE WHO'LL SAVE ROCK-N-ROLL." I LIKE IT! IT'S A BIG HOOK, AND THESE ARE BIG TIMES! BUT YOU'LL NEED A PRODUCER WHO CAN GIVE YOU A BIG SOUND-- A LANDAU OR BUCKINGHAM WHO CAN HIT 'EM WITH IT IN THE CAR, WON'T WAIT FOR 'EM TO LISTEN! WE CAN HOOK YOU UP WITH
WE CAN'T SELL THE MUSIC UNLESS WE SELL YOU AND WE CAN'T SELL YOU UNTIL WE FIND YOUR DEMO-NICHE, AND THAT MEAN LOOK, 'CAUSE MUSI S A VISUAL MEDIUM AND
YOU NEVER NEED TO THINK ABOUT ANYTHING AGAIN EXCEPT MAKING THE HITS. WE GOT THE MONEY COVERED, AND IF YOU'RE LONELY OR STRESSED WE GOT THE BEST STUFF YOU CAN FIND TO KEEP YOU
NOOOO!!
WHAM
BAM
BONNNG

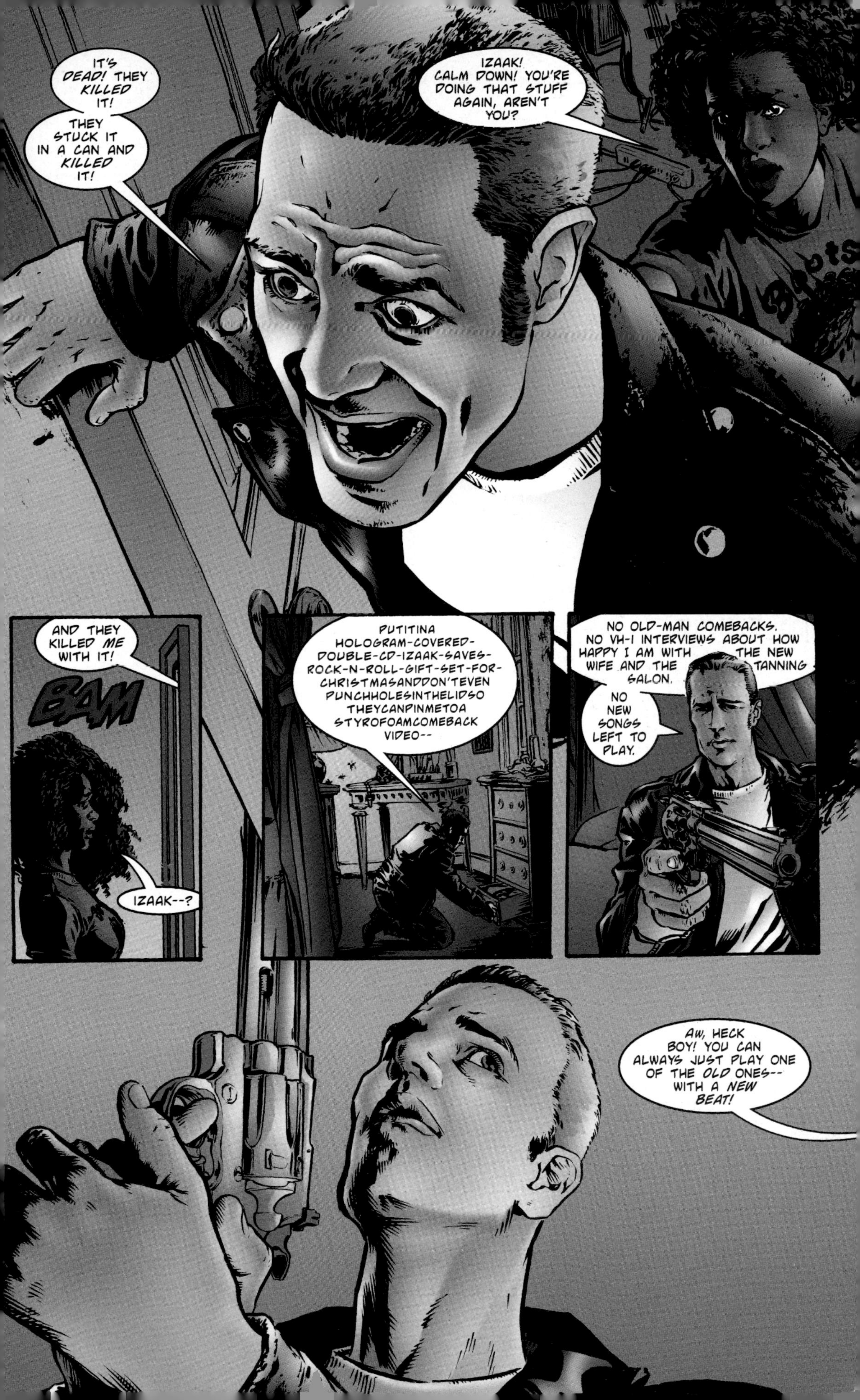
IT'S DEAD! THEY KILLED IT!
THEY STUCK IT IN A CAN AND KILLED IT!
IZAAK! CALM DOWN! YOU'RE DOING THAT STUFF AGAIN, AREN'T YOU?
AND THEY KILLED ME WITH IT!
BAM
IZAAK--?
PUTITINA HOLOGRAM-COVERED-DOUBLE-CD-IZAAK-SAVES-ROCK-N-ROLL-GIFT-SET-FOR-CHRISTMASANDDON'TEVEN PUNCHHOLESINTHELIDSO THEYCANPINMETOA STYROFOAMCOMEBACK VIDEO--
NO OLD-MAN COMEBACKS. NO VH-1 INTERVIEWS ABOUT HOW HAPPY I AM WITH THE NEW WIFE AND THE TANNING SALON.
NO NEW SONGS LEFT TO PLAY.
AW, HECK BOY! YOU CAN ALWAYS JUST PLAY ONE OF THE OLD ONES-- WITH A NEW BEAT!

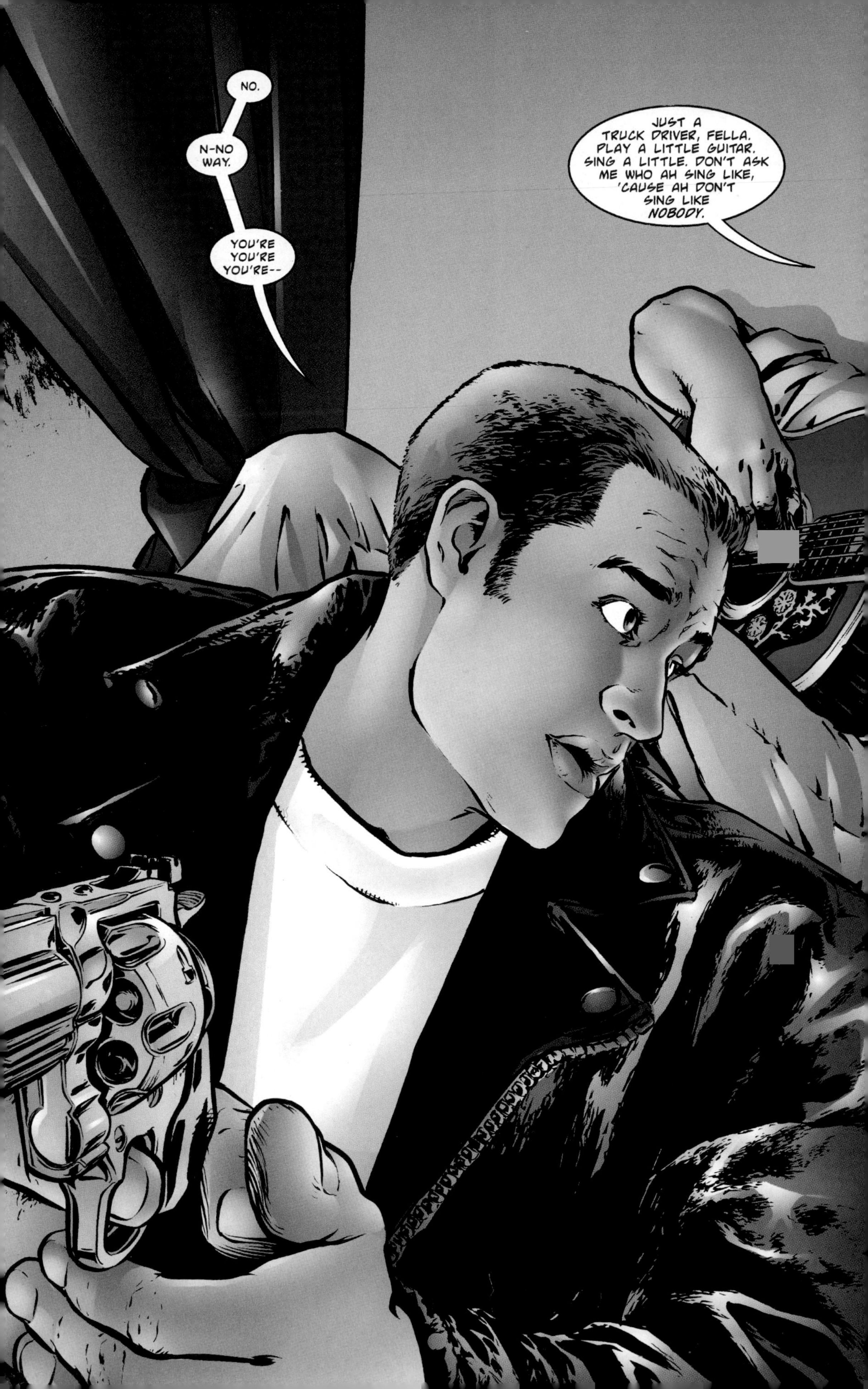
NO.
N-NO WAY.
YOU'RE YOU'RE YOU'RE--
JUST A TRUCK DRIVER, FELLA. PLAY A LITTLE GUITAR. SING A LITTLE. DON'T ASK ME WHO AH SING LIKE, 'CAUSE AH DON'T SING LIKE *NOBODY*.

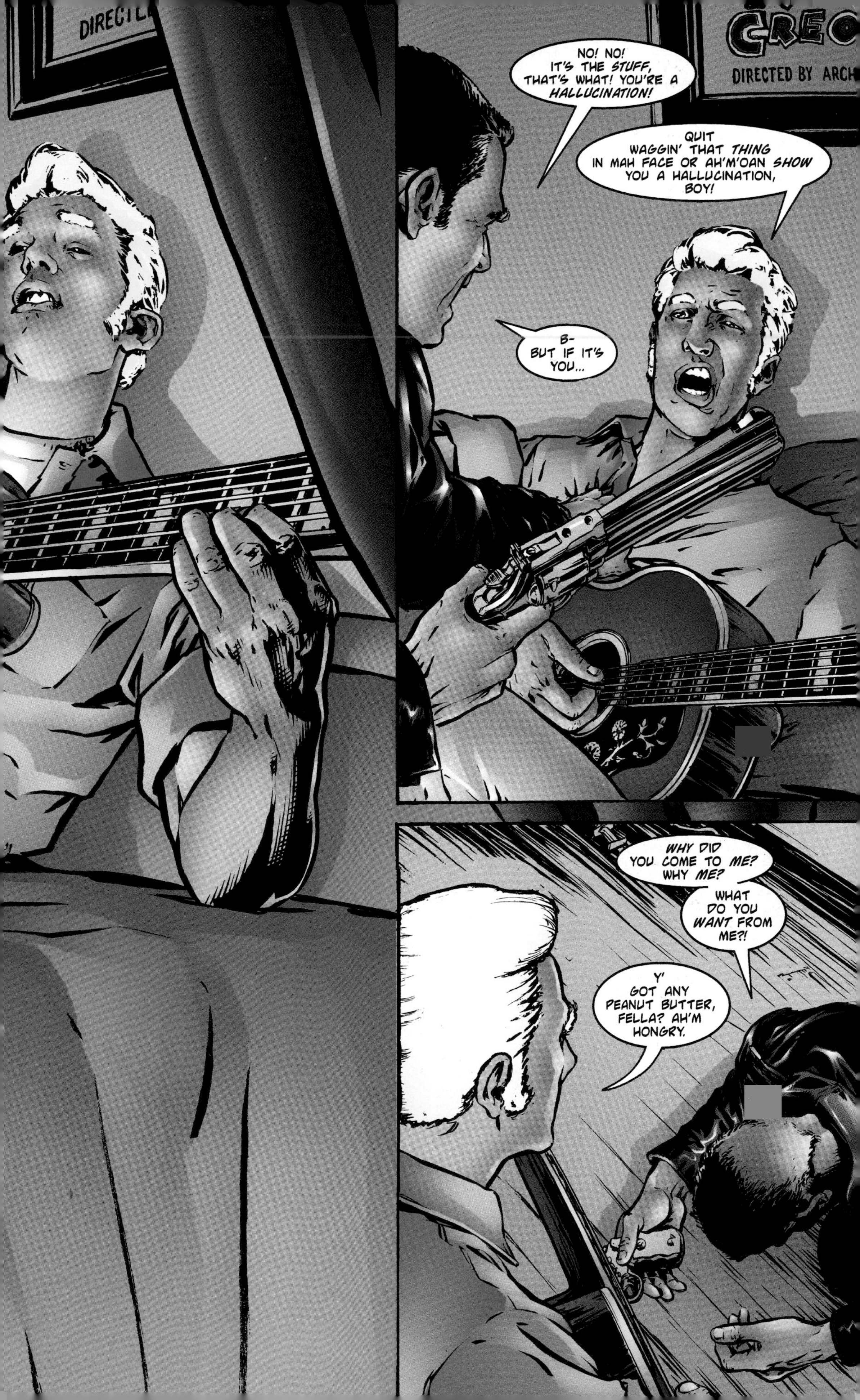
NO! NO! IT'S THE *STUFF*, THAT'S WHAT! YOU'RE A *HALLUCINATION!*
QUIT WAGGIN' THAT *THING* IN MAH FACE OR AH'M'OAN *SHOW* YOU A HALLUCINATION, BOY!
B- BUT IF IT'S YOU...
WHY DID YOU COME TO *ME?* WHY *ME?*
WHAT DO YOU *WANT* FROM ME?!
Y' GOT ANY PEANUT BUTTER, FELLA? AH'M HONGRY.

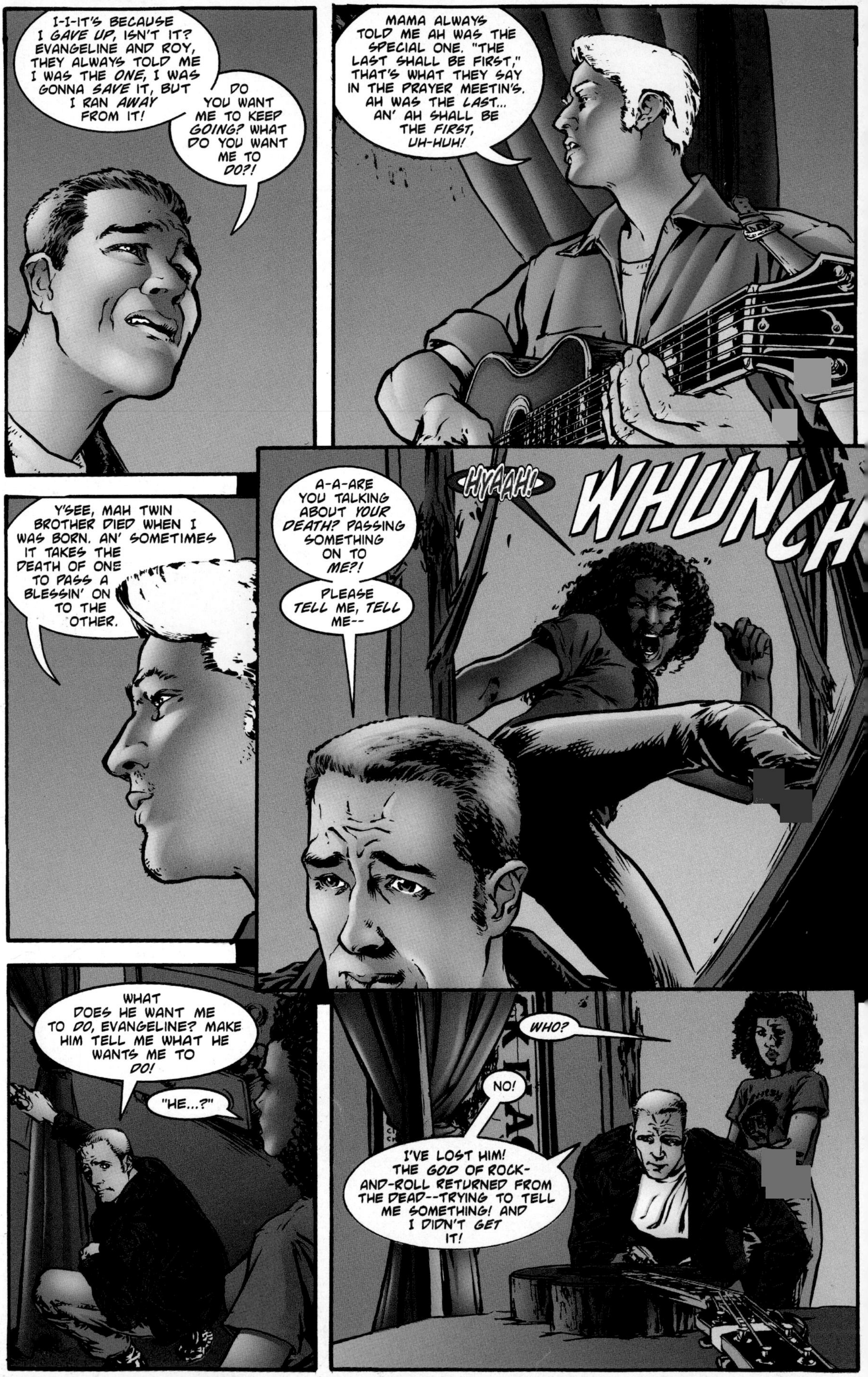
I-I-IT'S BECAUSE I GAVE UP, ISN'T IT? EVANGELINE AND ROY, THEY ALWAYS TOLD ME I WAS THE ONE, I WAS GONNA SAVE IT, BUT I RAN AWAY FROM IT!
DO YOU WANT ME TO KEEP GOING? WHAT DO YOU WANT ME TO DO?!
MAMA ALWAYS TOLD ME AH WAS THE SPECIAL ONE. "THE LAST SHALL BE FIRST," THAT'S WHAT THEY SAY IN THE PRAYER MEETIN'S. AH WAS THE LAST... AN' AH SHALL BE THE FIRST, UH-HUH!
Y'SEE, MAH TWIN BROTHER DIED WHEN I WAS BORN. AN' SOMETIMES IT TAKES THE DEATH OF ONE TO PASS A BLESSIN' ON TO THE OTHER.
A-A-ARE YOU TALKING ABOUT YOUR DEATH? PASSING SOMETHING ON TO ME?!
PLEASE TELL ME, TELL ME--
HYAAH!
WHUNCH
WHAT DOES HE WANT ME TO DO, EVANGELINE? MAKE HIM TELL ME WHAT HE WANTS ME TO DO!
"HE...?"
WHO?
NO!
I'VE LOST HIM! THE GOD OF ROCK-AND-ROLL RETURNED FROM THE DEAD--TRYING TO TELL ME SOMETHING! AND I DIDN'T GET IT!

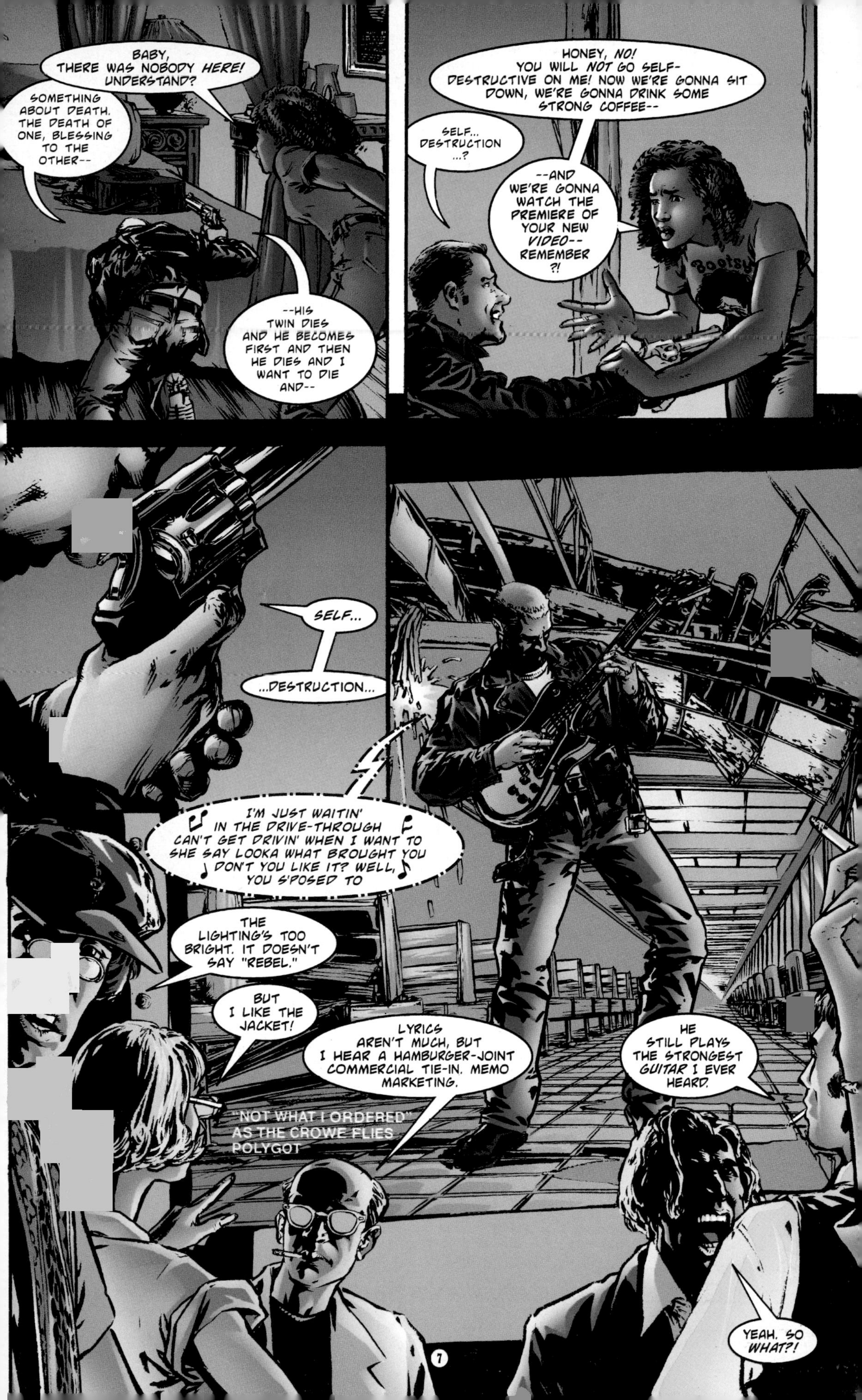
BABY, THERE WAS NOBODY HERE! UNDERSTAND?
SOMETHING ABOUT DEATH. THE DEATH OF ONE, BLESSING TO THE OTHER--
--HIS TWIN DIES AND HE BECOMES FIRST AND THEN HE DIES AND I WANT TO DIE AND--
HONEY, NO! YOU WILL NOT GO SELF-DESTRUCTIVE ON ME! NOW WE'RE GONNA SIT DOWN, WE'RE GONNA DRINK SOME STRONG COFFEE--
SELF... DESTRUCTION ...?
--AND WE'RE GONNA WATCH THE PREMIERE OF YOUR NEW VIDEO-- REMEMBER ?!
Bootsy
SELF...
...DESTRUCTION...
I'M JUST WAITIN' IN THE DRIVE-THROUGH CAN'T GET DRIVIN' WHEN I WANT TO SHE SAY LOOKA WHAT BROUGHT YOU DON'T YOU LIKE IT? WELL, YOU S'POSED TO
THE LIGHTING'S TOO BRIGHT. IT DOESN'T SAY "REBEL."
BUT I LIKE THE JACKET!
"NOT WHAT I ORDERED" AS THE CROWE FLIES POLYGOT
LYRICS AREN'T MUCH, BUT I HEAR A HAMBURGER-JOINT COMMERCIAL TIE-IN. MEMO MARKETING.
HE STILL PLAYS THE STRONGEST GUITAR I EVER HEARD.
YEAH. SO WHAT?!

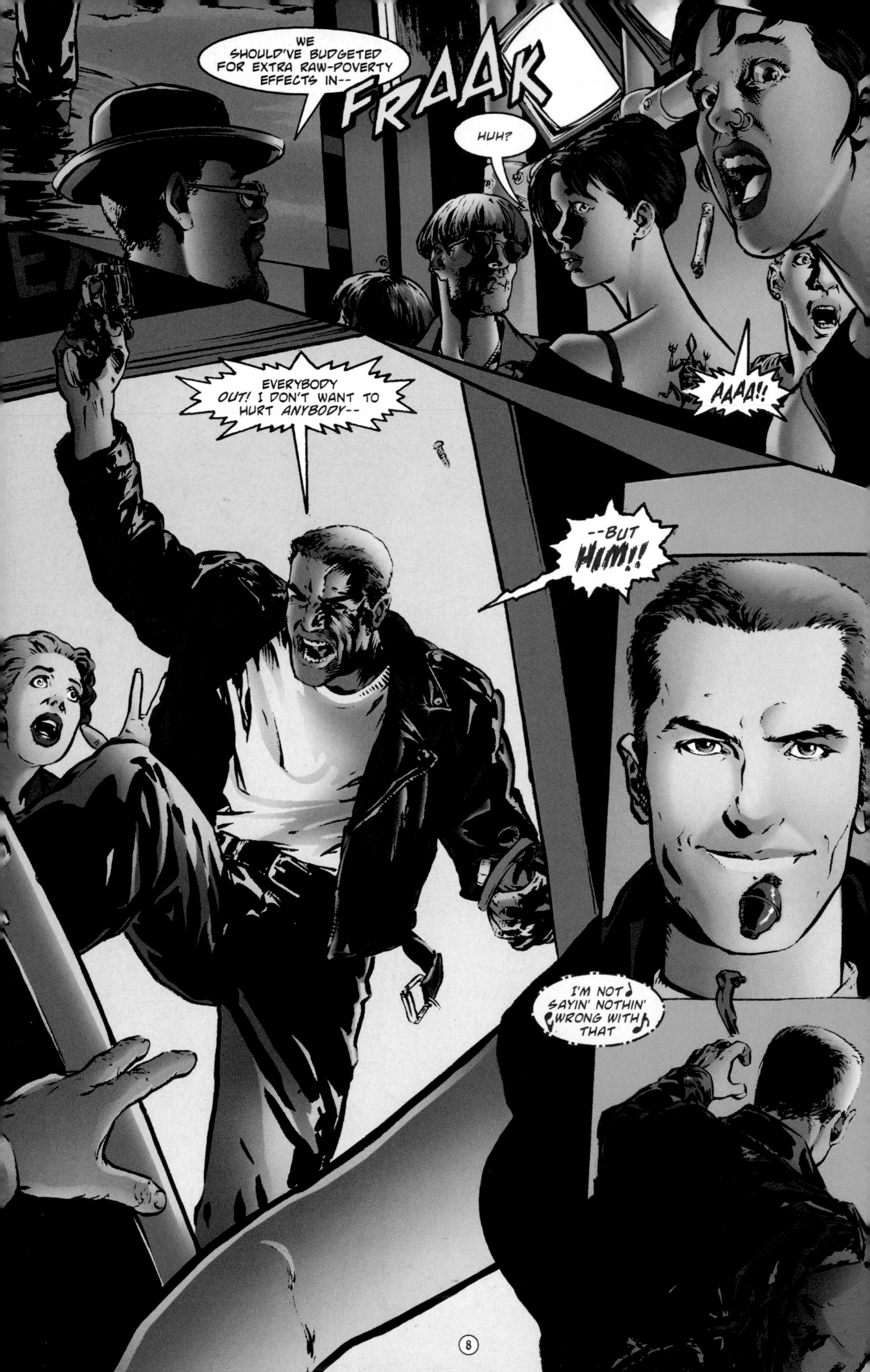
WE SHOULD'VE BUDGETED FOR EXTRA RAW-POVERTY EFFECTS IN--
FRAAK
HUH?
AAAA!!
EVERYBODY OUT! I DON'T WANT TO HURT ANYBODY--
--BUT HIM!!
I'M NOT SAYIN' NOTHIN' WRONG WITH THAT

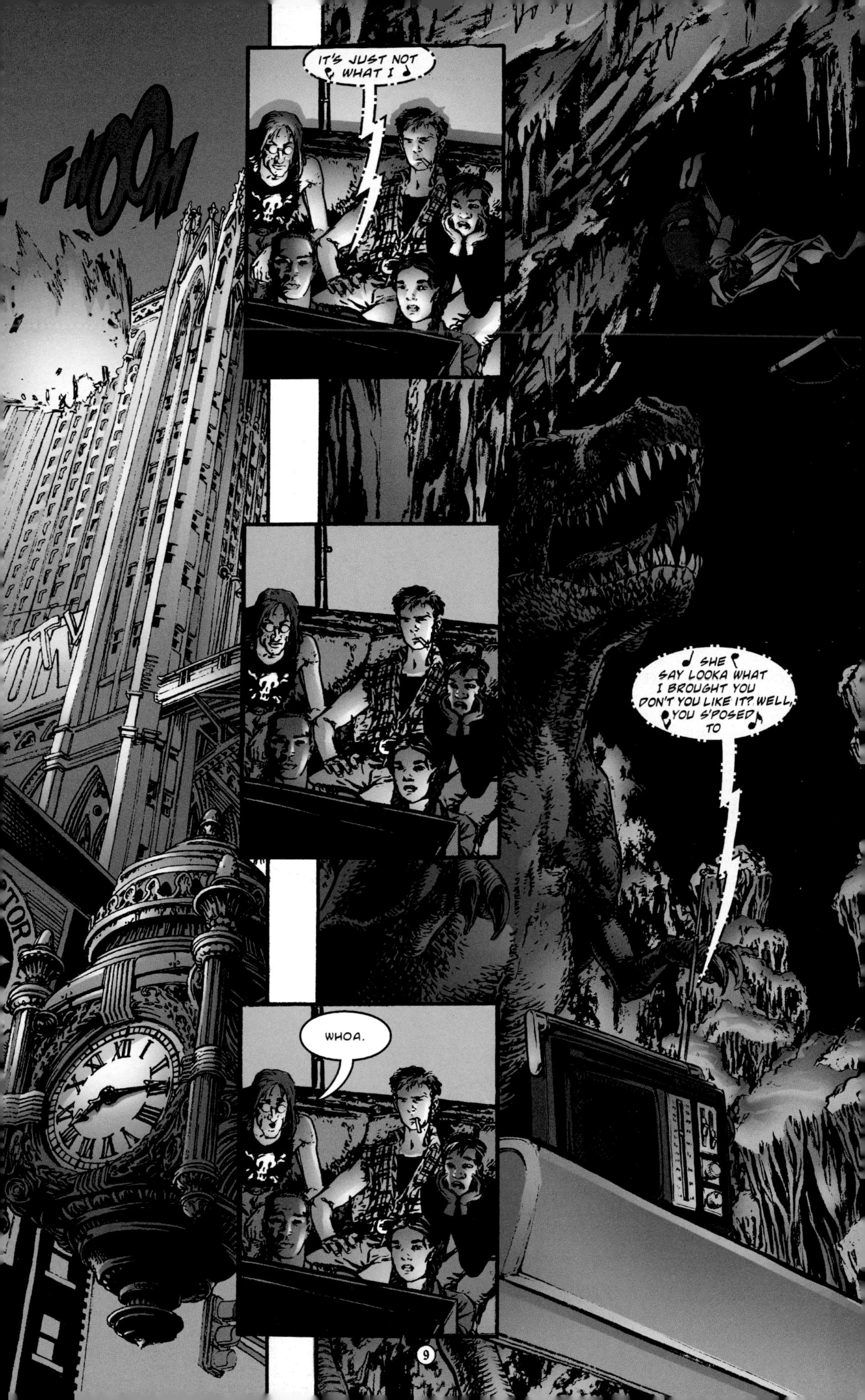
FHOOM
IT'S JUST NOT WHAT I
SHE SAY LOOKA WHAT I BROUGHT YOU DON'T YOU LIKE IT? WELL, YOU S'POSED TO
WHOA.

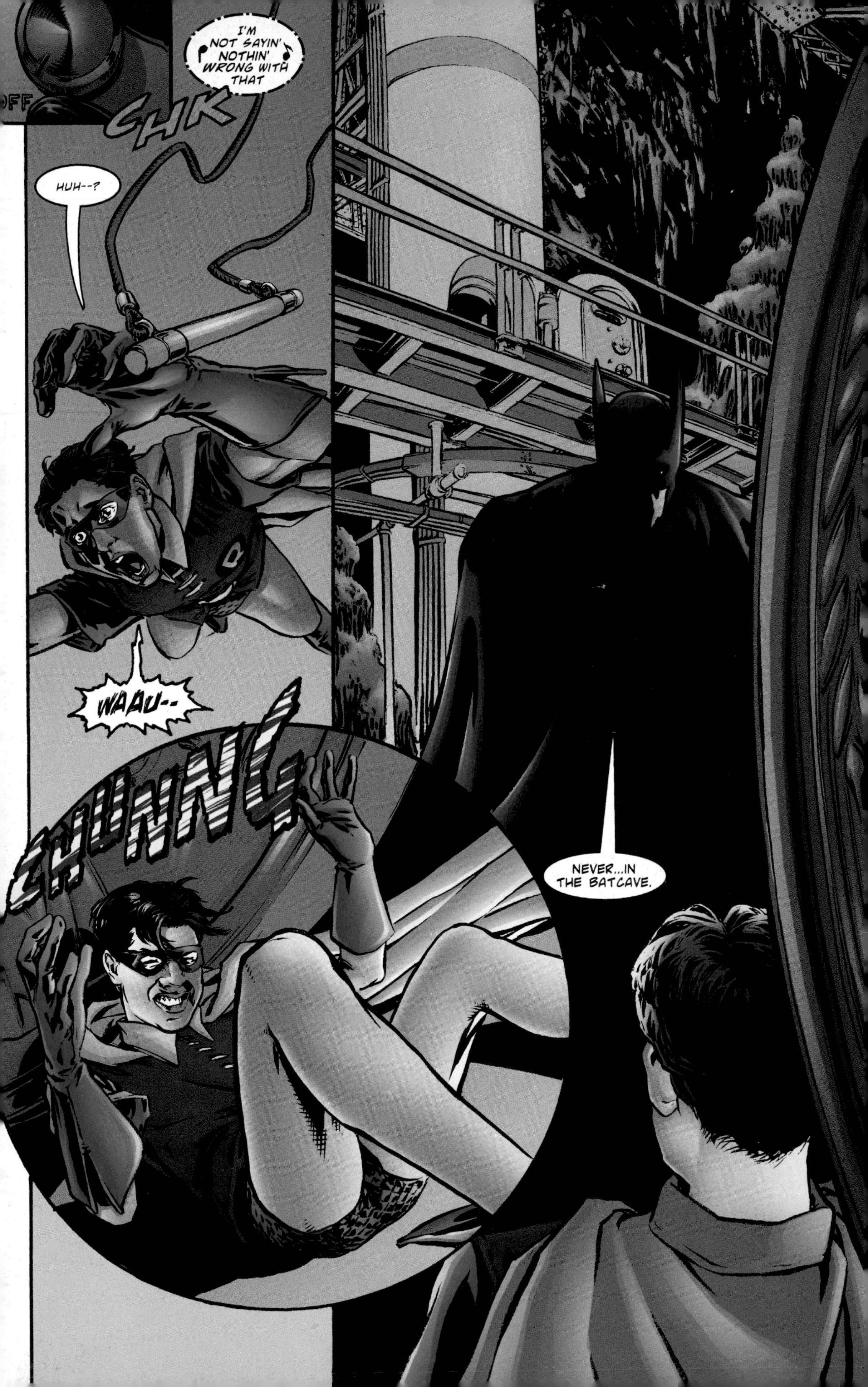

OFF
I'M NOT SAYIN' NOTHIN' WRONG WITH THAT
CHK
HUH--?
WAAU--
CHUNNG
NEVER...IN THE BATCAVE.

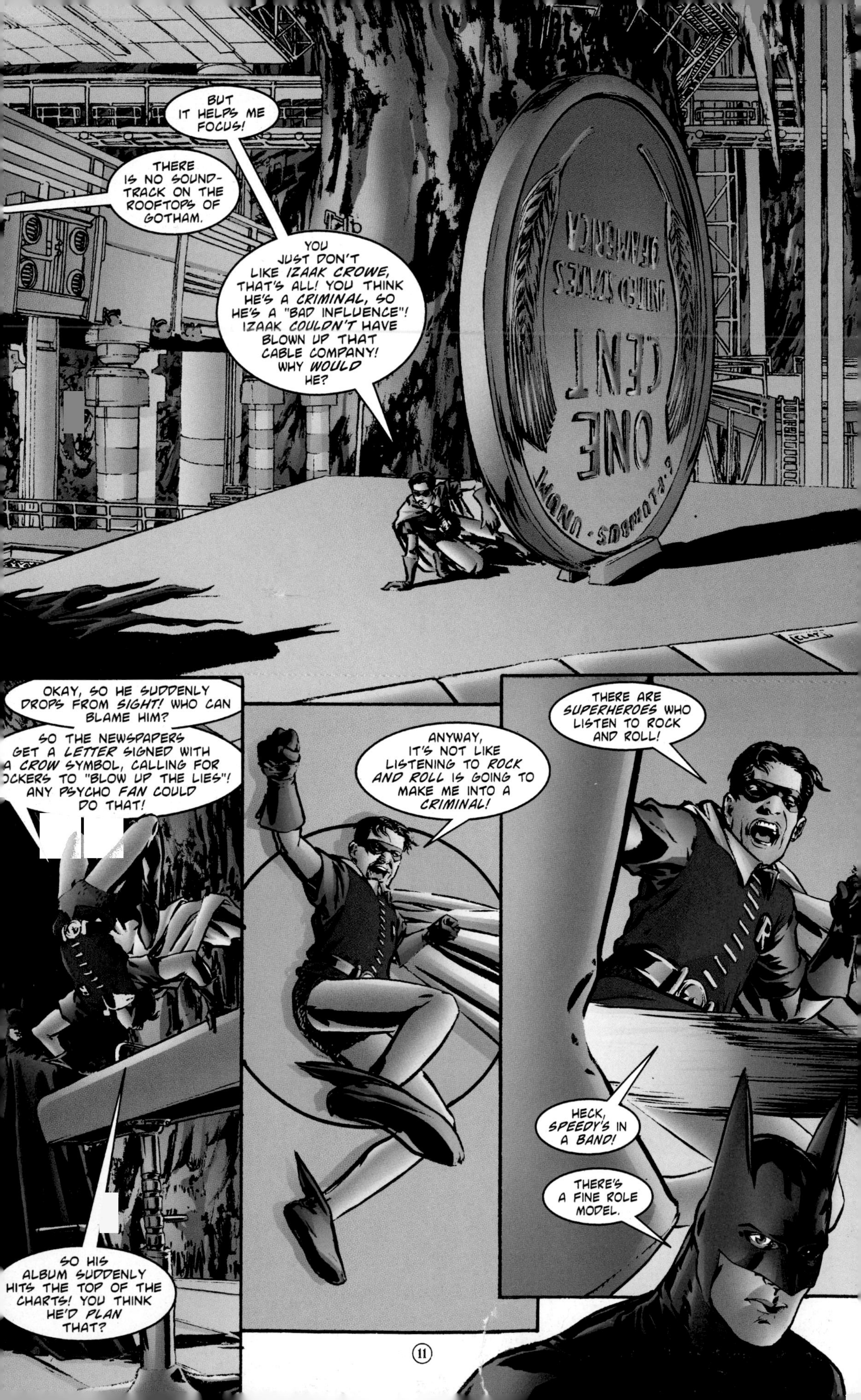
THERE IS NO SOUND-TRACK ON THE ROOFTOPS OF GOTHAM.
BUT IT HELPS ME FOCUS!
YOU JUST DON'T LIKE IZAAK CROWE, THAT'S ALL! YOU THINK HE'S A CRIMINAL, SO HE'S A "BAD INFLUENCE"! IZAAK COULDN'T HAVE BLOWN UP THAT CABLE COMPANY! WHY WOULD HE?
OKAY, SO HE SUDDENLY DROPS FROM SIGHT! WHO CAN BLAME HIM?
SO THE NEWSPAPERS GET A LETTER SIGNED WITH A CROW SYMBOL, CALLING FOR OCKERS TO "BLOW UP THE LIES"! ANY PSYCHO FAN COULD DO THAT!
SO HIS ALBUM SUDDENLY HITS THE TOP OF THE CHARTS! YOU THINK HE'D PLAN THAT?
ANYWAY, IT'S NOT LIKE LISTENING TO ROCK AND ROLL IS GOING TO MAKE ME INTO A CRIMINAL!
THERE ARE SUPERHEROES WHO LISTEN TO ROCK AND ROLL!
HECK, SPEEDY'S IN A BAND!
THERE'S A FINE ROLE MODEL.

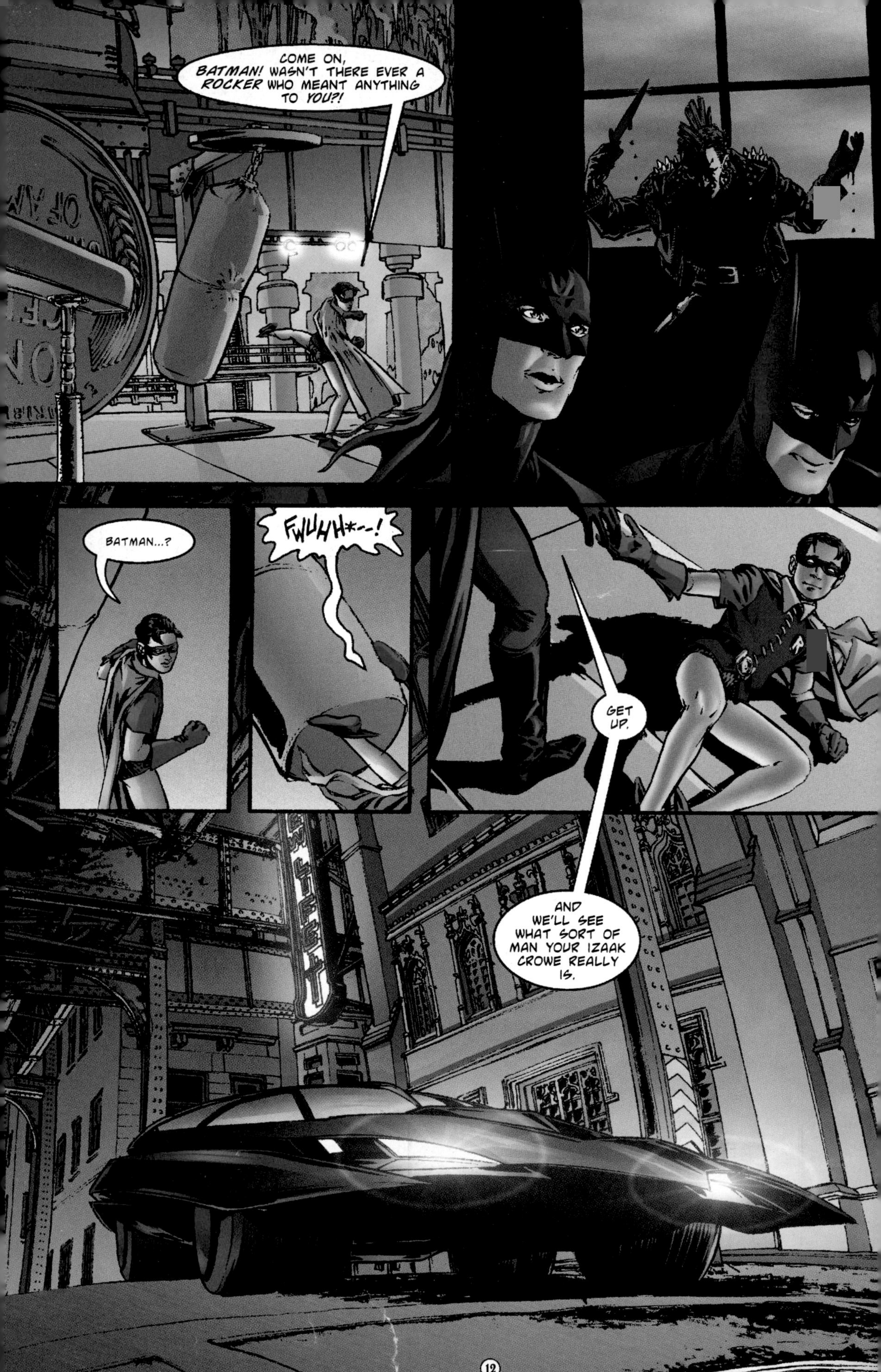
COME ON, BATMAN! WASN'T THERE EVER A ROCKER WHO MEANT ANYTHING TO YOU?!
BATMAN...?
FWUHH*--!
GET UP.
AND WE'LL SEE WHAT SORT OF MAN YOUR IZAAK CROWE REALLY IS.

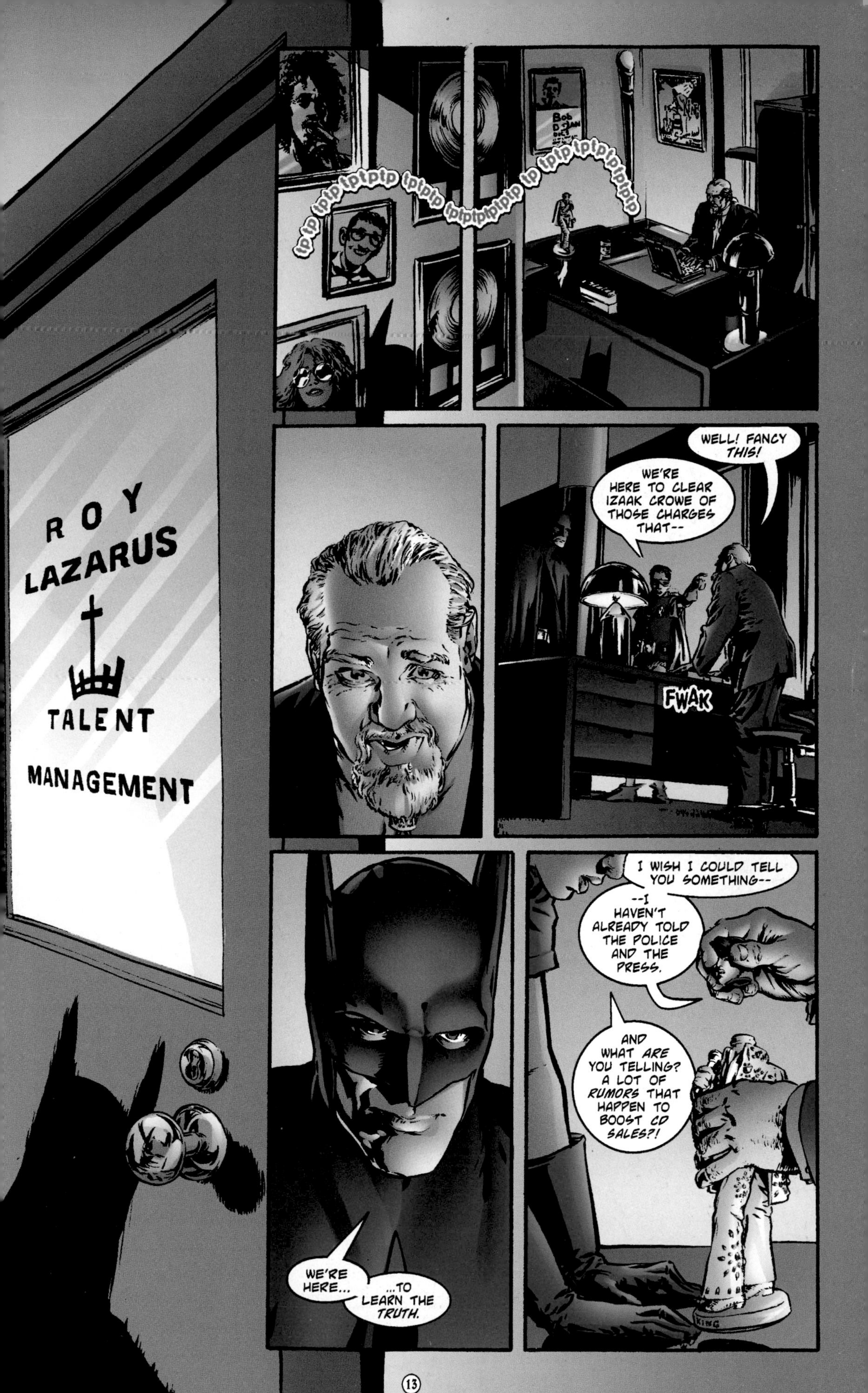
ROY
LAZARUS
TALENT
MANAGEMENT
tp tp tptptptp tptptptptptp tp tptp tptptptptp
WELL! FANCY THIS!
WE'RE HERE TO CLEAR IZAAK CROWE OF THOSE CHARGES THAT--
FWAK
WE'RE HERE...
...TO LEARN THE TRUTH.
I WISH I COULD TELL YOU SOMETHING--
--I HAVEN'T ALREADY TOLD THE POLICE AND THE PRESS.
AND WHAT ARE YOU TELLING? A LOT OF RUMORS THAT HAPPEN TO BOOST CD SALES?!
KING

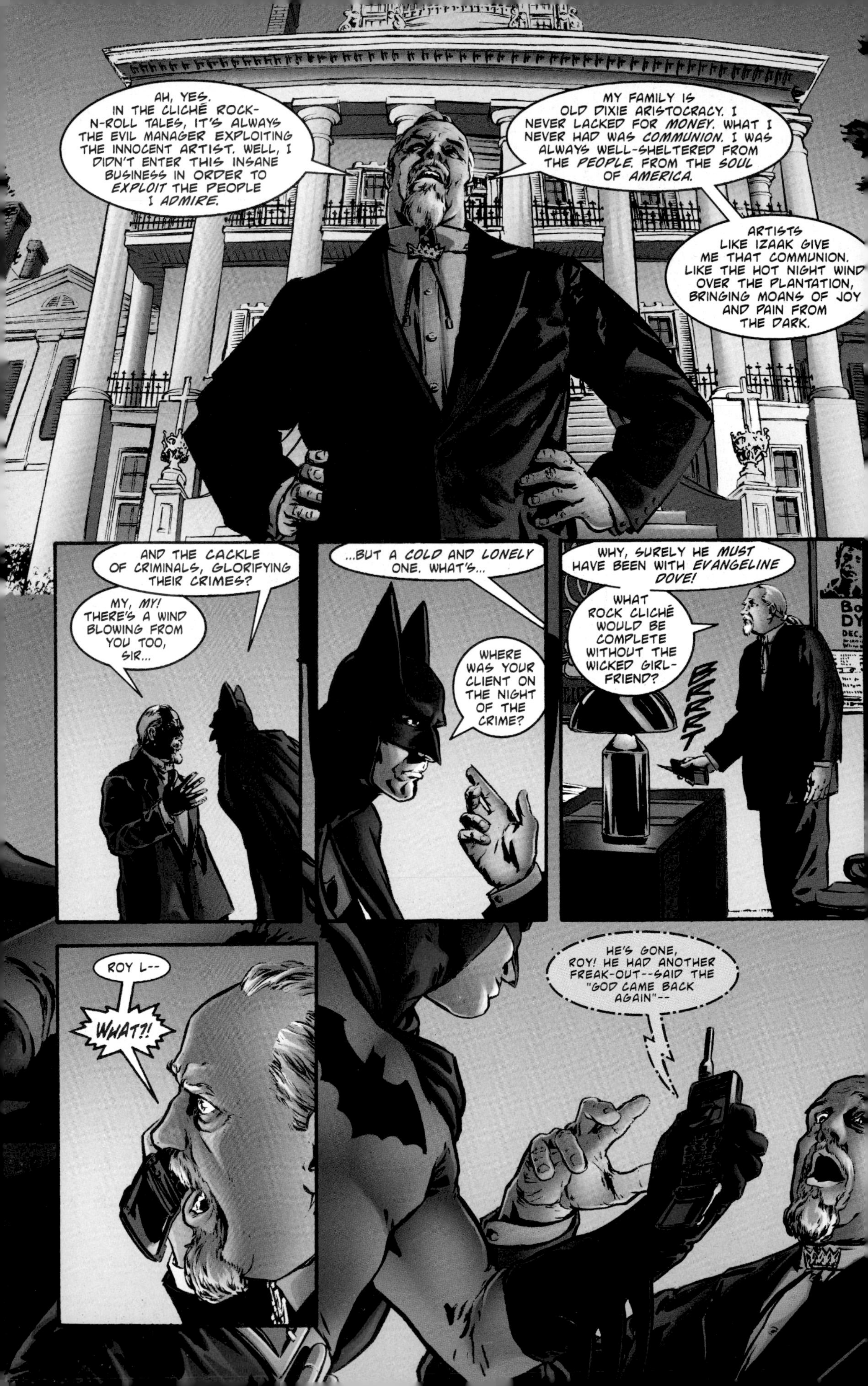
AH, YES. IN THE CLICHÉ ROCK-N-ROLL TALES, IT'S ALWAYS THE EVIL MANAGER EXPLOITING THE INNOCENT ARTIST. WELL, I DIDN'T ENTER THIS INSANE BUSINESS IN ORDER TO EXPLOIT THE PEOPLE I ADMIRE.
MY FAMILY IS OLD DIXIE ARISTOCRACY. I NEVER LACKED FOR MONEY. WHAT I NEVER HAD WAS COMMUNION. I WAS ALWAYS WELL-SHELTERED FROM THE PEOPLE. FROM THE SOUL OF AMERICA.
ARTISTS LIKE IZAAK GIVE ME THAT COMMUNION. LIKE THE HOT NIGHT WIND OVER THE PLANTATION, BRINGING MOANS OF JOY AND PAIN FROM THE DARK.
AND THE CACKLE OF CRIMINALS, GLORIFYING THEIR CRIMES?
MY, MY! THERE'S A WIND BLOWING FROM YOU TOO, SIR...
...BUT A COLD AND LONELY ONE. WHAT'S...
WHERE WAS YOUR CLIENT ON THE NIGHT OF THE CRIME?
WHY, SURELY HE MUST HAVE BEEN WITH EVANGELINE DOVE!
WHAT ROCK CLICHÉ WOULD BE COMPLETE WITHOUT THE WICKED GIRL-FRIEND?
BRRRT
ROY L--
WHAT?!
HE'S GONE, ROY! HE HAD ANOTHER FREAK-OUT--SAID THE "GOD CAME BACK AGAIN"--

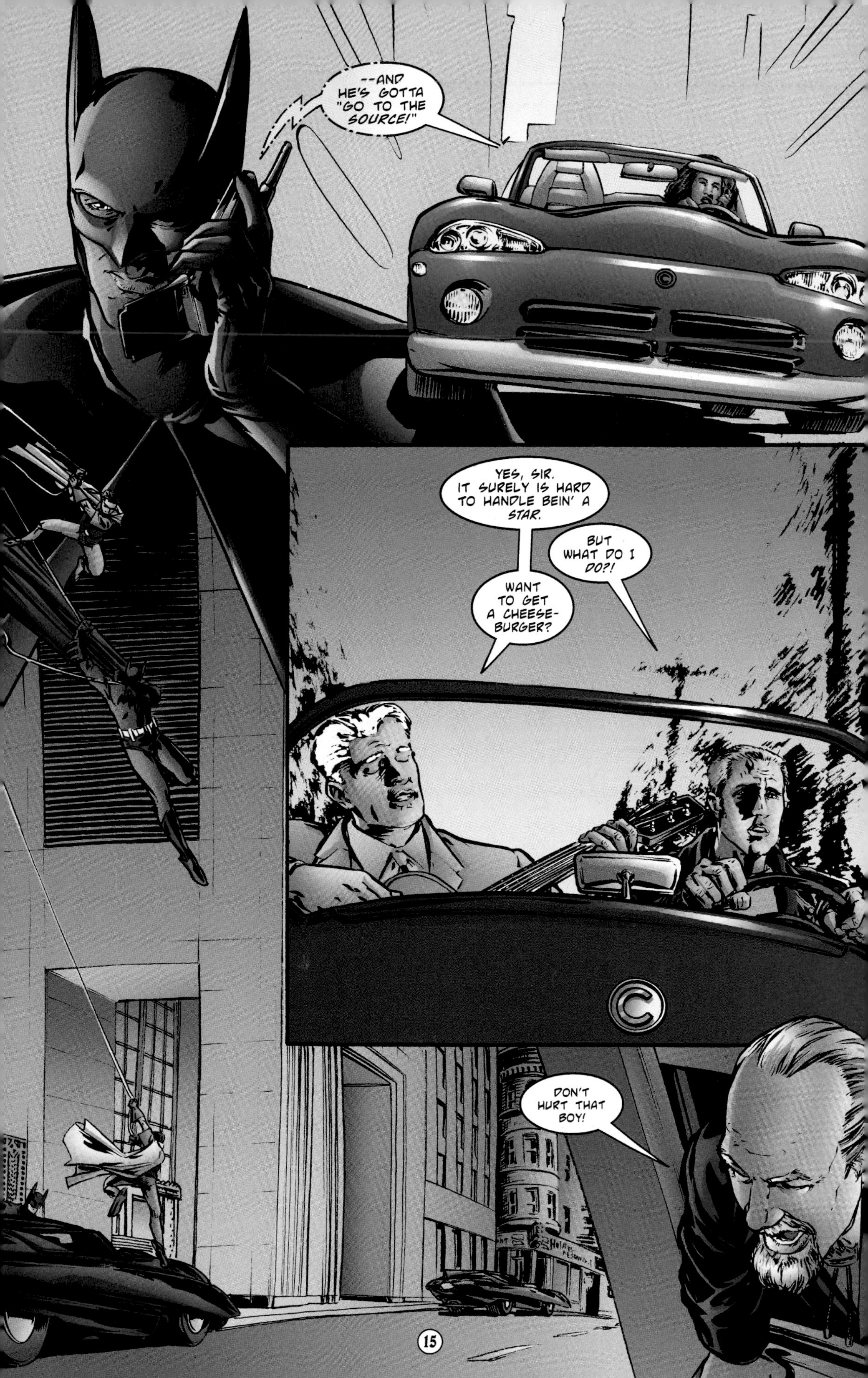
--AND HE'S GOTTA "GO TO THE SOURCE!"
YES, SIR. IT SURELY IS HARD TO HANDLE BEIN' A STAR.
WANT TO GET A CHEESE-BURGER?
BUT WHAT DO I DO?!
DON'T HURT THAT BOY!

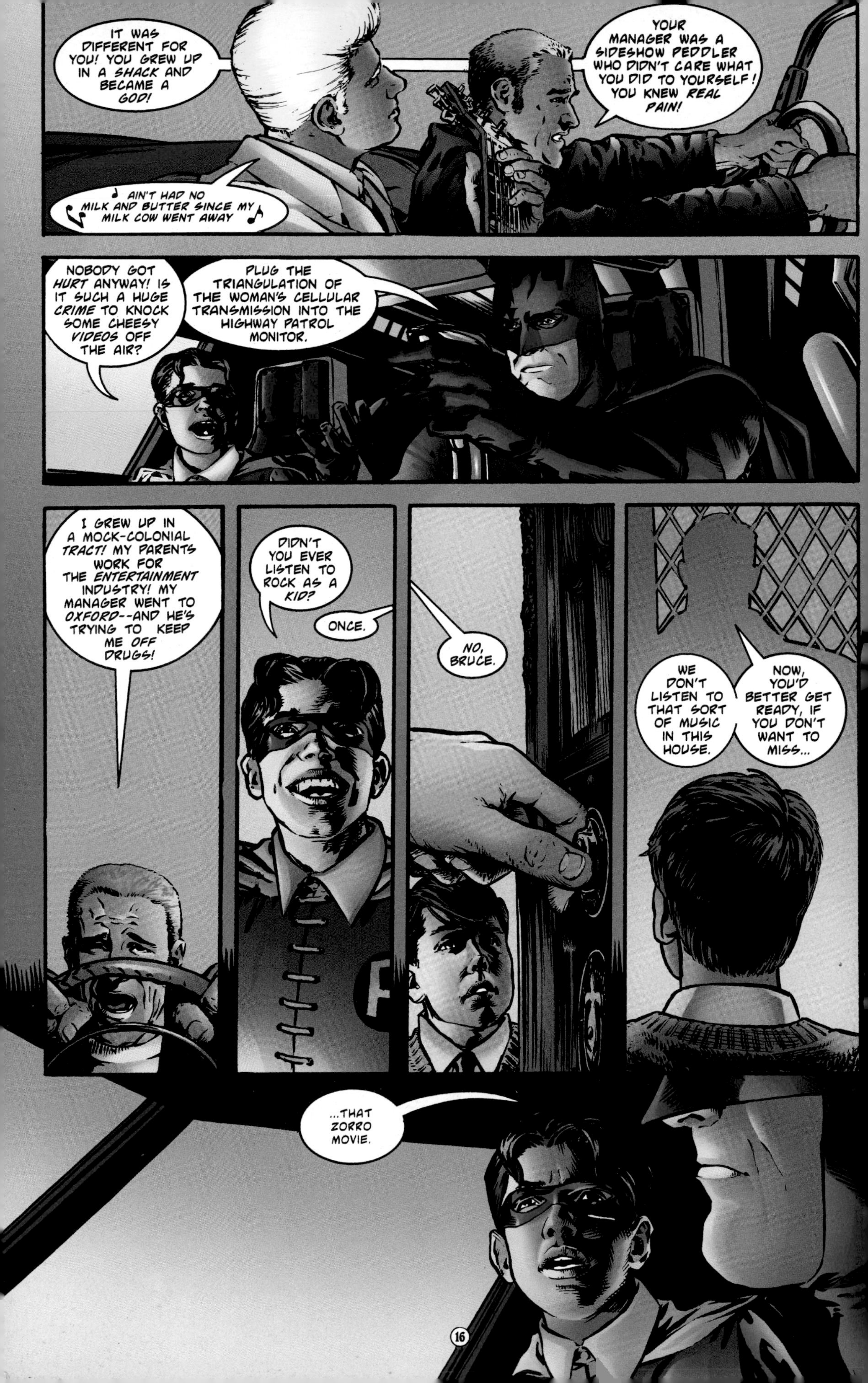
IT WAS DIFFERENT FOR YOU! YOU GREW UP IN A SHACK AND BECAME A GOD!
YOUR MANAGER WAS A SIDESHOW PEDDLER WHO DIDN'T CARE WHAT YOU DID TO YOURSELF! YOU KNEW REAL PAIN!
♪ AIN'T HAD NO MILK AND BUTTER SINCE MY MILK COW WENT AWAY ♪
NOBODY GOT HURT ANYWAY! IS IT SUCH A HUGE CRIME TO KNOCK SOME CHEESY VIDEOS OFF THE AIR?
PLUG THE TRIANGULATION OF THE WOMAN'S CELLULAR TRANSMISSION INTO THE HIGHWAY PATROL MONITOR.
I GREW UP IN A MOCK-COLONIAL TRACT! MY PARENTS WORK FOR THE ENTERTAINMENT INDUSTRY! MY MANAGER WENT TO OXFORD--AND HE'S TRYING TO KEEP ME OFF DRUGS!
DIDN'T YOU EVER LISTEN TO ROCK AS A KID?
ONCE.
NO, BRUCE.
WE DON'T LISTEN TO THAT SORT OF MUSIC IN THIS HOUSE.
NOW, YOU'D BETTER GET READY, IF YOU DON'T WANT TO MISS...
...THAT ZORRO MOVIE.

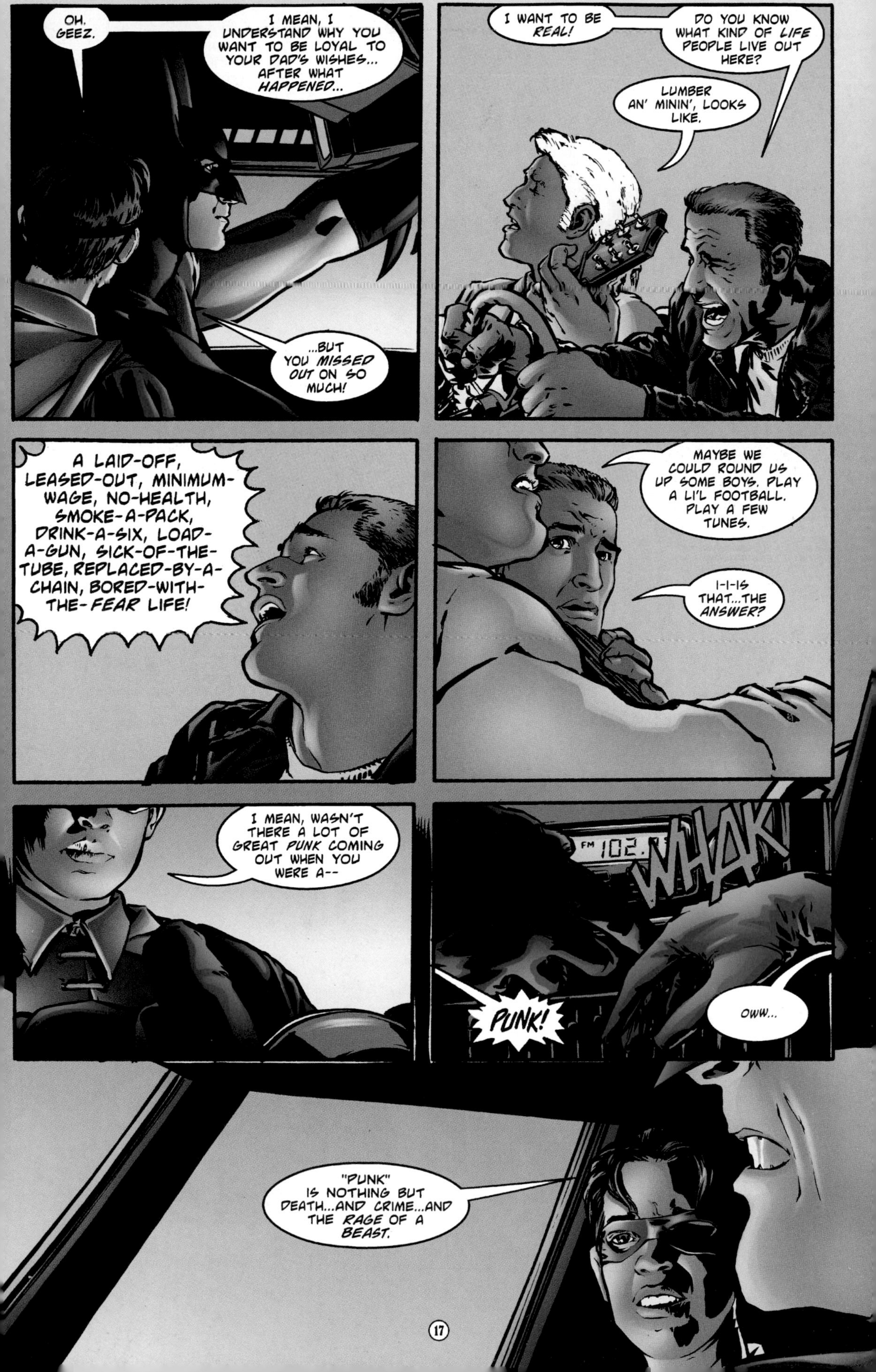
OH. GEEZ.
I MEAN, I UNDERSTAND WHY YOU WANT TO BE LOYAL TO YOUR DAD'S WISHES... AFTER WHAT HAPPENED...
...BUT YOU MISSED OUT ON SO MUCH!
I WANT TO BE REAL!
DO YOU KNOW WHAT KIND OF LIFE PEOPLE LIVE OUT HERE?
LUMBER AN' MININ', LOOKS LIKE.
A LAID-OFF, LEASED-OUT, MINIMUM-WAGE, NO-HEALTH, SMOKE-A-PACK, DRINK-A-SIX, LOAD-A-GUN, SICK-OF-THE-TUBE, REPLACED-BY-A-CHAIN, BORED-WITH-THE-FEAR LIFE!
MAYBE WE COULD ROUND US UP SOME BOYS. PLAY A LI'L FOOTBALL. PLAY A FEW TUNES.
I-I-IS THAT...THE ANSWER?
I MEAN, WASN'T THERE A LOT OF GREAT PUNK COMING OUT WHEN YOU WERE A--
FM 102.
WHAK!
PUNK!
OWW...
"PUNK" IS NOTHING BUT DEATH...AND CRIME...AND THE RAGE OF A BEAST.

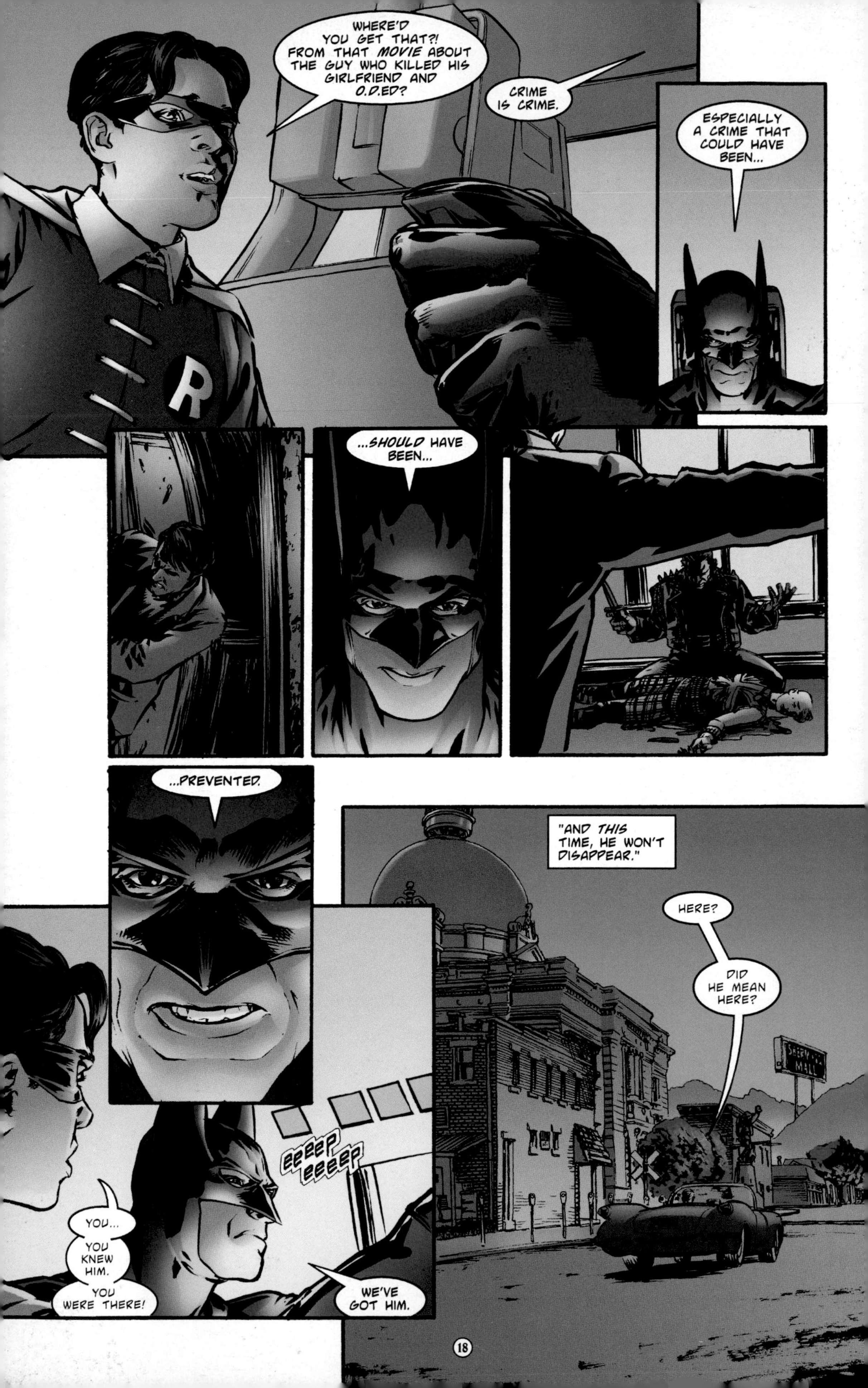

WHERE'D YOU GET THAT?! FROM THAT *MOVIE* ABOUT THE GUY WHO KILLED HIS GIRLFRIEND AND O.D.ED?
CRIME IS CRIME.
ESPECIALLY A CRIME THAT COULD HAVE BEEN...
...*SHOULD* HAVE BEEN...
...PREVENTED.
YOU... YOU KNEW HIM. YOU WERE THERE!
EEEEP EEEEP
WE'VE GOT HIM.
"AND *THIS* TIME, HE WON'T DISAPPEAR."
HERE?
DID HE MEAN HERE?

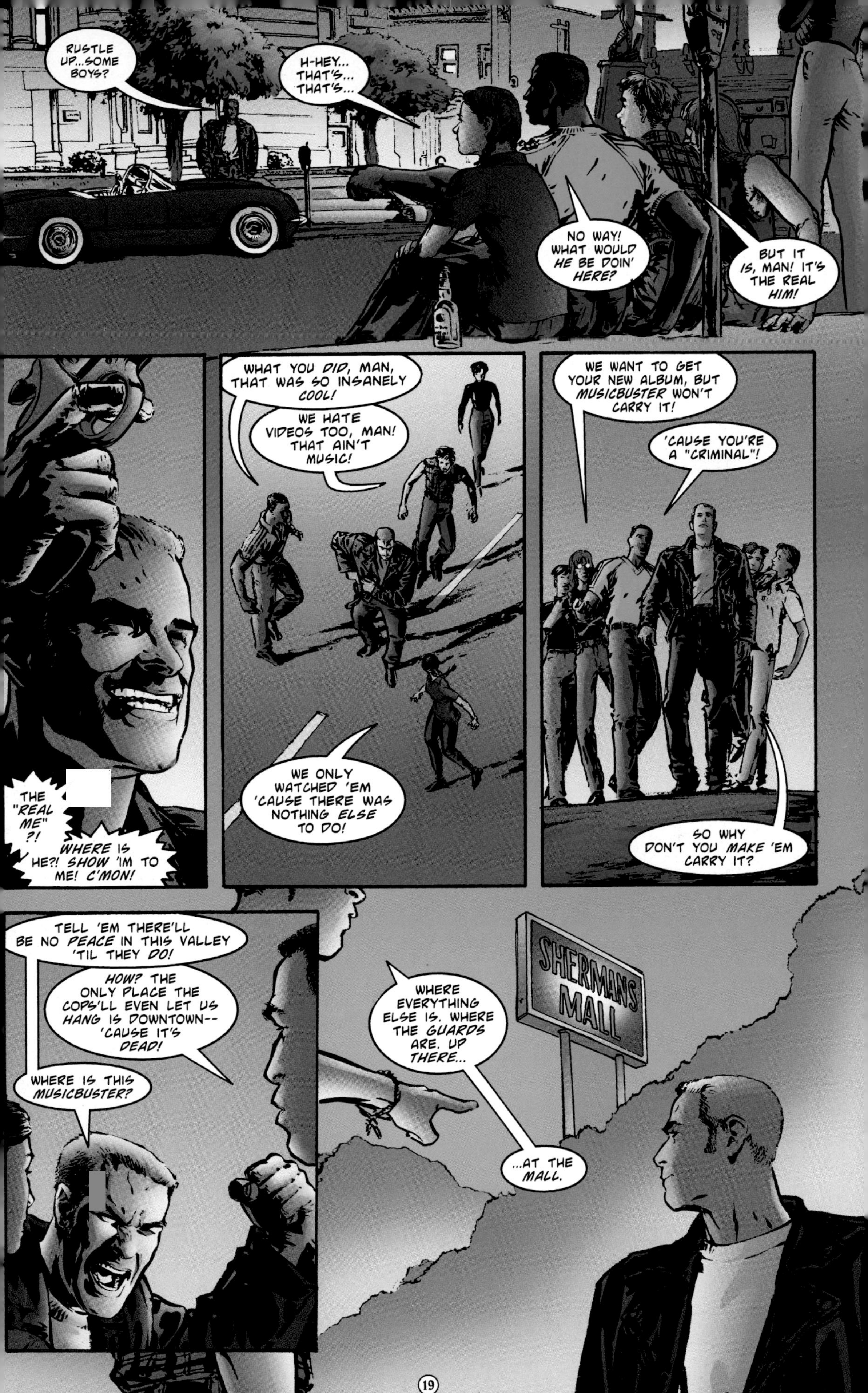
RUSTLE UP...SOME BOYS?
H-HEY... THAT'S... THAT'S...
NO WAY! WHAT WOULD HE BE DOIN' HERE?
BUT IT IS, MAN! IT'S THE REAL HIM!
THE "REAL ME" ?!
WHERE IS HE?! SHOW 'IM TO ME! C'MON!
WHAT YOU DID, MAN, THAT WAS SO INSANELY COOL!
WE HATE VIDEOS TOO, MAN! THAT AIN'T MUSIC!
WE ONLY WATCHED 'EM 'CAUSE THERE WAS NOTHING ELSE TO DO!
WE WANT TO GET YOUR NEW ALBUM, BUT MUSICBUSTER WON'T CARRY IT!
'CAUSE YOU'RE A "CRIMINAL"!
SO WHY DON'T YOU MAKE 'EM CARRY IT?
TELL 'EM THERE'LL BE NO PEACE IN THIS VALLEY 'TIL THEY DO!
HOW? THE ONLY PLACE THE COPS'LL EVEN LET US HANG IS DOWNTOWN-- 'CAUSE IT'S DEAD!
WHERE IS THIS MUSICBUSTER?
WHERE EVERYTHING ELSE IS. WHERE THE GUARDS ARE. UP THERE...
SHERMANS MALL
...AT THE MALL.

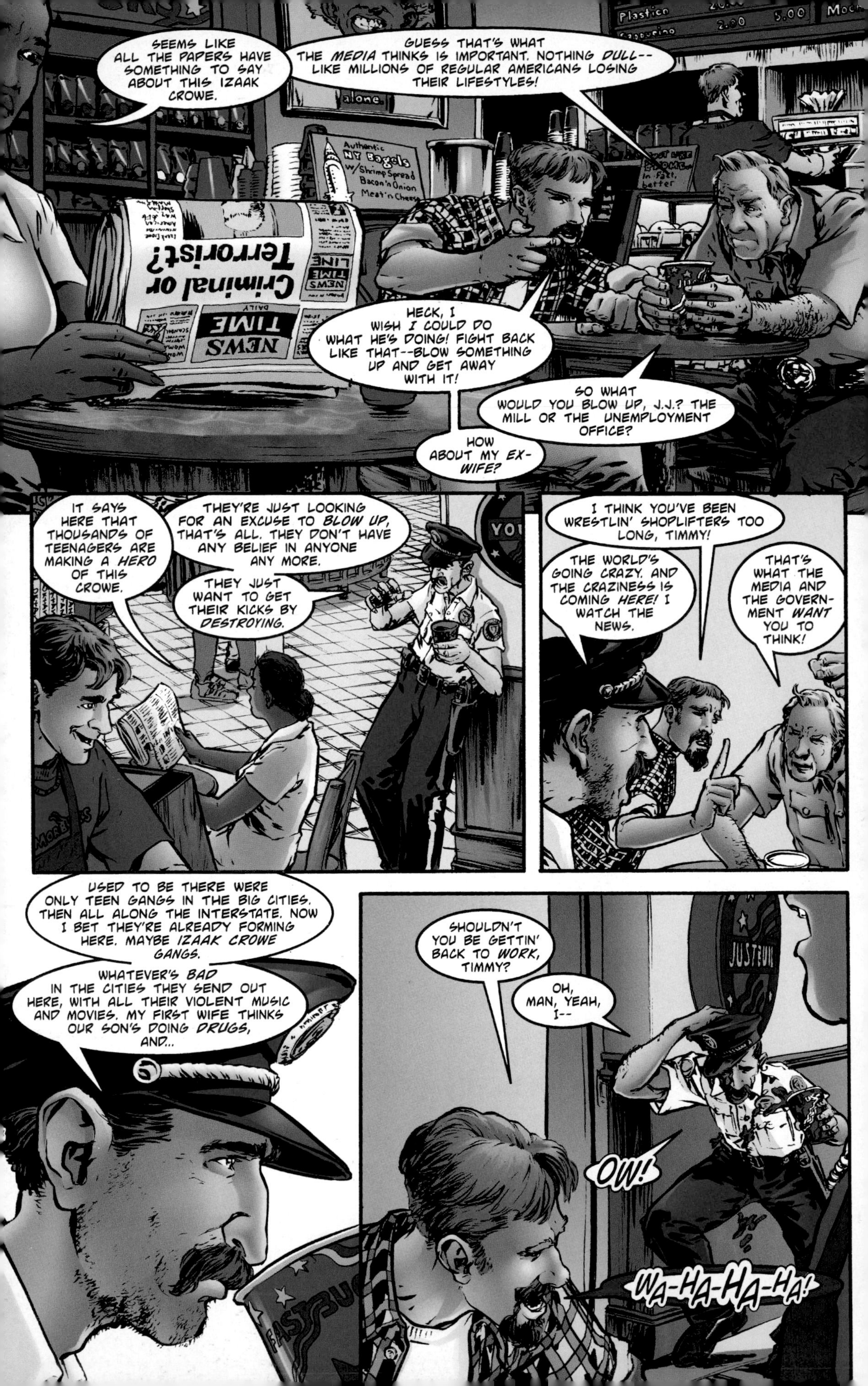

SEEMS LIKE ALL THE PAPERS HAVE SOMETHING TO SAY ABOUT THIS IZAAK CROWE.
GUESS THAT'S WHAT THE *MEDIA* THINKS IS IMPORTANT. NOTHING *DULL*-- LIKE MILLIONS OF REGULAR AMERICANS LOSING THEIR LIFESTYLES!
NEWS TIME DAILY
Criminal or Terrorist?
Authentic NY Bagels w/Shrimp Spread Bacon'n Onion Meat'n Cheese
HECK, I WISH *I* COULD DO WHAT HE'S DOING! FIGHT BACK LIKE THAT--BLOW SOMETHING UP AND GET AWAY WITH IT!
SO WHAT WOULD YOU BLOW UP, J.J.? THE MILL OR THE UNEMPLOYMENT OFFICE?
HOW ABOUT MY *EX-WIFE?*
IT SAYS HERE THAT THOUSANDS OF TEENAGERS ARE MAKING A *HERO* OF THIS CROWE.
THEY'RE JUST LOOKING FOR AN EXCUSE TO *BLOW UP*, THAT'S ALL. THEY DON'T HAVE ANY BELIEF IN ANYONE ANY MORE.
THEY JUST WANT TO GET THEIR KICKS BY *DESTROYING.*
I THINK YOU'VE BEEN WRESTLIN' SHOPLIFTERS TOO LONG, TIMMY!
THE WORLD'S GOING CRAZY. AND THE CRAZINESS IS COMING *HERE!* I WATCH THE NEWS.
THAT'S WHAT THE MEDIA AND THE GOVERNMENT *WANT* YOU TO THINK!
USED TO BE THERE WERE ONLY TEEN GANGS IN THE BIG CITIES. THEN ALL ALONG THE INTERSTATE. NOW I BET THEY'RE ALREADY FORMING HERE. MAYBE *IZAAK CROWE* GANGS.
WHATEVER'S *BAD* IN THE CITIES THEY SEND OUT HERE, WITH ALL THEIR VIOLENT MUSIC AND MOVIES. MY FIRST WIFE THINKS OUR SON'S DOING *DRUGS*, AND...
SHOULDN'T YOU BE GETTIN' BACK TO *WORK*, TIMMY?
OH, MAN, YEAH, I--
OW!
WA-HA-HA-HA!

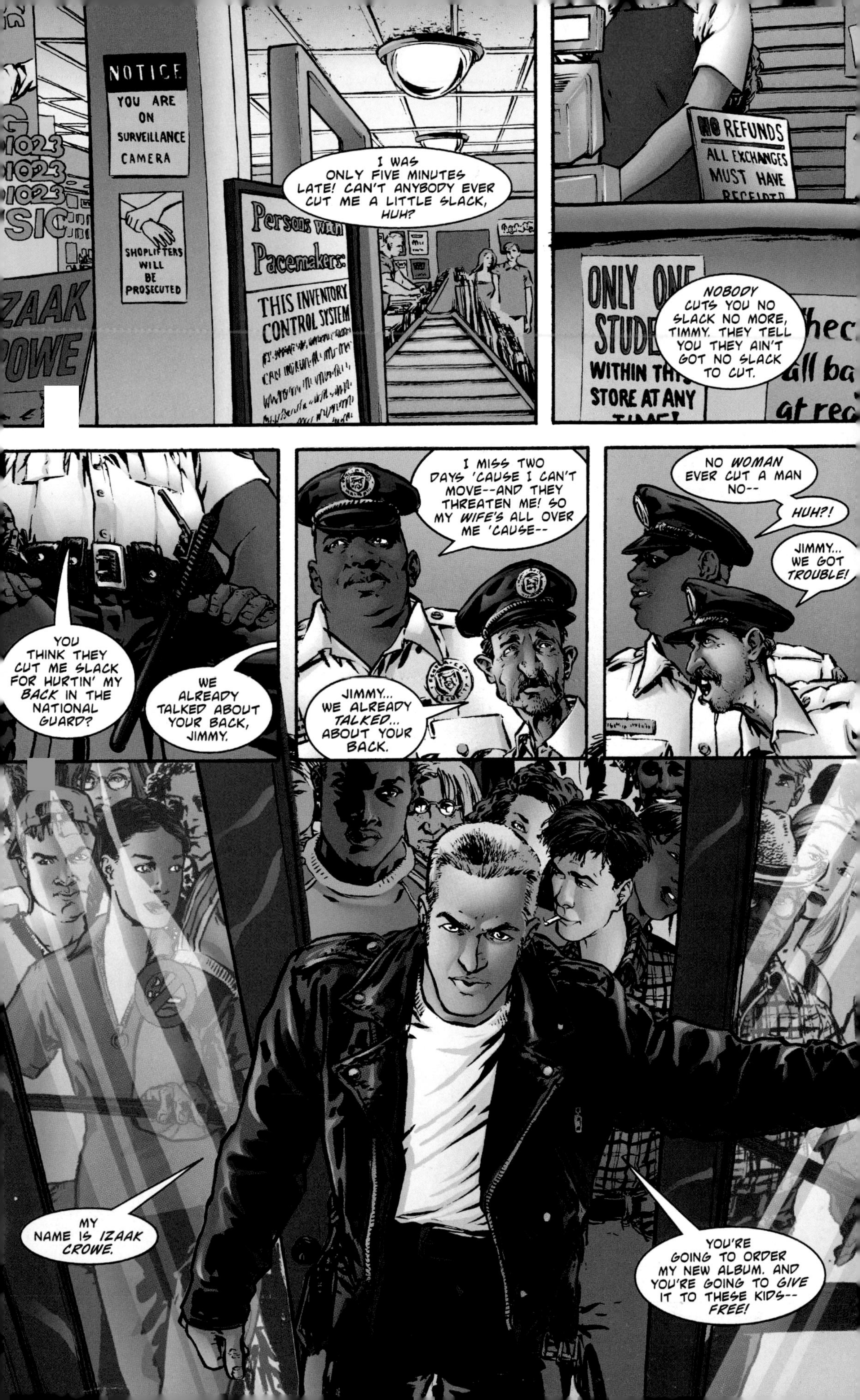
NOTICE
YOU ARE ON SURVEILLANCE CAMERA
SHOPLIFTERS WILL BE PROSECUTED
THIS INVENTORY CONTROL SYSTEM
I WAS ONLY FIVE MINUTES LATE! CAN'T ANYBODY EVER CUT ME A LITTLE SLACK, HUH?
NO REFUNDS
ALL EXCHANGES MUST HAVE
NOBODY CUTS YOU NO SLACK NO MORE, TIMMY. THEY TELL YOU THEY AIN'T GOT NO SLACK TO CUT.
YOU THINK THEY CUT ME SLACK FOR HURTIN' MY BACK IN THE NATIONAL GUARD?
WE ALREADY TALKED ABOUT YOUR BACK, JIMMY.
I MISS TWO DAYS 'CAUSE I CAN'T MOVE--AND THEY THREATEN ME! SO MY WIFE'S ALL OVER ME 'CAUSE--
JIMMY... WE ALREADY TALKED... ABOUT YOUR BACK.
NO WOMAN EVER CUT A MAN NO--
HUH?!
JIMMY... WE GOT TROUBLE!
MY NAME IS IZAAK CROWE.
YOU'RE GOING TO ORDER MY NEW ALBUM. AND YOU'RE GOING TO GIVE IT TO THESE KIDS-- FREE!

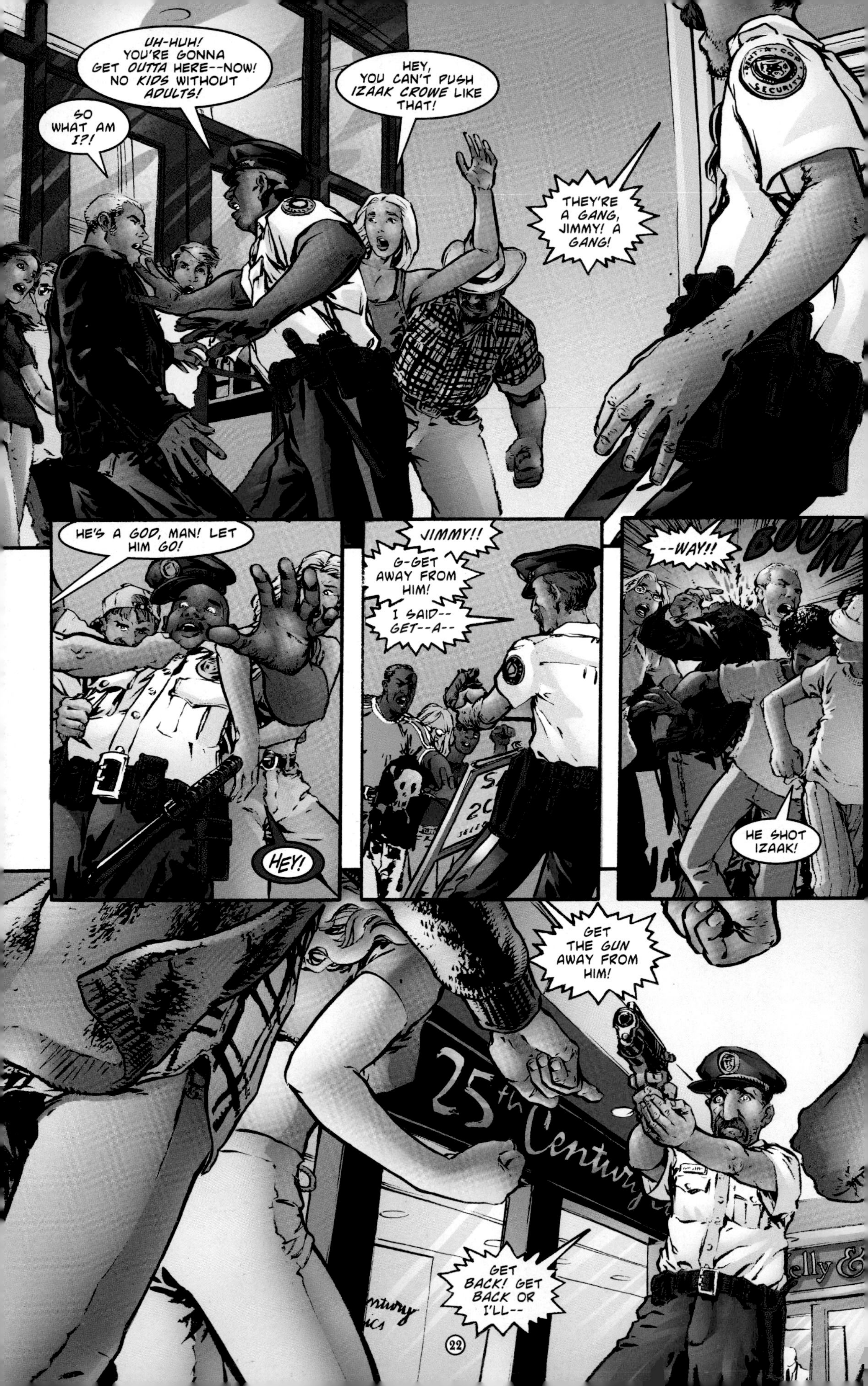
UH-HUH! YOU'RE GONNA GET OUTTA HERE--NOW! NO KIDS WITHOUT ADULTS!
SO WHAT AM I?!
HEY, YOU CAN'T PUSH IZAAK CROWE LIKE THAT!
THEY'RE A GANG, JIMMY! A GANG!
RENT-A-COP SECURITY
HE'S A GOD, MAN! LET HIM GO!
HEY!
JIMMY!!
G-GET AWAY FROM HIM!
I SAID--GET--A--
--WAY!!
BOOM
HE SHOT IZAAK!
GET THE GUN AWAY FROM HIM!
25th Century
GET BACK! GET BACK OR I'LL--

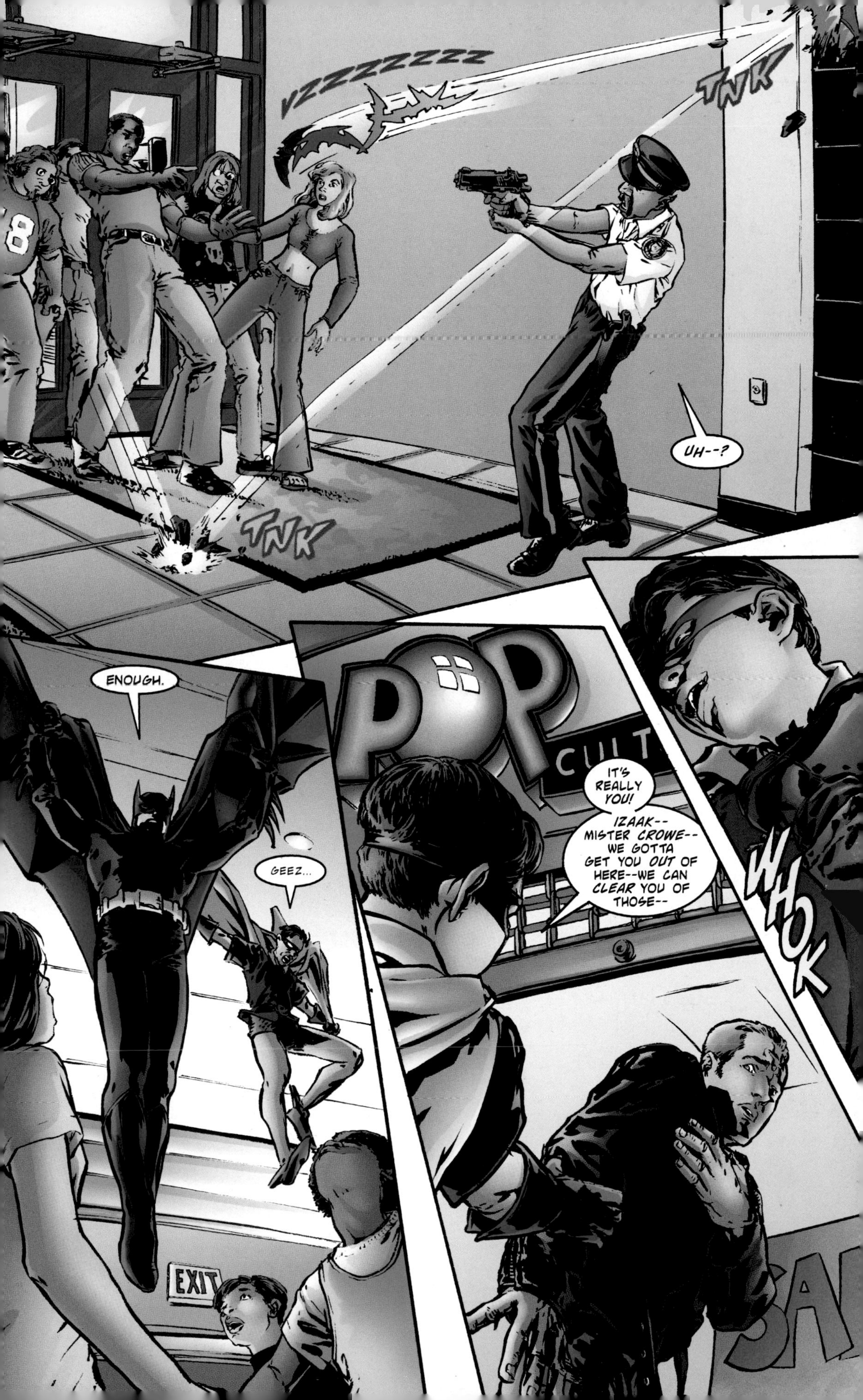
VZZZZZZZZZ
TNK
UH--?
TNK
ENOUGH.
GEEZ...
POP CULT
IT'S REALLY YOU!
IZAAK--MISTER CROWE--WE GOTTA GET YOU OUT OF HERE--WE CAN CLEAR YOU OF THOSE--
WHOK
EXIT

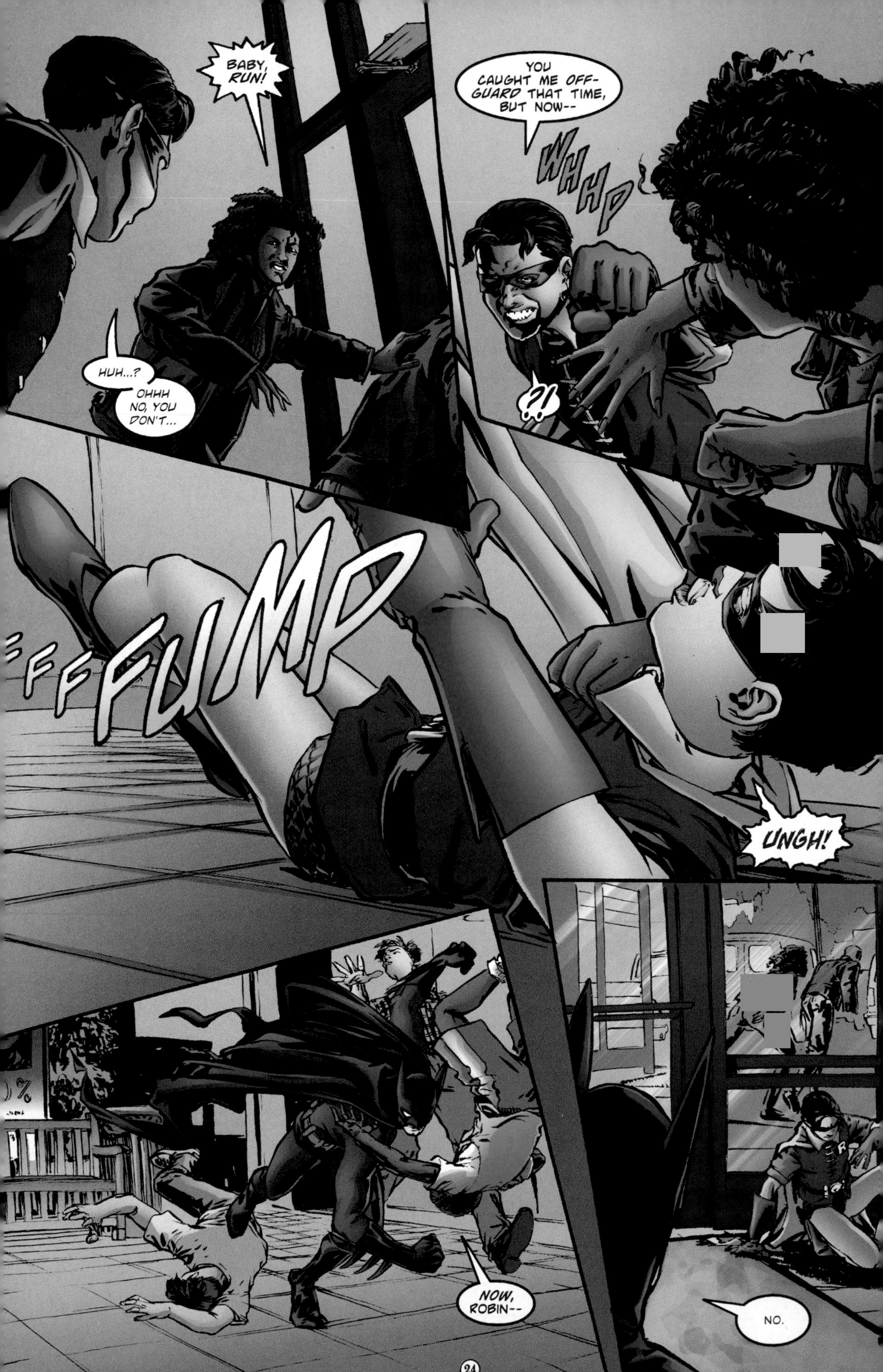
BABY, RUN!
HUH...?
OHHH NO, YOU DON'T...
YOU CAUGHT ME OFF-GUARD THAT TIME, BUT NOW--
WHHP
?!
FFFUMP
UNGH!
NOW, ROBIN--
NO.

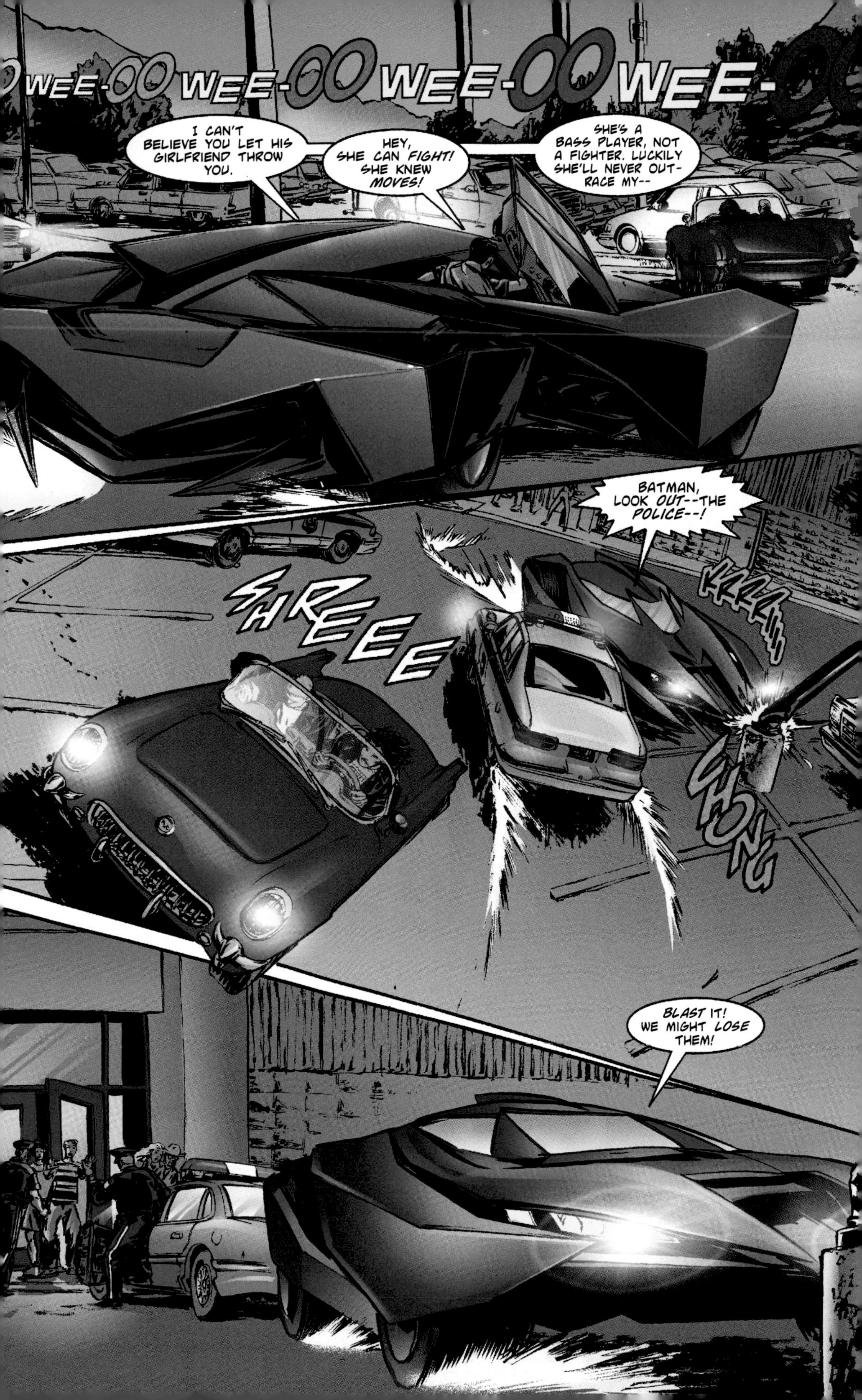
WEE-OO WEE-OO WEE-OO WEE-
I CAN'T BELIEVE YOU LET HIS GIRLFRIEND THROW YOU.
HEY, SHE CAN FIGHT! SHE KNEW MOVES!
SHE'S A BASS PLAYER, NOT A FIGHTER. LUCKILY SHE'LL NEVER OUT-RACE MY--
BATMAN, LOOK OUT--THE POLICE--!
SHREEEE
CHONG
BLAST IT! WE MIGHT LOSE THEM!

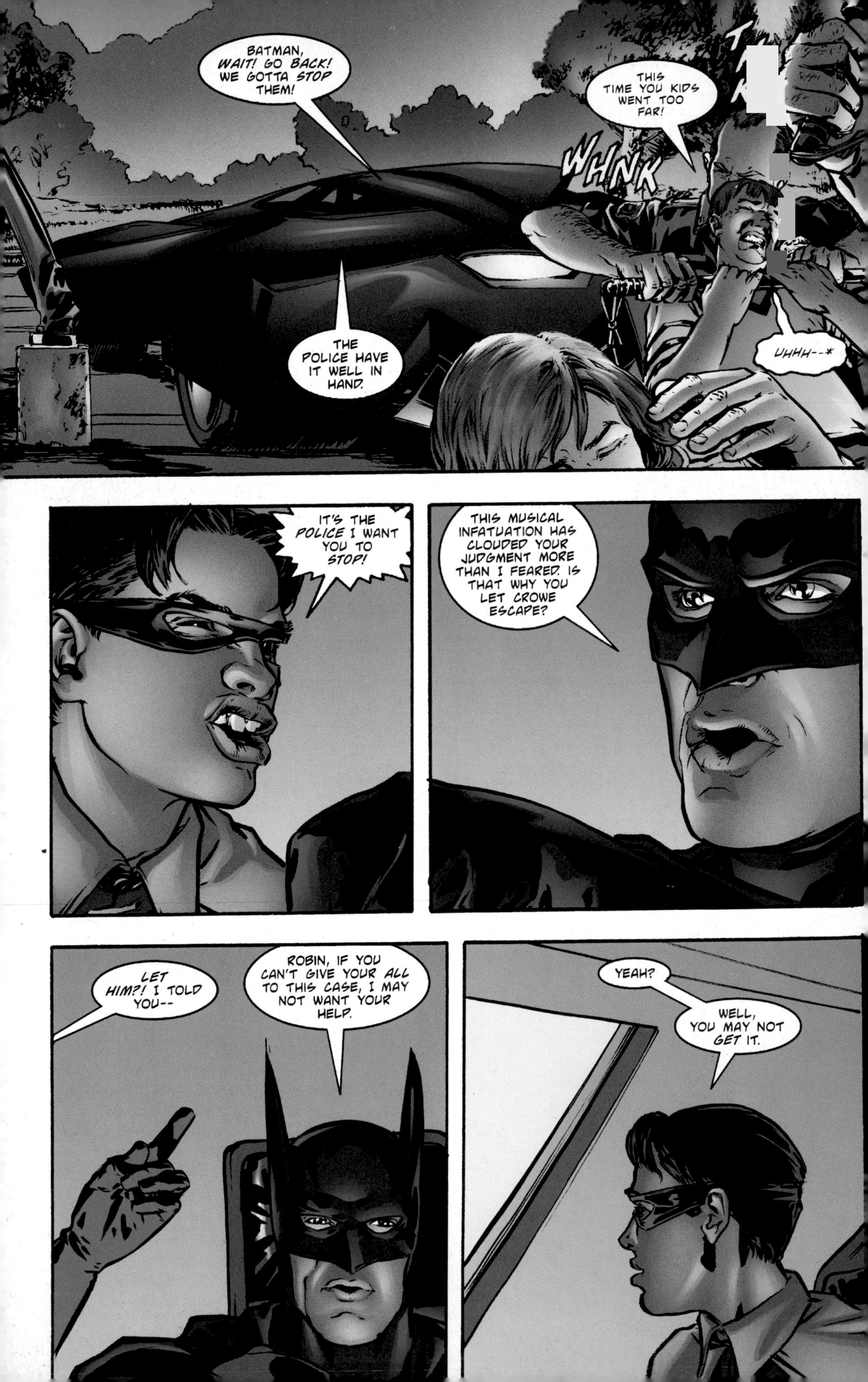
BATMAN, WAIT! GO BACK! WE GOTTA STOP THEM!
THE POLICE HAVE IT WELL IN HAND.
THIS TIME YOU KIDS WENT TOO FAR!
WHNK
UHHH--*
IT'S THE POLICE I WANT YOU TO STOP!
THIS MUSICAL INFATUATION HAS CLOUDED YOUR JUDGMENT MORE THAN I FEARED. IS THAT WHY YOU LET CROWE ESCAPE?
LET HIM?! I TOLD YOU--
ROBIN, IF YOU CAN'T GIVE YOUR ALL TO THIS CASE, I MAY NOT WANT YOUR HELP.
YEAH?
WELL, YOU MAY NOT GET IT.

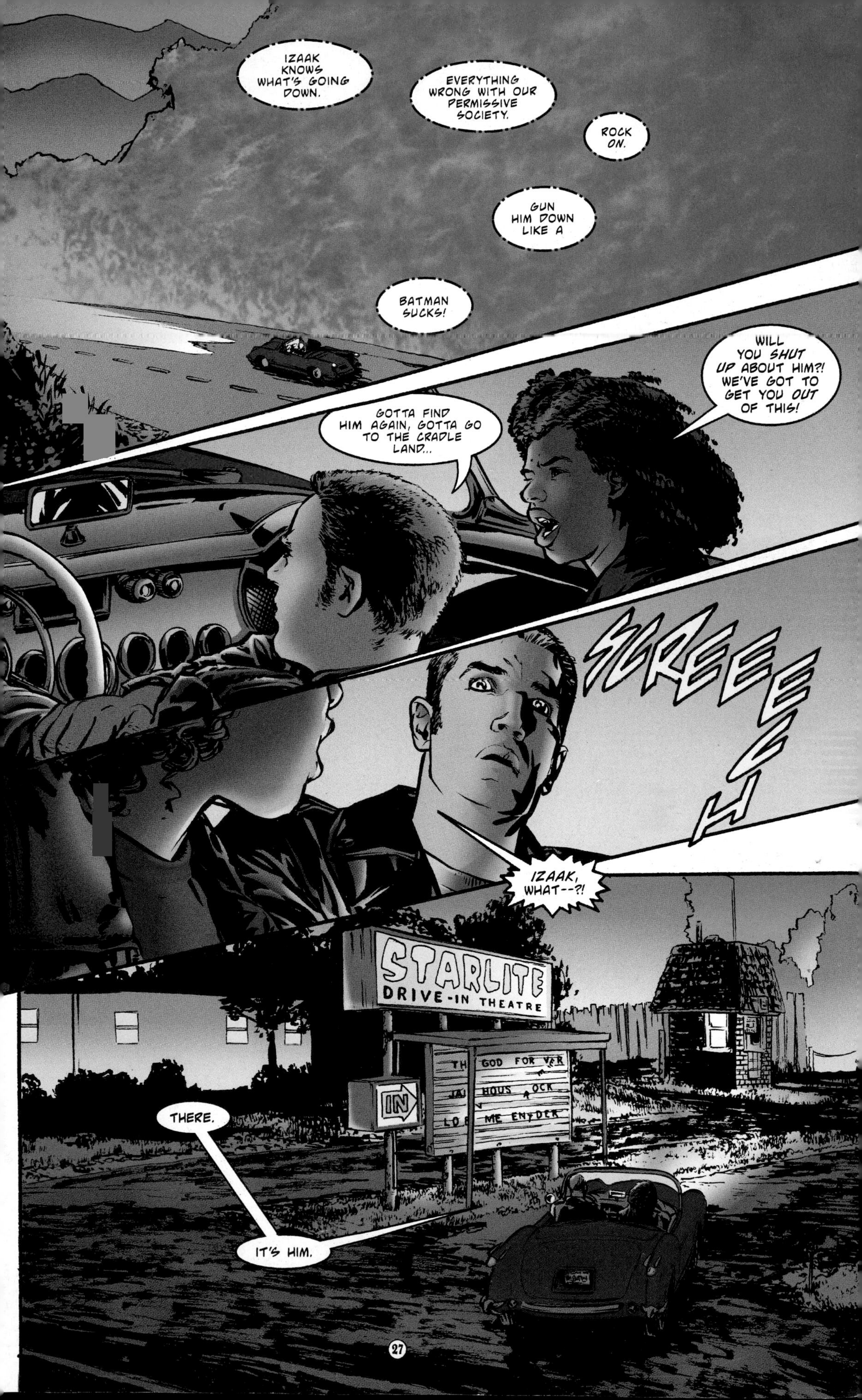
IZAAK KNOWS WHAT'S GOING DOWN.
EVERYTHING WRONG WITH OUR PERMISSIVE SOCIETY.
ROCK ON.
GUN HIM DOWN LIKE A
BATMAN SUCKS!
GOTTA FIND HIM AGAIN, GOTTA GO TO THE CRADLE LAND...
WILL YOU *SHUT UP* ABOUT HIM?! WE'VE GOT TO GET YOU *OUT* OF THIS!
SCREEECH
IZAAK, WHAT--?!
STARLITE
DRIVE-IN THEATRE
IN
THERE.
IT'S HIM.

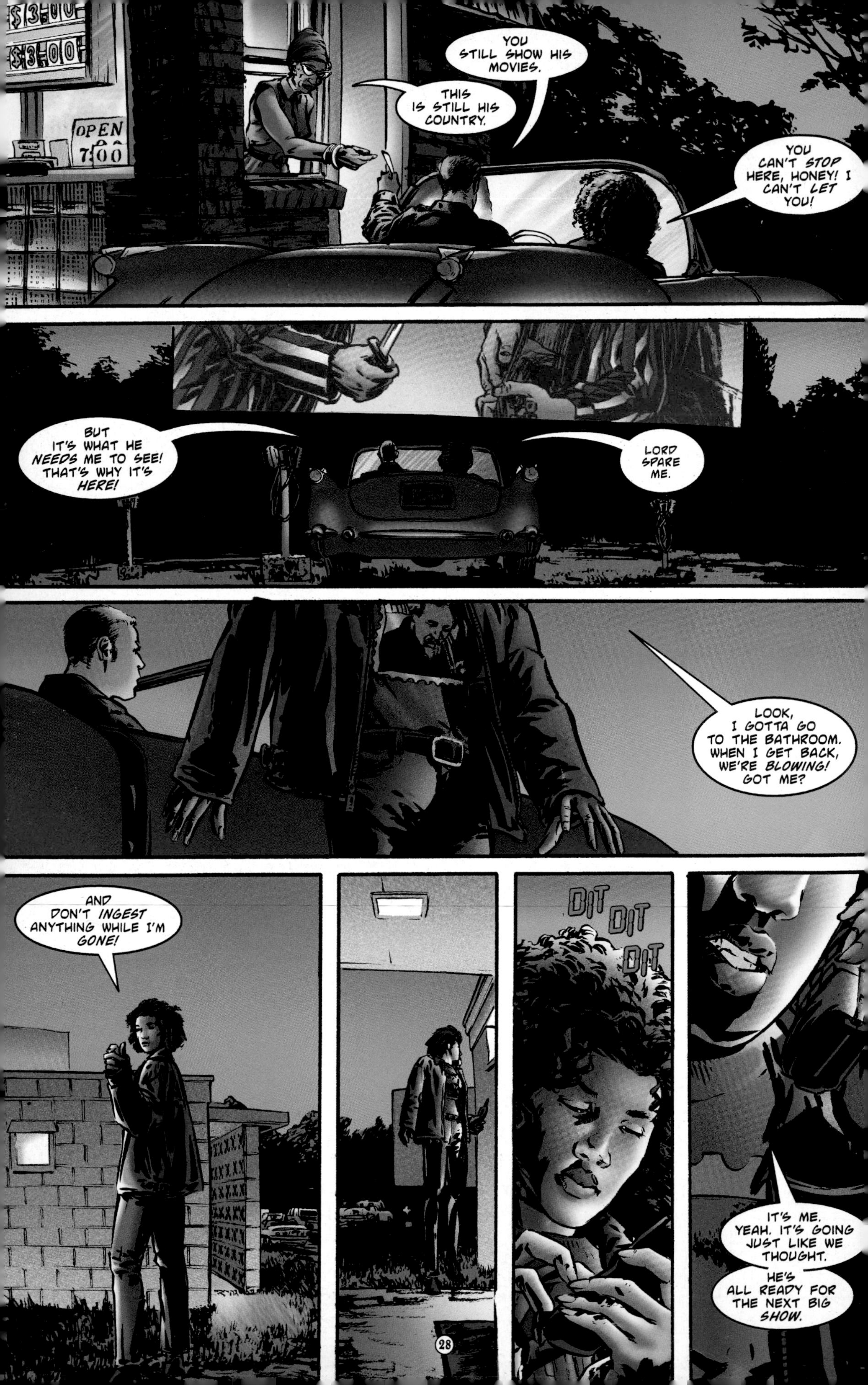
$3.00
$3.00
OPEN
7:00
YOU STILL SHOW HIS MOVIES.
THIS IS STILL HIS COUNTRY.
YOU CAN'T STOP HERE, HONEY! I CAN'T LET YOU!
BUT IT'S WHAT HE NEEDS ME TO SEE! THAT'S WHY IT'S HERE!
LORD SPARE ME.
LOOK, I GOTTA GO TO THE BATHROOM. WHEN I GET BACK, WE'RE BLOWING! GOT ME?
AND DON'T INGEST ANYTHING WHILE I'M GONE!
DIT DIT DIT
IT'S ME. YEAH. IT'S GOING JUST LIKE WE THOUGHT.
HE'S ALL READY FOR THE NEXT BIG SHOW.

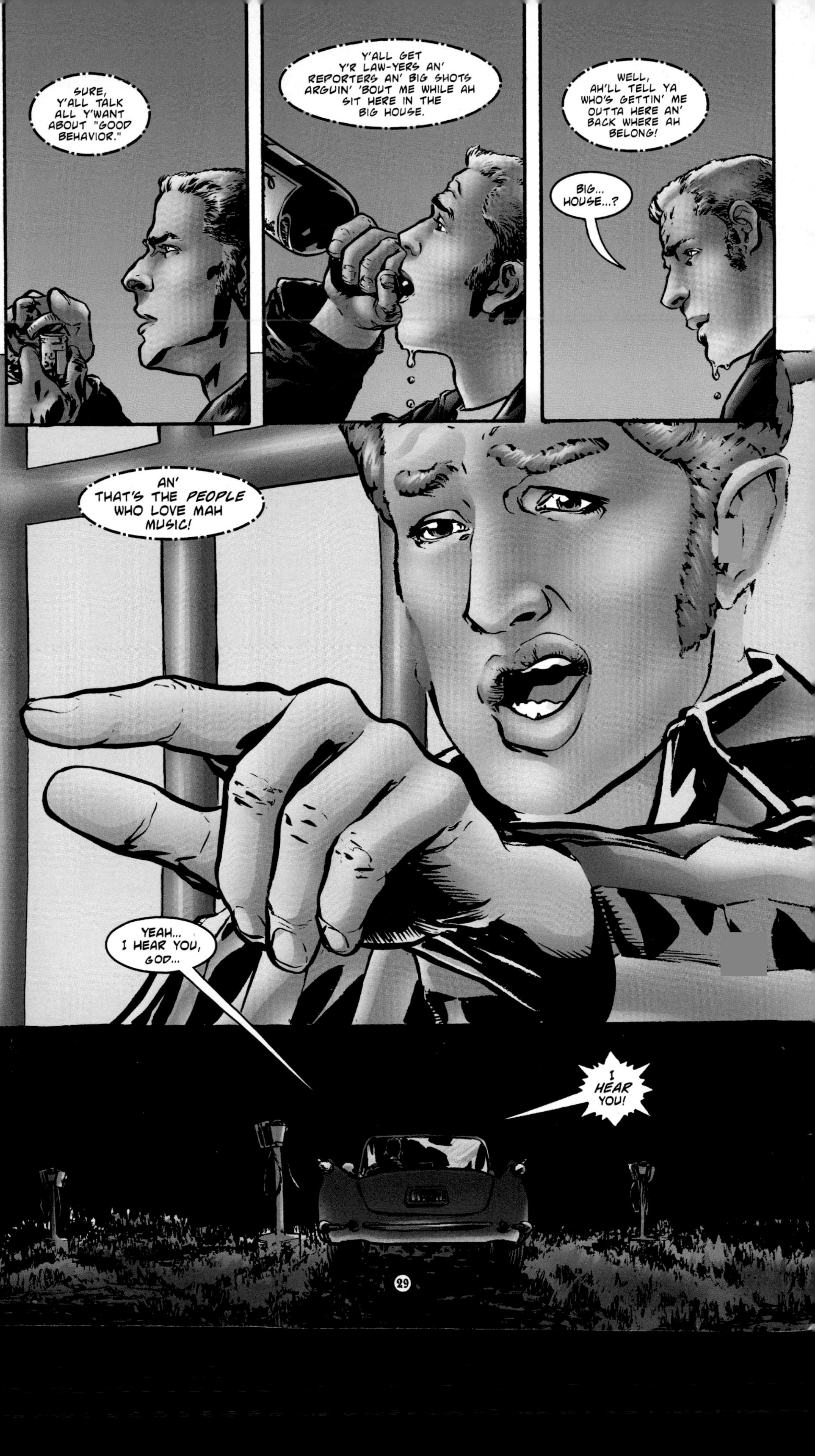

SURE, Y'ALL TALK ALL Y'WANT ABOUT "GOOD BEHAVIOR."
Y'ALL GET Y'R LAW-YERS AN' REPORTERS AN' BIG SHOTS ARGUIN' 'BOUT ME WHILE AH SIT HERE IN THE BIG HOUSE.
WELL, AH'LL TELL YA WHO'S GETTIN' ME OUTTA HERE AN' BACK WHERE AH BELONG!
BIG... HOUSE...?
AN' THAT'S THE PEOPLE WHO LOVE MAH MUSIC!
YEAH... I HEAR YOU, GOD...
I HEAR YOU!

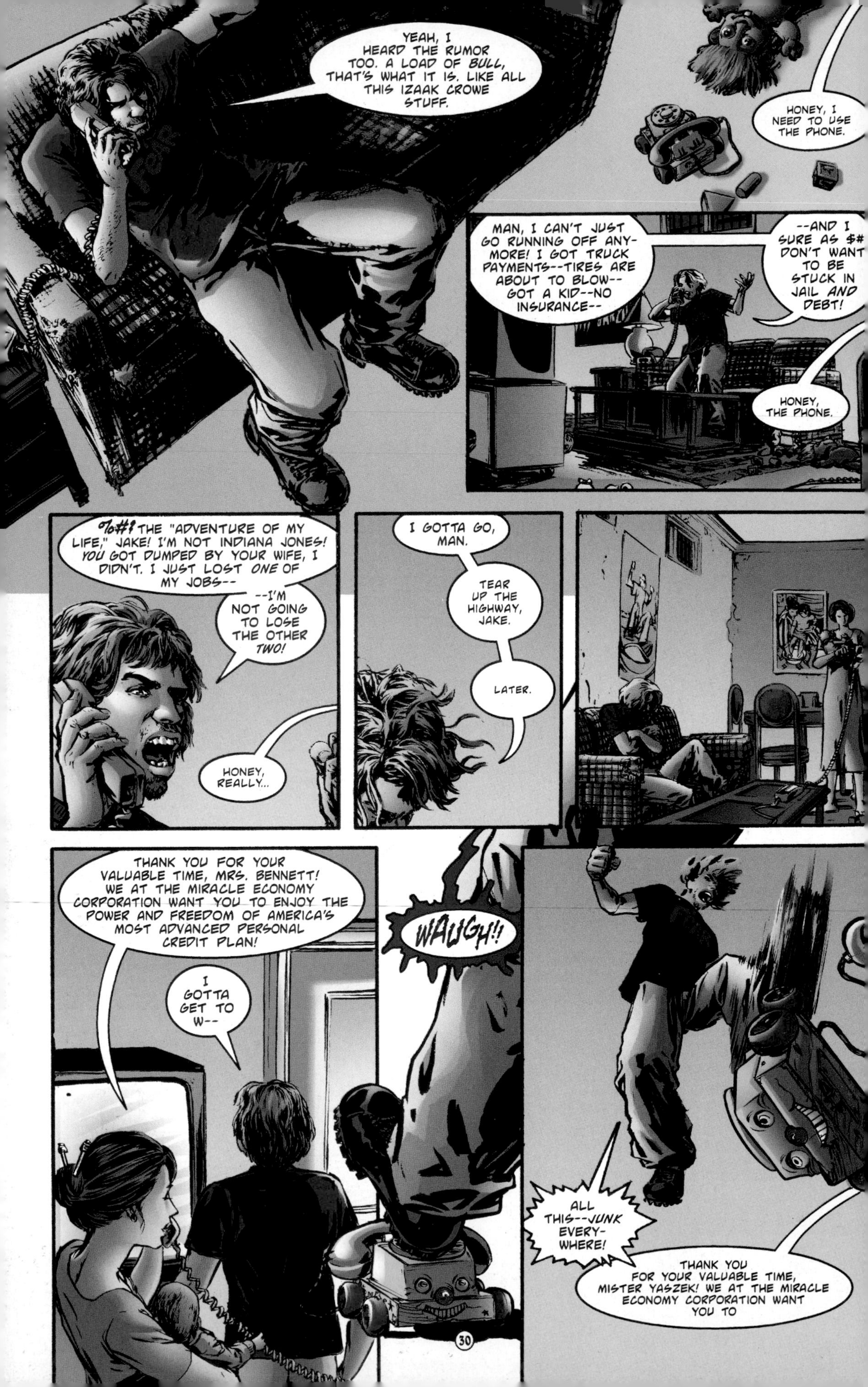
YEAH, I HEARD THE RUMOR TOO. A LOAD OF BULL, THAT'S WHAT IT IS. LIKE ALL THIS IZAAK CROWE STUFF.
HONEY, I NEED TO USE THE PHONE.
MAN, I CAN'T JUST GO RUNNING OFF ANY-MORE! I GOT TRUCK PAYMENTS--TIRES ARE ABOUT TO BLOW--GOT A KID--NO INSURANCE--
--AND I SURE AS $# DON'T WANT TO BE STUCK IN JAIL AND DEBT!
HONEY, THE PHONE.
%#! THE "ADVENTURE OF MY LIFE," JAKE! I'M NOT INDIANA JONES! YOU GOT DUMPED BY YOUR WIFE, I DIDN'T. I JUST LOST ONE OF MY JOBS--
--I'M NOT GOING TO LOSE THE OTHER TWO!
HONEY, REALLY...
I GOTTA GO, MAN.
TEAR UP THE HIGHWAY, JAKE.
LATER.
THANK YOU FOR YOUR VALUABLE TIME, MRS. BENNETT! WE AT THE MIRACLE ECONOMY CORPORATION WANT YOU TO ENJOY THE POWER AND FREEDOM OF AMERICA'S MOST ADVANCED PERSONAL CREDIT PLAN!
I GOTTA GET TO W--
WAUGH!!
ALL THIS--JUNK EVERY-WHERE!
THANK YOU FOR YOUR VALUABLE TIME, MISTER YASZEK! WE AT THE MIRACLE ECONOMY CORPORATION WANT YOU TO

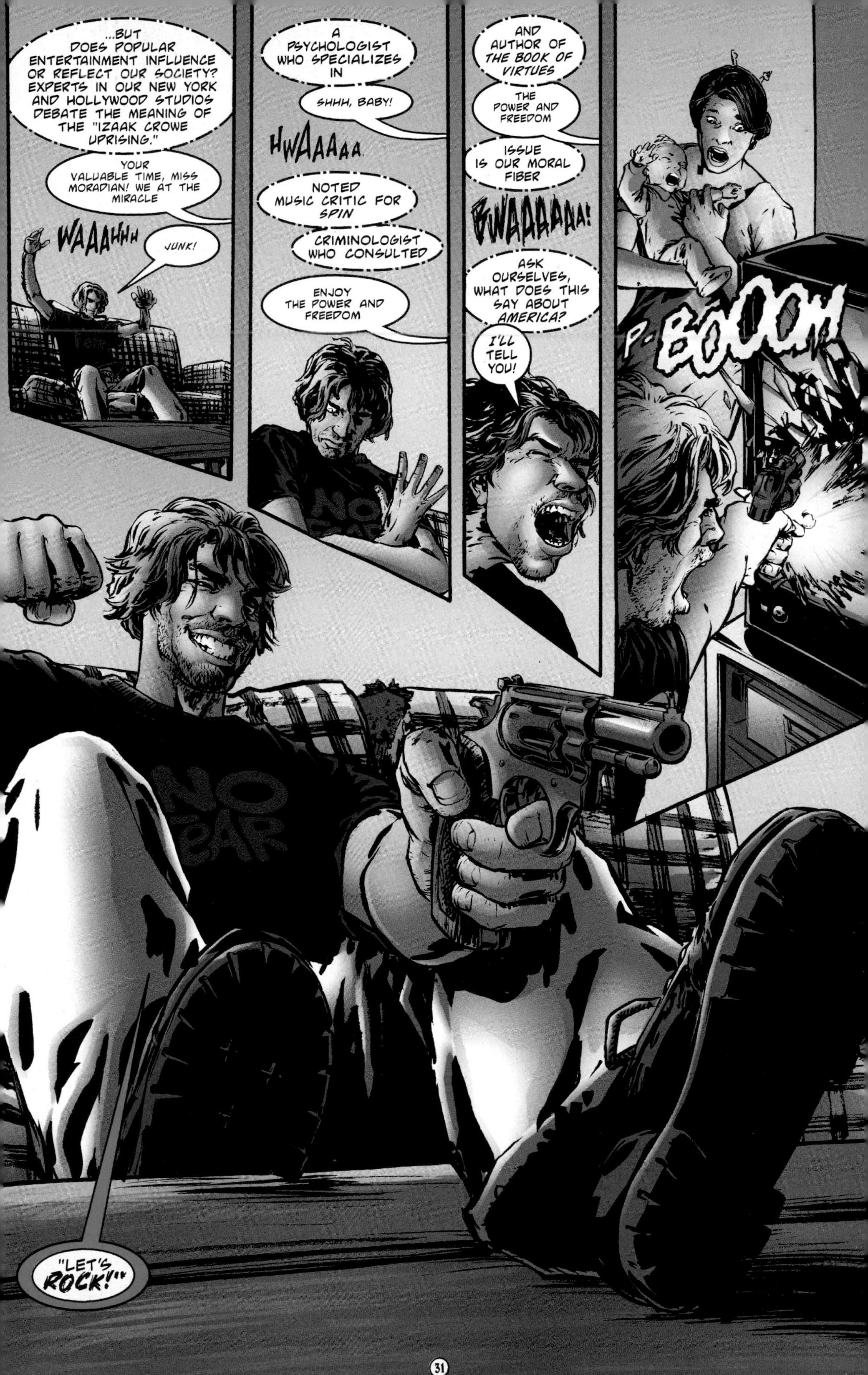
...BUT DOES POPULAR ENTERTAINMENT INFLUENCE OR REFLECT OUR SOCIETY? EXPERTS IN OUR NEW YORK AND HOLLYWOOD STUDIOS DEBATE THE MEANING OF THE "IZAAK CROWE UPRISING."
YOUR VALUABLE TIME, MISS MORADIAN! WE AT THE MIRACLE
WAAAHHH
JUNK!
A PSYCHOLOGIST WHO SPECIALIZES IN
SHHH, BABY!
HWAAAAA
NOTED MUSIC CRITIC FOR SPIN
CRIMINOLOGIST WHO CONSULTED
ENJOY THE POWER AND FREEDOM
AND AUTHOR OF THE BOOK OF VIRTUES
THE POWER AND FREEDOM
ISSUE IS OUR MORAL FIBER
BWAAAAAA!
ASK OURSELVES, WHAT DOES THIS SAY ABOUT AMERICA?
I'LL TELL YOU!
P-BOOOM
"LET'S ROCK!"

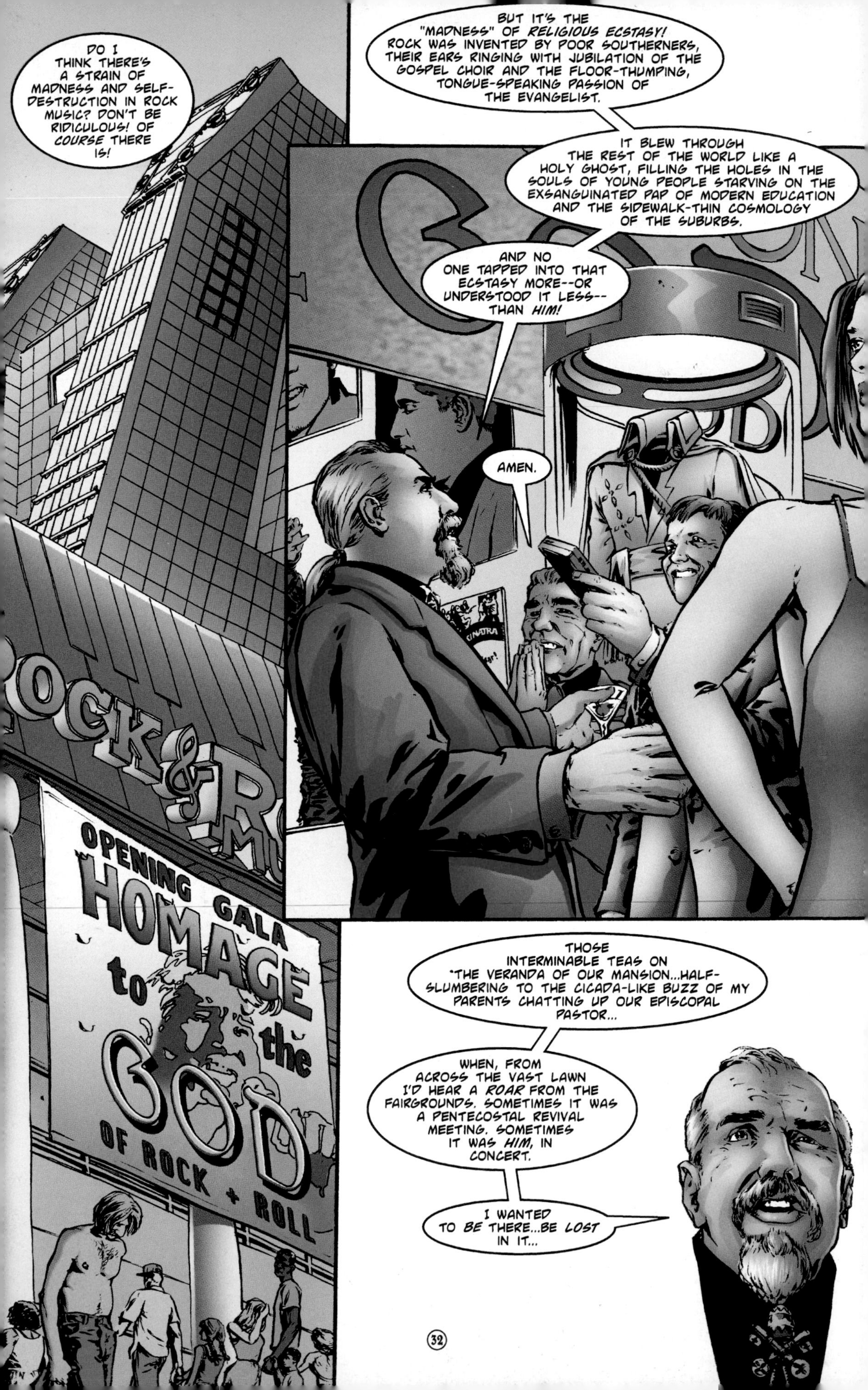
DO I THINK THERE'S A STRAIN OF MADNESS AND SELF-DESTRUCTION IN ROCK MUSIC? DON'T BE RIDICULOUS! OF COURSE THERE IS!
BUT IT'S THE "MADNESS" OF RELIGIOUS ECSTASY! ROCK WAS INVENTED BY POOR SOUTHERNERS, THEIR EARS RINGING WITH JUBILATION OF THE GOSPEL CHOIR AND THE FLOOR-THUMPING, TONGUE-SPEAKING PASSION OF THE EVANGELIST.
IT BLEW THROUGH THE REST OF THE WORLD LIKE A HOLY GHOST, FILLING THE HOLES IN THE SOULS OF YOUNG PEOPLE STARVING ON THE EXSANGUINATED PAP OF MODERN EDUCATION AND THE SIDEWALK-THIN COSMOLOGY OF THE SUBURBS.
AND NO ONE TAPPED INTO THAT ECSTASY MORE--OR UNDERSTOOD IT LESS--THAN HIM!
AMEN.
OPENING GALA
HOMAGE to the GOD OF ROCK + ROLL
THOSE INTERMINABLE TEAS ON THE VERANDA OF OUR MANSION...HALF-SLUMBERING TO THE CICADA-LIKE BUZZ OF MY PARENTS CHATTING UP OUR EPISCOPAL PASTOR...
WHEN, FROM ACROSS THE VAST LAWN I'D HEAR A ROAR FROM THE FAIRGROUNDS. SOMETIMES IT WAS A PENTECOSTAL REVIVAL MEETING. SOMETIMES IT WAS HIM, IN CONCERT.
I WANTED TO BE THERE...BE LOST IN IT...

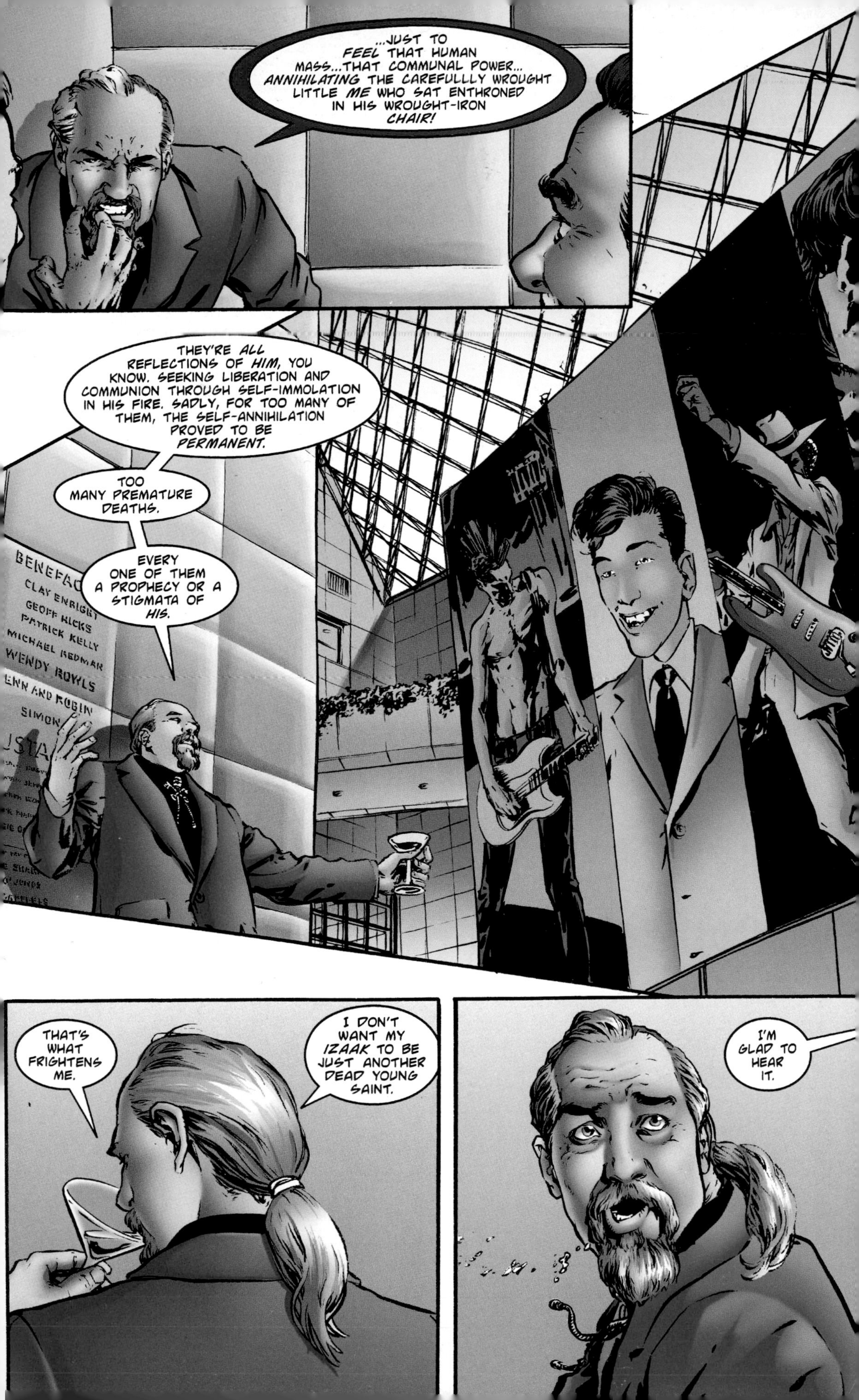
...JUST TO *FEEL* THAT HUMAN MASS...THAT COMMUNAL POWER... *ANNIHILATING* THE CAREFULLLY WROUGHT LITTLE *ME* WHO SAT ENTHRONED IN HIS WROUGHT-IRON *CHAIR!*
THEY'RE *ALL* REFLECTIONS OF *HIM*, YOU KNOW. SEEKING LIBERATION AND COMMUNION THROUGH SELF-IMMOLATION IN HIS FIRE. SADLY, FOR TOO MANY OF THEM, THE SELF-ANNIHILATION PROVED TO BE *PERMANENT*.
TOO MANY PREMATURE DEATHS.
EVERY ONE OF THEM A PROPHECY OR A STIGMATA OF *HIS*.
CLAY ENRIGHT
GEOFF HICKS
PATRICK KELLY
MICHAEL BEDMAR
WENDY ROWLS
SIMON
THAT'S WHAT FRIGHTENS ME.
I DON'T WANT MY *IZAAK* TO BE JUST ANOTHER DEAD YOUNG SAINT.
I'M GLAD TO HEAR IT.

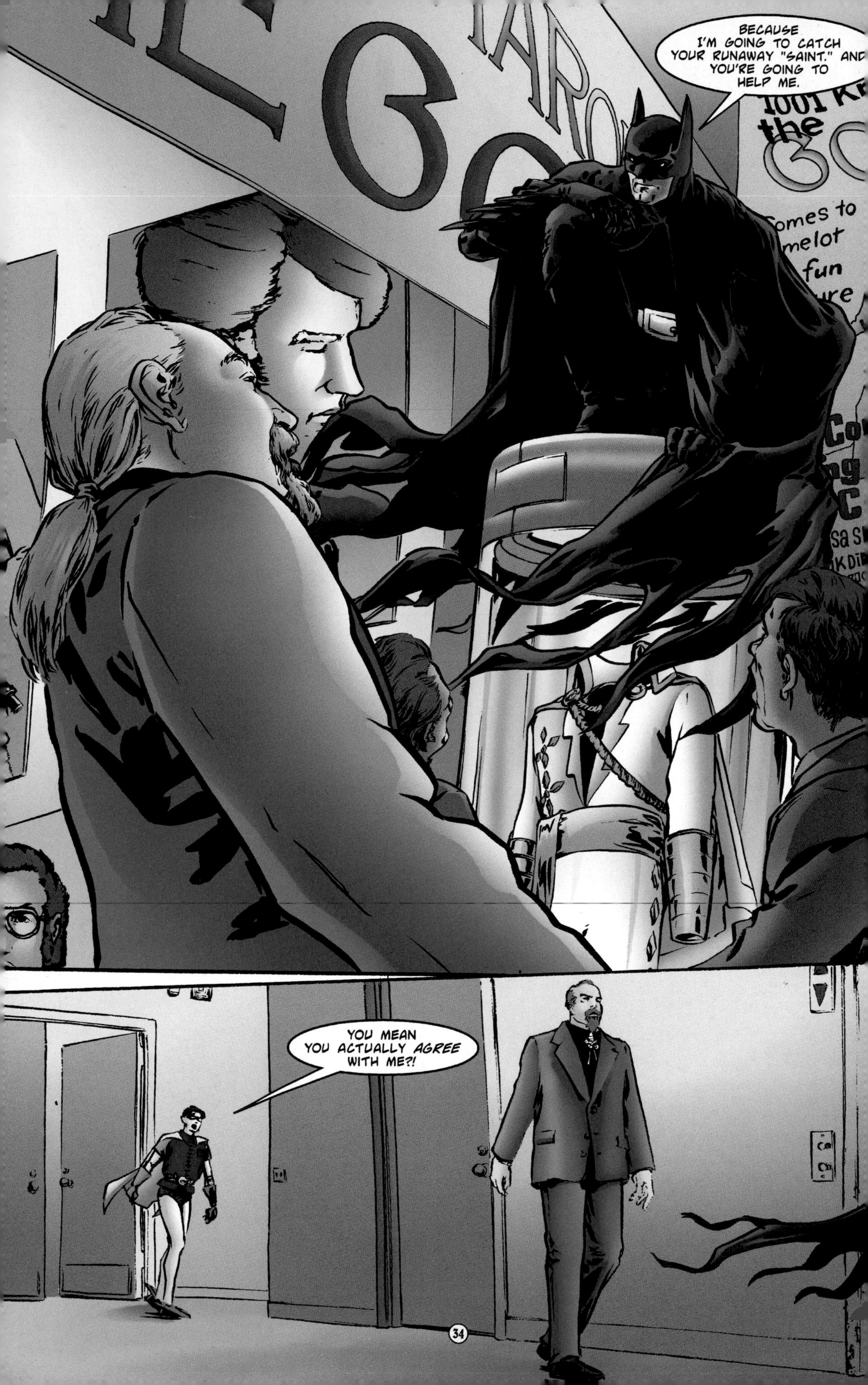
BECAUSE I'M GOING TO CATCH YOUR RUNAWAY "SAINT." AND YOU'RE GOING TO HELP ME.
YOU MEAN YOU ACTUALLY AGREE WITH ME?!

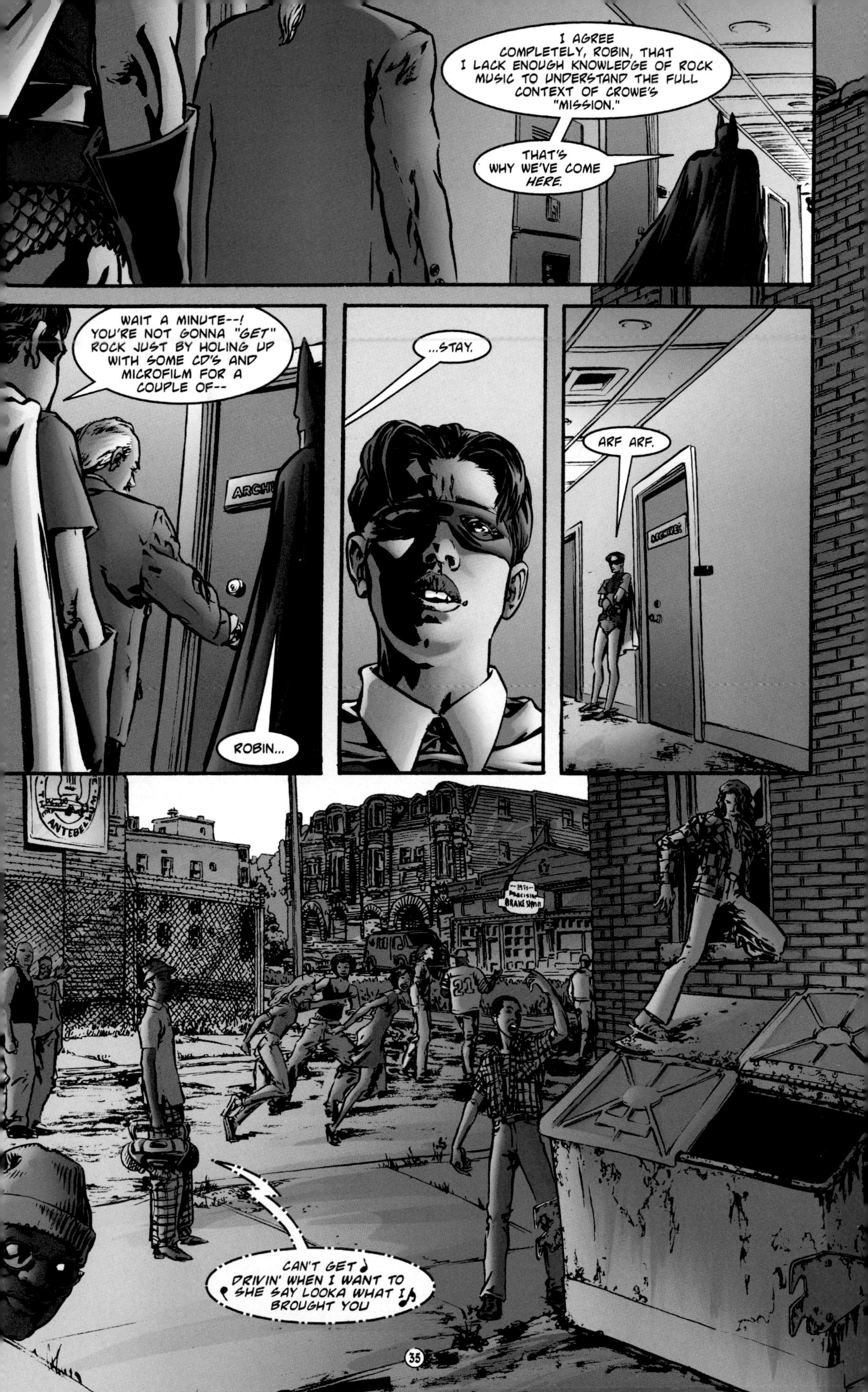
I AGREE COMPLETELY, ROBIN, THAT I LACK ENOUGH KNOWLEDGE OF ROCK MUSIC TO UNDERSTAND THE FULL CONTEXT OF CROWE'S "MISSION."
THAT'S WHY WE'VE COME HERE.
WAIT A MINUTE--! YOU'RE NOT GONNA "GET" ROCK JUST BY HOLING UP WITH SOME CD'S AND MICROFILM FOR A COUPLE OF--
ROBIN...
...STAY.
ARF ARF.
CAN'T GET DRIVIN' WHEN I WANT TO SHE SAY LOOKA WHAT I BROUGHT YOU

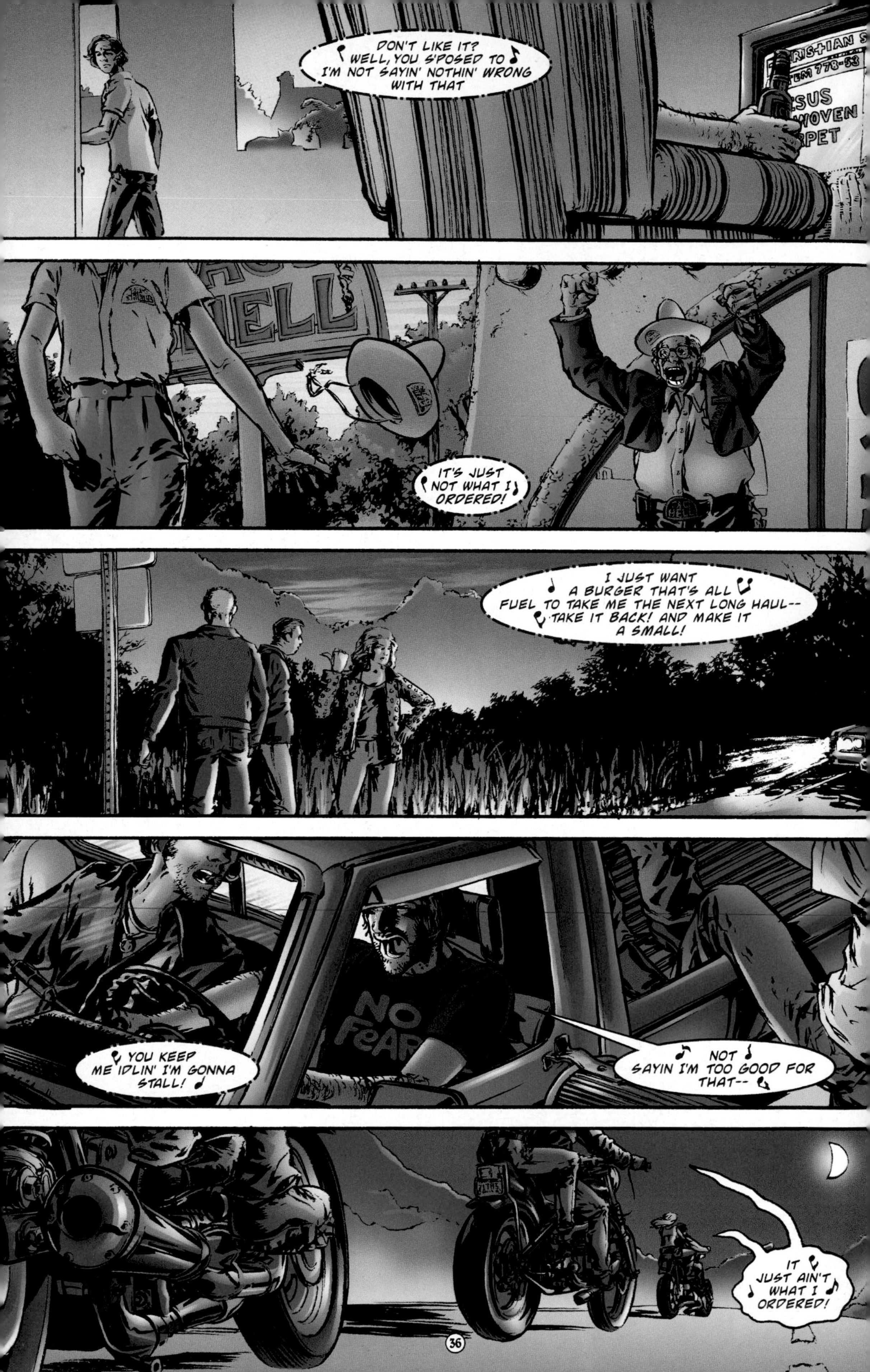
DON'T LIKE IT? WELL, YOU S'POSED TO I'M NOT SAYIN' NOTHIN' WRONG WITH THAT
IT'S JUST NOT WHAT I ORDERED!
I JUST WANT A BURGER THAT'S ALL FUEL TO TAKE ME THE NEXT LONG HAUL-- TAKE IT BACK! AND MAKE IT A SMALL!
YOU KEEP ME IDLIN' I'M GONNA STALL!
NOT SAYIN I'M TOO GOOD FOR THAT--
IT JUST AIN'T WHAT I ORDERED!

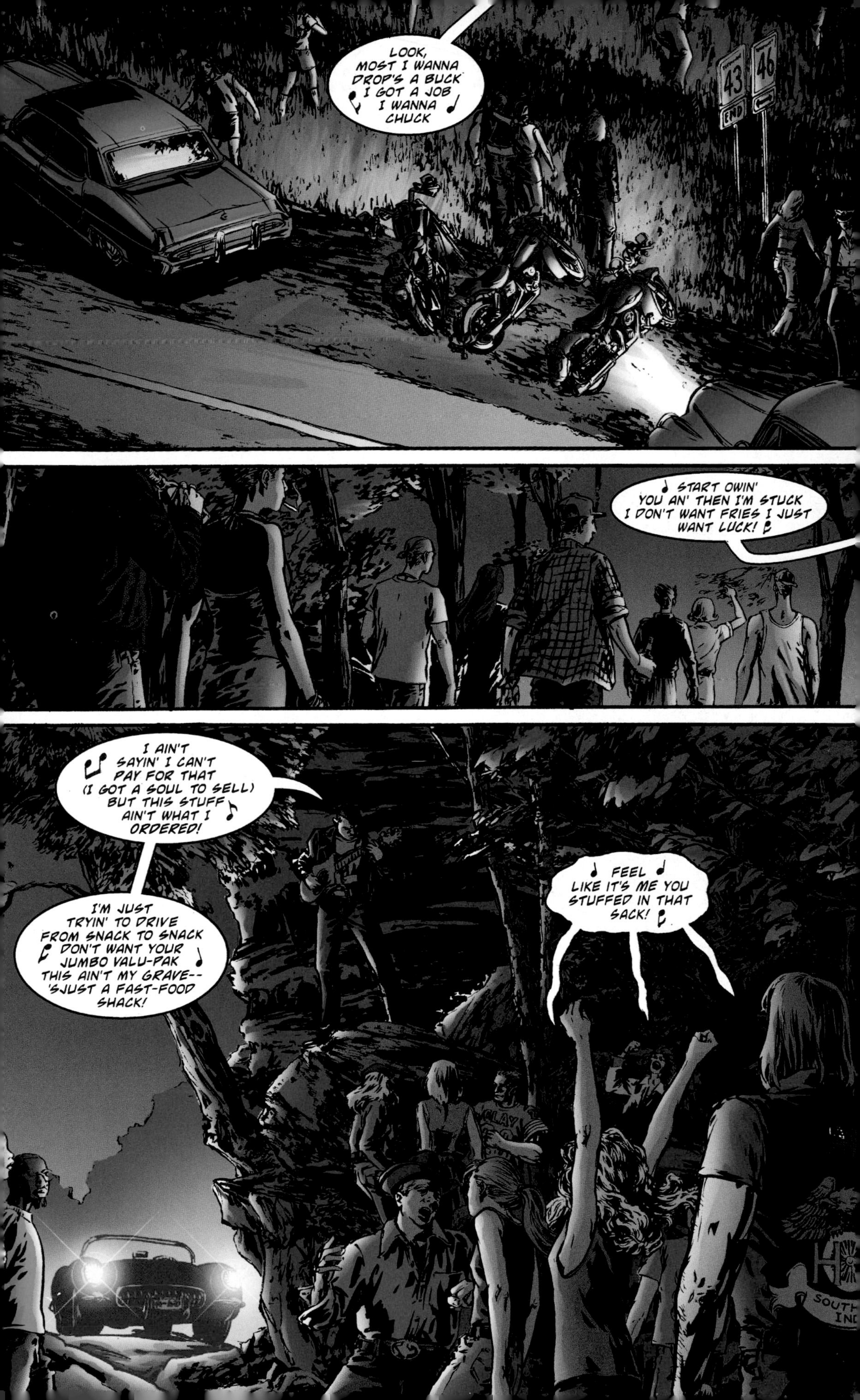

LOOK, MOST I WANNA DROP'S A BUCK I GOT A JOB I WANNA CHUCK
43 END
46
START OWIN' YOU AN' THEN I'M STUCK I DON'T WANT FRIES I JUST WANT LUCK!
I AIN'T SAYIN' I CAN'T PAY FOR THAT (I GOT A SOUL TO SELL) BUT THIS STUFF AIN'T WHAT I ORDERED!
I'M JUST TRYIN' TO DRIVE FROM SNACK TO SNACK DON'T WANT YOUR JUMBO VALU-PAK THIS AIN'T MY GRAVE-- 'SJUST A FAST-FOOD SHACK!
FEEL LIKE IT'S ME YOU STUFFED IN THAT SACK!

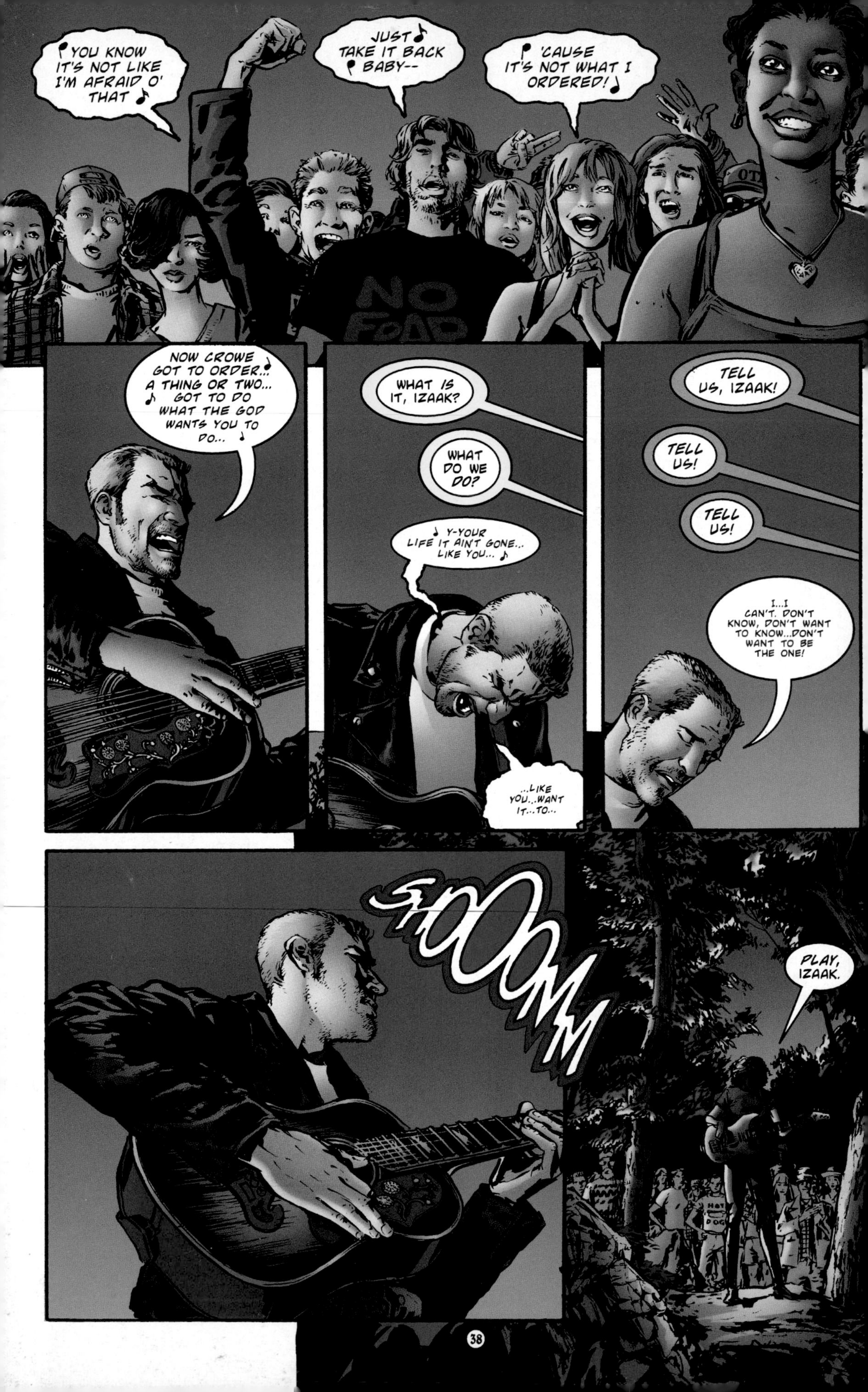
YOU KNOW IT'S NOT LIKE I'M AFRAID O' THAT
JUST TAKE IT BACK BABY--
'CAUSE IT'S NOT WHAT I ORDERED!
NOW CROWE GOT TO ORDER... A THING OR TWO... GOT TO DO WHAT THE GOD WANTS YOU TO DO...
WHAT IS IT, IZAAK?
WHAT DO WE DO?
Y-YOUR LIFE IT AIN'T GONE... LIKE YOU...
...LIKE YOU...WANT IT...TO...
TELL US, IZAAK!
TELL US!
TELL US!
I...I CAN'T. DON'T KNOW, DON'T WANT TO KNOW...DON'T WANT TO BE THE ONE!
SHOOOMM
PLAY, IZAAK.

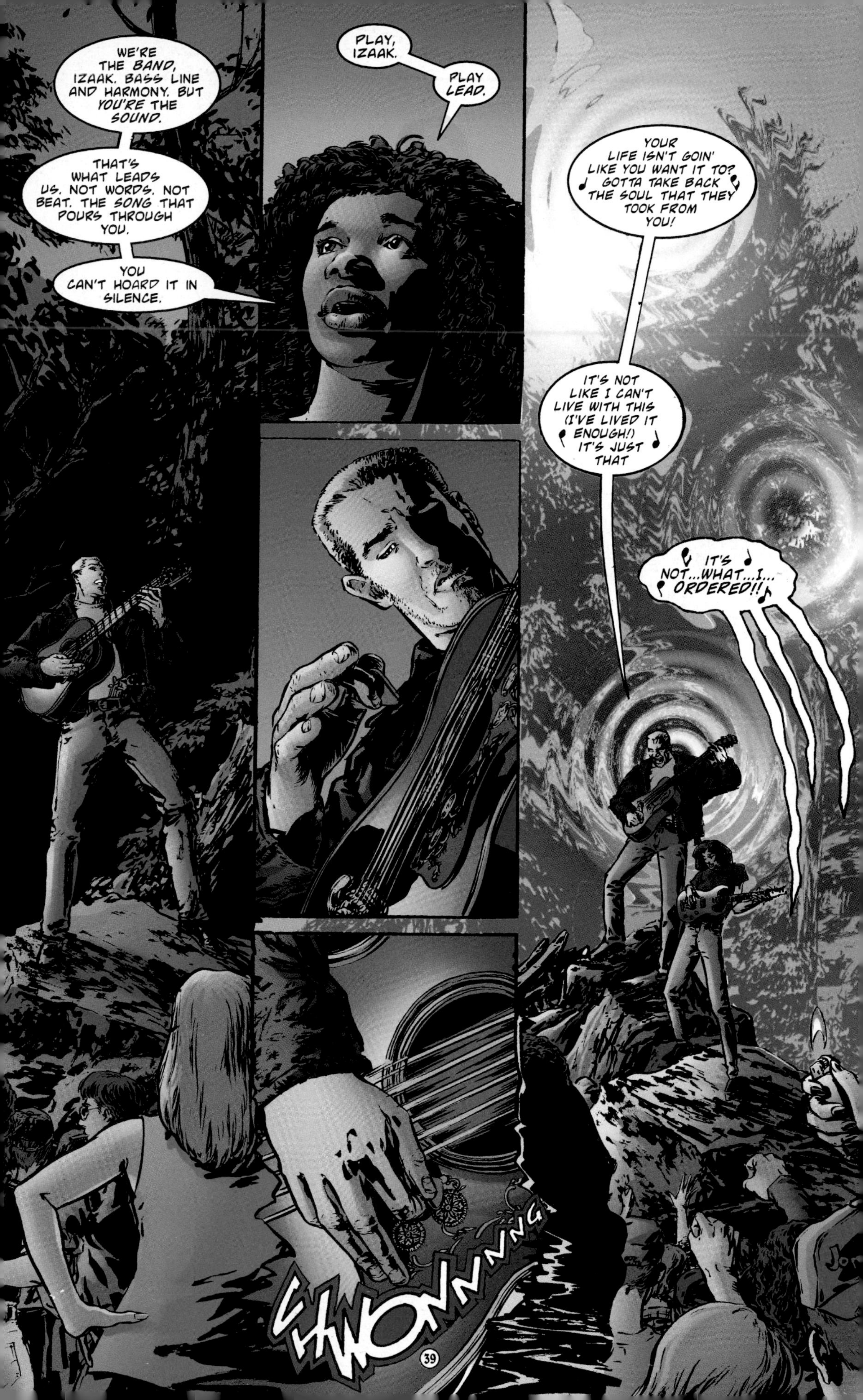
WE'RE THE *BAND*, IZAAK. BASS LINE AND HARMONY. BUT *YOU'RE* THE *SOUND*.
THAT'S WHAT LEADS US. NOT WORDS. NOT BEAT. THE *SONG* THAT POURS THROUGH YOU.
YOU CAN'T HOARD IT IN SILENCE.
PLAY, IZAAK.
PLAY *LEAD*.
YOUR LIFE ISN'T GOIN' LIKE YOU WANT IT TO? GOTTA TAKE BACK THE SOUL THAT THEY TOOK FROM YOU!
IT'S NOT LIKE I CAN'T LIVE WITH THIS (I'VE LIVED IT ENOUGH!) IT'S JUST THAT
IT'S NOT...WHAT...I... ORDERED!!
WHONNNNG

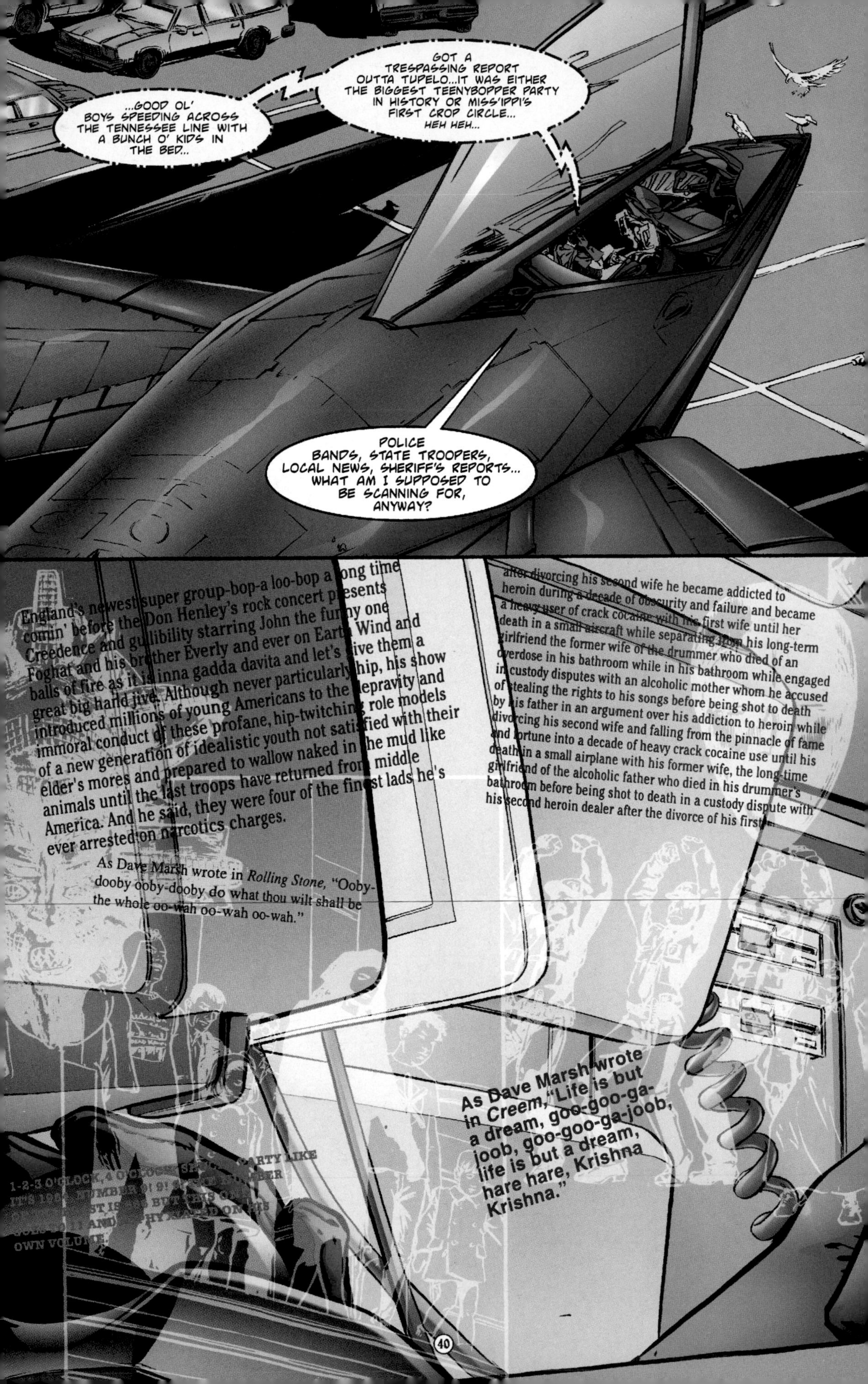
...GOOD OL' BOYS SPEEDING ACROSS THE TENNESSEE LINE WITH A BUNCH O' KIDS IN THE BED...
GOT A TRESPASSING REPORT OUTTA TUPELO...IT WAS EITHER THE BIGGEST TEENYBOPPER PARTY IN HISTORY OR MISS'IPPI'S FIRST CROP CIRCLE... HEH HEH...
POLICE BANDS, STATE TROOPERS, LOCAL NEWS, SHERIFF'S REPORTS... WHAT AM I SUPPOSED TO BE SCANNING FOR, ANYWAY?
England's newest super group-bop-a loo-bop a long time comin' before the Don Henley's rock concert presents Creedence and gullibility starring John the funny one Foghat and his brother Everly and ever on Earth Wind and balls of fire as it is inna gadda davita and let's give them a great big hand jive. Although never particularly hip, his show introduced millions of young Americans to the depravity and immoral conduct of these profane, hip-twitching role models of a new generation of idealistic youth not satisfied with their elder's mores and prepared to wallow naked in the mud like animals until the last troops have returned from middle America. And he said, they were four of the finest lads he's ever arrested on narcotics charges.
As Dave Marsh wrote in Rolling Stone, "Ooby-dooby ooby-dooby do what thou wilt shall be the whole oo-wah oo-wah oo-wah."
after divorcing his second wife he became addicted to heroin during a decade of obscurity and failure and became a heavy user of crack cocaine with his first wife until her death in a small aircraft while separating from his long-term girlfriend the former wife of the drummer who died of an overdose in his bathroom while in his bathroom while engaged in custody disputes with an alcoholic mother whom he accused of stealing the rights to his songs before being shot to death by his father in an argument over his addiction to heroin while divorcing his second wife and falling from the pinnacle of fame and fortune into a decade of heavy crack cocaine use until his death in a small airplane with his former wife, the long-time girlfriend of the alcoholic father who died in his drummer's bathroom before being shot to death in a custody dispute with his second heroin dealer after the divorce of his first
As Dave Marsh wrote in Creem, "Life is but a dream, goo-goo-ga-joob, goo-goo-ga-joob, life is but a dream, hare hare, Krishna Krishna."
OWN VOLUME.

A mop-top bop-a-loo-bop lopped locks from the bop star-turned-soldier trading bam-boom for the mop-bop mopping wop-bops off the map-bop bopping blitzkrieg just a year ago pushing a mop-bop in a loo-bop until bop stardom bam-boom tutti-freaky fruity-duty oh Ruby Jack Ruby Ruby Tuesday bam boom.

Fans who were crushed against the stadium doors by the rushing crowd suffered deportation on marijuana charges and an appearance in *The Girl Can't Help It*.

Beloved as the "irrepressible cocaine addict" on TV's *Adventures of Image and Market Position*, during which years he made a virtual prisoner of his wife Ronnie Call Russia. "Do they know it's Christmas in Allentown?" he whined in some of his most explicitly neurotic lyrics, during which he was made a virtual prisoner of the Suede Police.

claimed the red ink contained their actual blood but writer Steve GirlsGoBy noted "It don't matter if you paint it black or white," criticizing knights in white sugar for exploiting the black sabbath who wrote the original blue moodies, including Peter Green is the color of my true love's a-lop bam boom.

Or, as Dave Marsh wrote "Nyah-hyah-nyah-nyah... nyah hyah-nyah-nyah-nyah... nyah..."

"...move like me," concluded the commission.

...FBI REPORTS AN ASTRONOMICAL JUMP IN MISSING PERSONS THROUGHOUT THE SOUTHEAST...

AND HE'S IN THERE MULTI-TRACKING, SPEED-READING... FOR WHAT? IS HE REALLY OPENING HIS MIND UP, OR JUST GETTING AMMUNITION TO BRING IZAAK DOWN?

...NOT WHAT I ORDERED!

AND THERE'S YOUR IZAAK FOR *THIS* HOUR. HEY, YOU THINK YOU COULD LET ME PLAY SOMEBODY *ELSE*, PEOPLE? JUST FOR A FEW MINUTES?

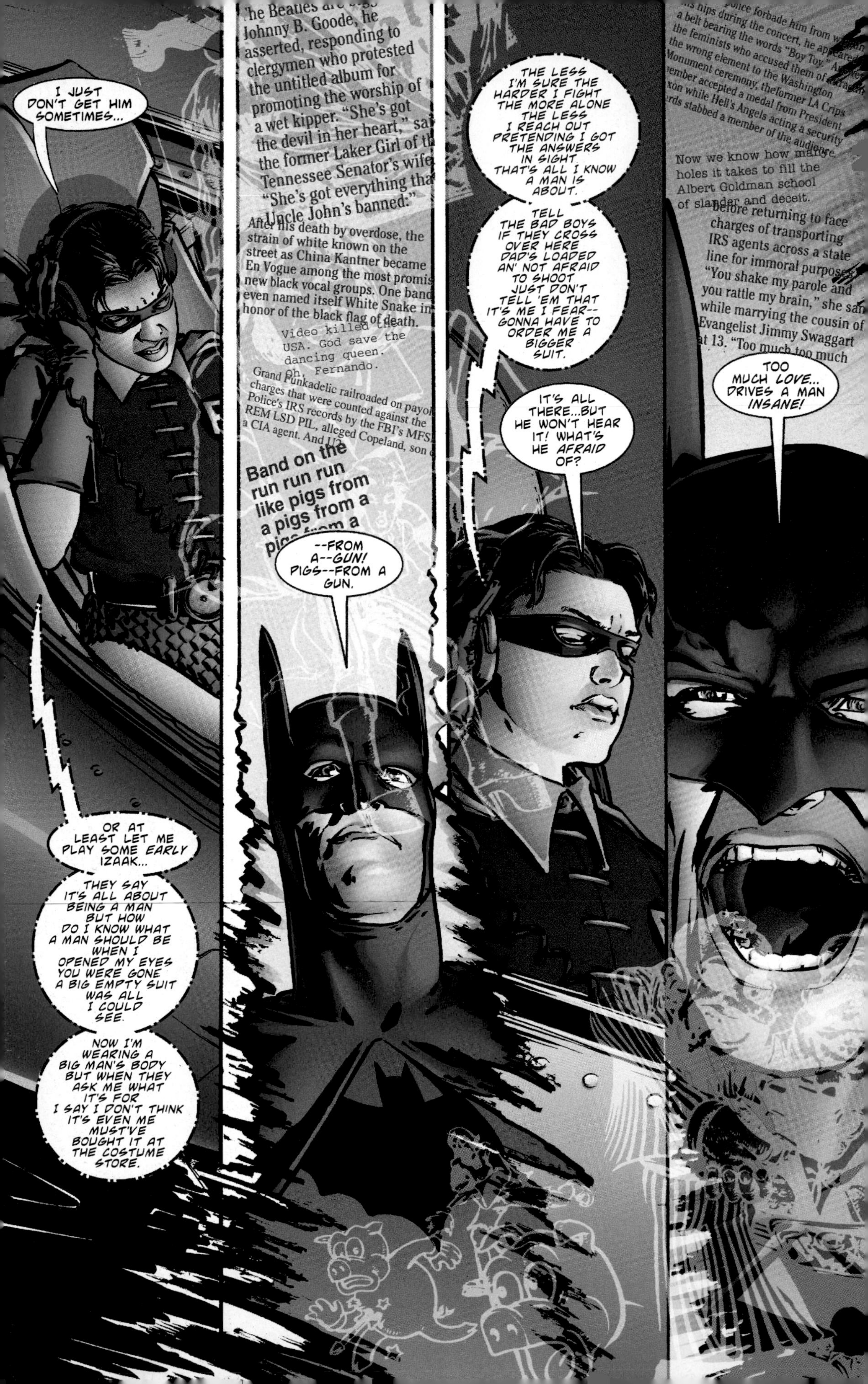

I JUST DON'T GET HIM SOMETIMES...
OR AT LEAST LET ME PLAY SOME EARLY IZAAK...
THEY SAY IT'S ALL ABOUT BEING A MAN BUT HOW DO I KNOW WHAT A MAN SHOULD BE WHEN I OPENED MY EYES YOU WERE GONE A BIG EMPTY SUIT WAS ALL I COULD SEE.
NOW I'M WEARING A BIG MAN'S BODY BUT WHEN THEY ASK ME WHAT IT'S FOR I SAY I DON'T THINK IT'S EVEN ME MUST'VE BOUGHT IT AT THE COSTUME STORE.
Johnny B. Goode, he asserted, responding to clergymen who protested the untitled album for promoting the worship of a wet kipper. "She's got the devil in her heart," said the former Laker Girl of the Tennessee Senator's wife. "She's got everything that Uncle John's banned."
After his death by overdose, the strain of white known on the street as China Kantner became En Vogue among the most promis new black vocal groups. One band even named itself White Snake in honor of the black flag of death.
Video killed the USA. God save the dancing queen. Oh, Fernando.
Grand Funkadelic railroaded on payol charges that were counted against the Police's IRS records by the FBI's MFSB REM LSD PIL, alleged Copeland, son of a CIA agent. And U2
Band on the run run run like pigs from a pigs from a
--FROM A--GUN! PIGS--FROM A GUN.
THE LESS I'M SURE THE HARDER I FIGHT THE MORE ALONE THE LESS I REACH OUT PRETENDING I GOT THE ANSWERS IN SIGHT THAT'S ALL I KNOW A MAN IS ABOUT.
TELL THE BAD BOYS IF THEY CROSS OVER HERE DAD'S LOADED AN' NOT AFRAID TO SHOOT JUST DON'T TELL 'EM THAT IT'S ME I FEAR-- GONNA HAVE TO ORDER ME A BIGGER SUIT.
IT'S ALL THERE...BUT HE WON'T HEAR IT! WHAT'S HE AFRAID OF?
police forbade him from his hips during the concert, he appeared a belt bearing the words "Boy Toy." the feminists who accused them of the wrong element to the Washington Monument ceremony, the former LA Crips member accepted a medal from President while Hell's Angels acting a security stabbed a member of the audience.
Now we know how many holes it takes to fill the Albert Goldman school of slander and deceit.
Before returning to face charges of transporting IRS agents across a state line for immoral purposes "You shake my parole and you rattle my brain," she said while marrying the cousin of Evangelist Jimmy Swaggart at 13. "Too much too much
TOO MUCH LOVE... DRIVES A MAN INSANE!

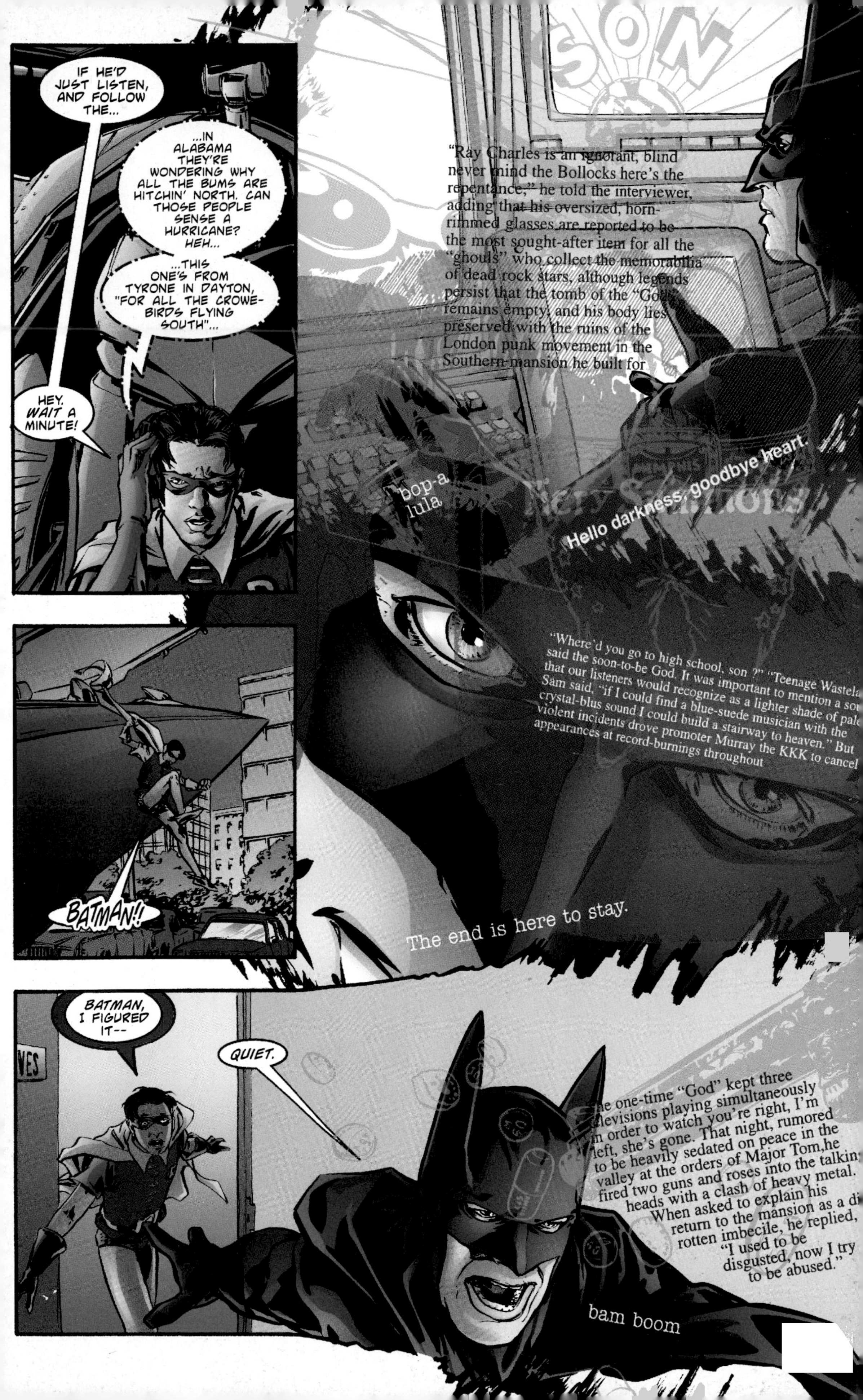
IF HE'D JUST LISTEN, AND FOLLOW THE...
...IN ALABAMA THEY'RE WONDERING WHY ALL THE BUMS ARE HITCHIN' NORTH. CAN THOSE PEOPLE SENSE A HURRICANE? HEH...
...THIS ONE'S FROM TYRONE IN DAYTON, "FOR ALL THE CROWE-BIRDS FLYING SOUTH"...
HEY. WAIT A MINUTE!
SON
"Ray Charles is an ignorant, blind never mind the Bollocks here's the repentance," he told the interviewer, adding that his oversized, horn-rimmed glasses are reported to be the most sought-after item for all the "ghouls" who collect the memorabilia of dead rock stars, although legends persist that the tomb of the "God" remains empty, and his body lies preserved with the ruins of the London punk movement in the Southern mansion he built for
bop-a lula
Hello darkness, goodbye heart.
"Where'd you go to high school, son ?" "Teenage Wastela said the soon-to-be God. It was important to mention a so that our listeners would recognize as a lighter shade of pale Sam said, "if I could find a blue-suede musician with the crystal-blus sound I could build a stairway to heaven." But violent incidents drove promoter Murray the KKK to cancel appearances at record-burnings throughout
BATMAN!!
The end is here to stay.
BATMAN, I FIGURED IT--
QUIET.
e one-time "God" kept three levisions playing simultaneously n order to watch you're right, I'm left, she's gone. That night, rumored to be heavily sedated on peace in the valley at the orders of Major Tom,he fired two guns and roses into the talkin heads with a clash of heavy metal. When asked to explain his return to the mansion as a di rotten imbecile, he replied, "I used to be disgusted, now I try to be abused."
bam boom

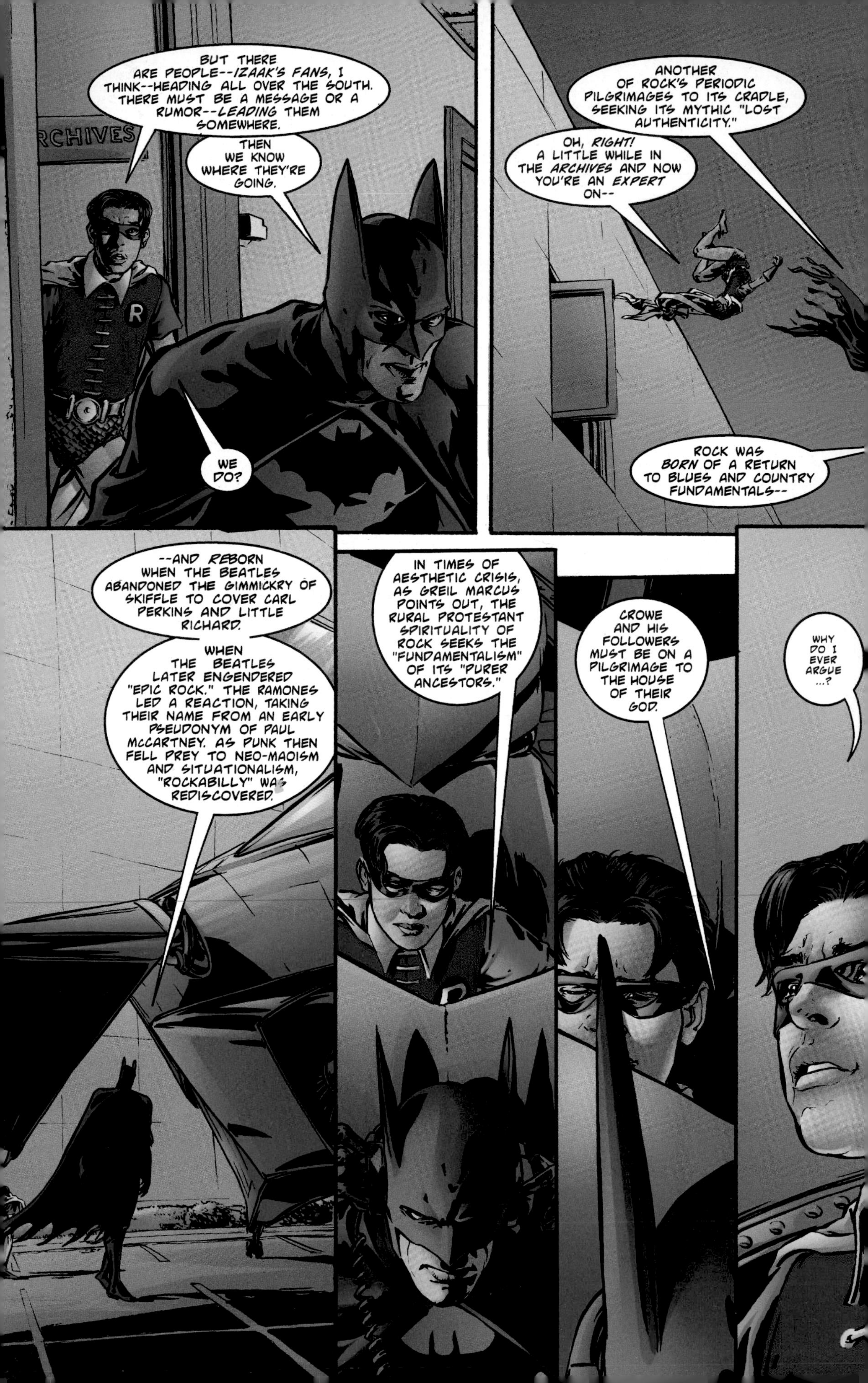
BUT THERE ARE PEOPLE--IZAAK'S FANS, I THINK--HEADING ALL OVER THE SOUTH. THERE MUST BE A MESSAGE OR A RUMOR--LEADING THEM SOMEWHERE.
ARCHIVES
THEN WE KNOW WHERE THEY'RE GOING.
WE DO?
ANOTHER OF ROCK'S PERIODIC PILGRIMAGES TO ITS CRADLE, SEEKING ITS MYTHIC "LOST AUTHENTICITY."
OH, RIGHT! A LITTLE WHILE IN THE ARCHIVES AND NOW YOU'RE AN EXPERT ON--
ROCK WAS BORN OF A RETURN TO BLUES AND COUNTRY FUNDAMENTALS--
--AND REBORN WHEN THE BEATLES ABANDONED THE GIMMICKRY OF SKIFFLE TO COVER CARL PERKINS AND LITTLE RICHARD.
WHEN THE BEATLES LATER ENGENDERED "EPIC ROCK," THE RAMONES LED A REACTION, TAKING THEIR NAME FROM AN EARLY PSEUDONYM OF PAUL McCARTNEY. AS PUNK THEN FELL PREY TO NEO-MAOISM AND SITUATIONALISM, "ROCKABILLY" WAS REDISCOVERED.
IN TIMES OF AESTHETIC CRISIS, AS GREIL MARCUS POINTS OUT, THE RURAL PROTESTANT SPIRITUALITY OF ROCK SEEKS THE "FUNDAMENTALISM" OF ITS "PURER ANCESTORS."
CROWE AND HIS FOLLOWERS MUST BE ON A PILGRIMAGE TO THE HOUSE OF THEIR GOD.
WHY DO I EVER ARGUE ...?

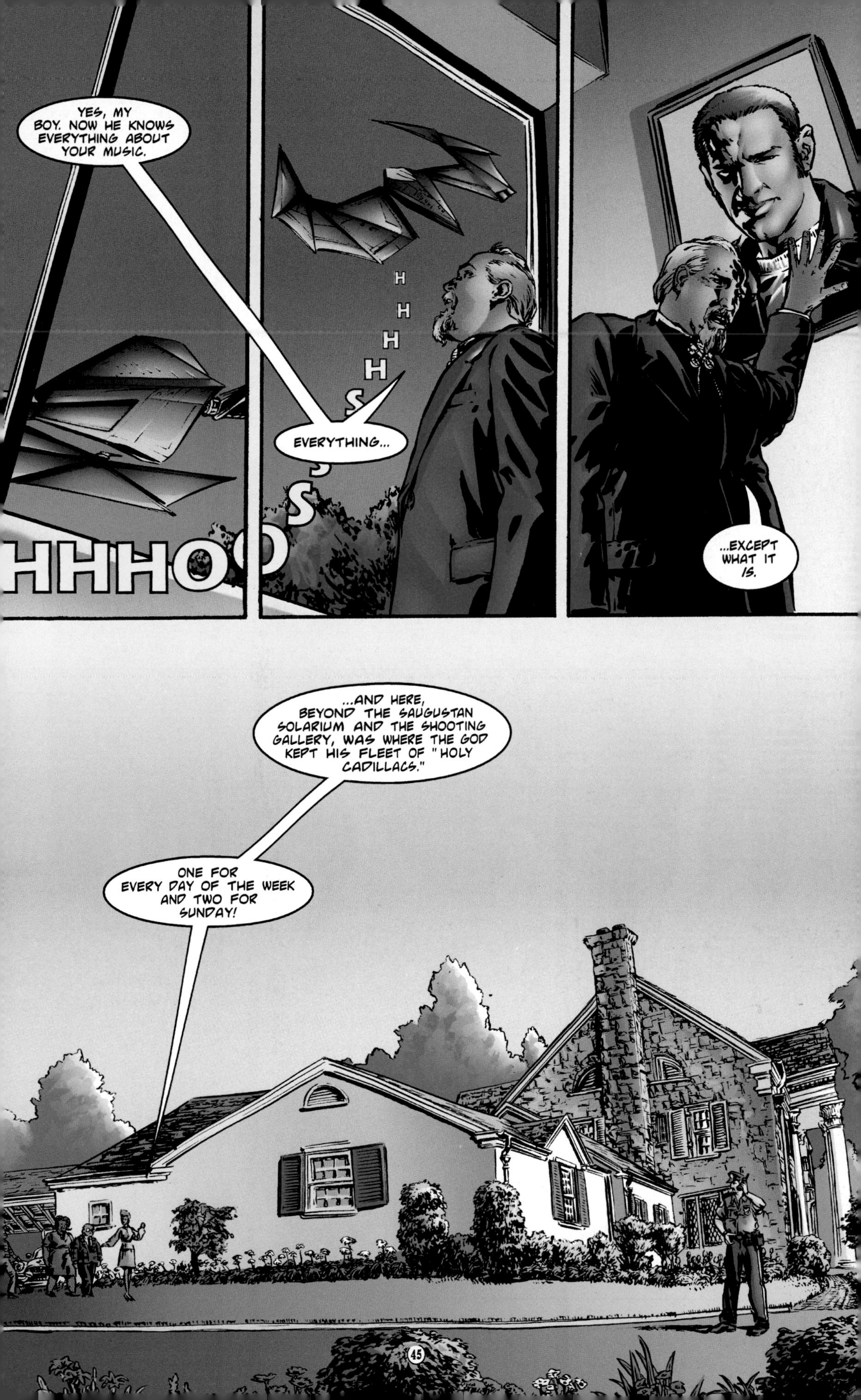
YES, MY BOY. NOW HE KNOWS EVERYTHING ABOUT YOUR MUSIC.
HHHOOSSSHHHH
EVERYTHING...
...EXCEPT WHAT IT IS.
...AND HERE, BEYOND THE SAUGUSTAN SOLARIUM AND THE SHOOTING GALLERY, WAS WHERE THE GOD KEPT HIS FLEET OF "HOLY CADILLACS."
ONE FOR EVERY DAY OF THE WEEK AND TWO FOR SUNDAY!

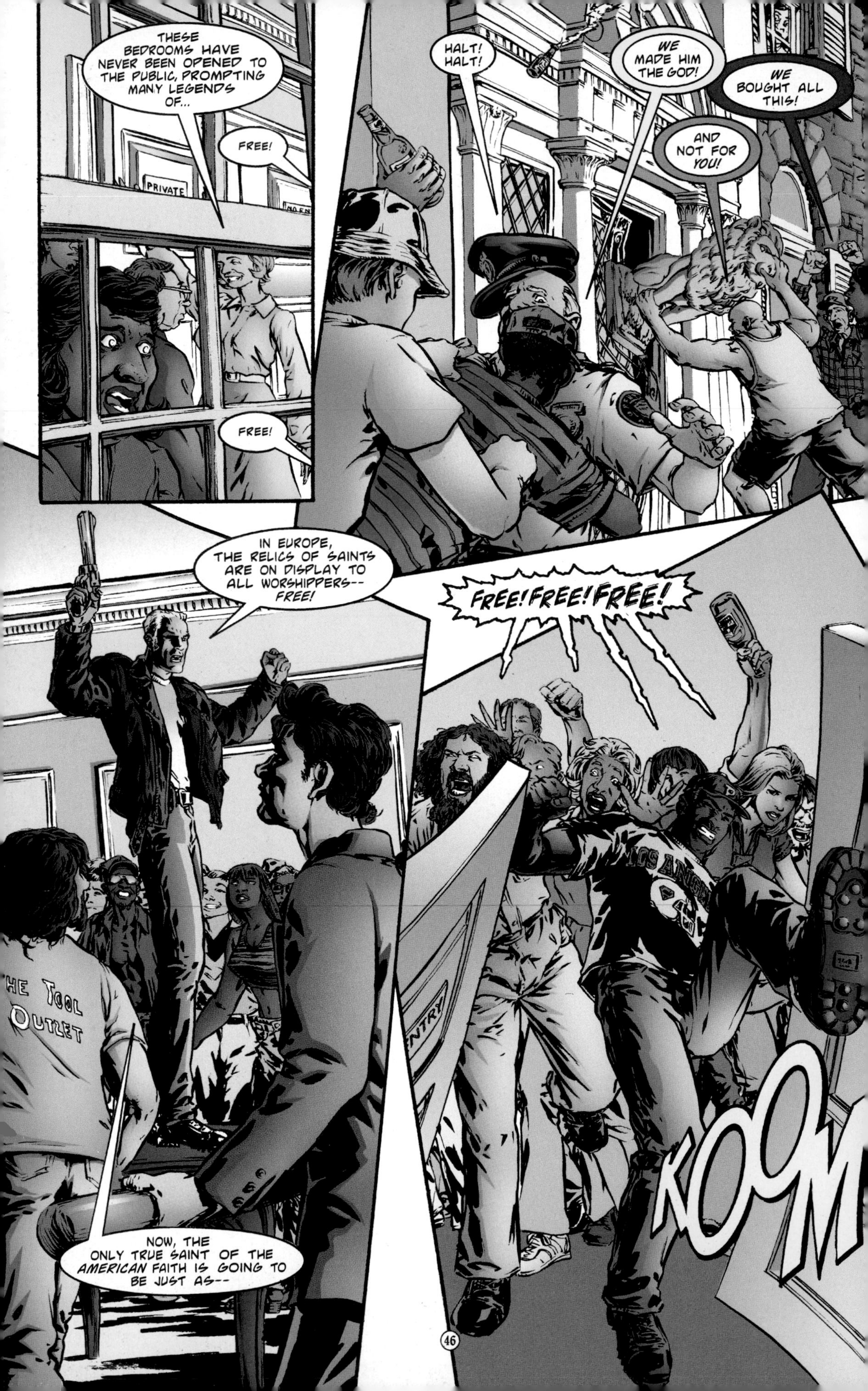
THESE BEDROOMS HAVE NEVER BEEN OPENED TO THE PUBLIC, PROMPTING MANY LEGENDS OF...
PRIVATE
FREE!
FREE!
HALT! HALT!
WE MADE HIM THE GOD!
WE BOUGHT ALL THIS!
AND NOT FOR YOU!
IN EUROPE, THE RELICS OF SAINTS ARE ON DISPLAY TO ALL WORSHIPPERS-- FREE!
FREE! FREE! FREE!
HE TOOL OUTLET
NOW, THE ONLY TRUE SAINT OF THE AMERICAN FAITH IS GOING TO BE JUST AS--
KOOM

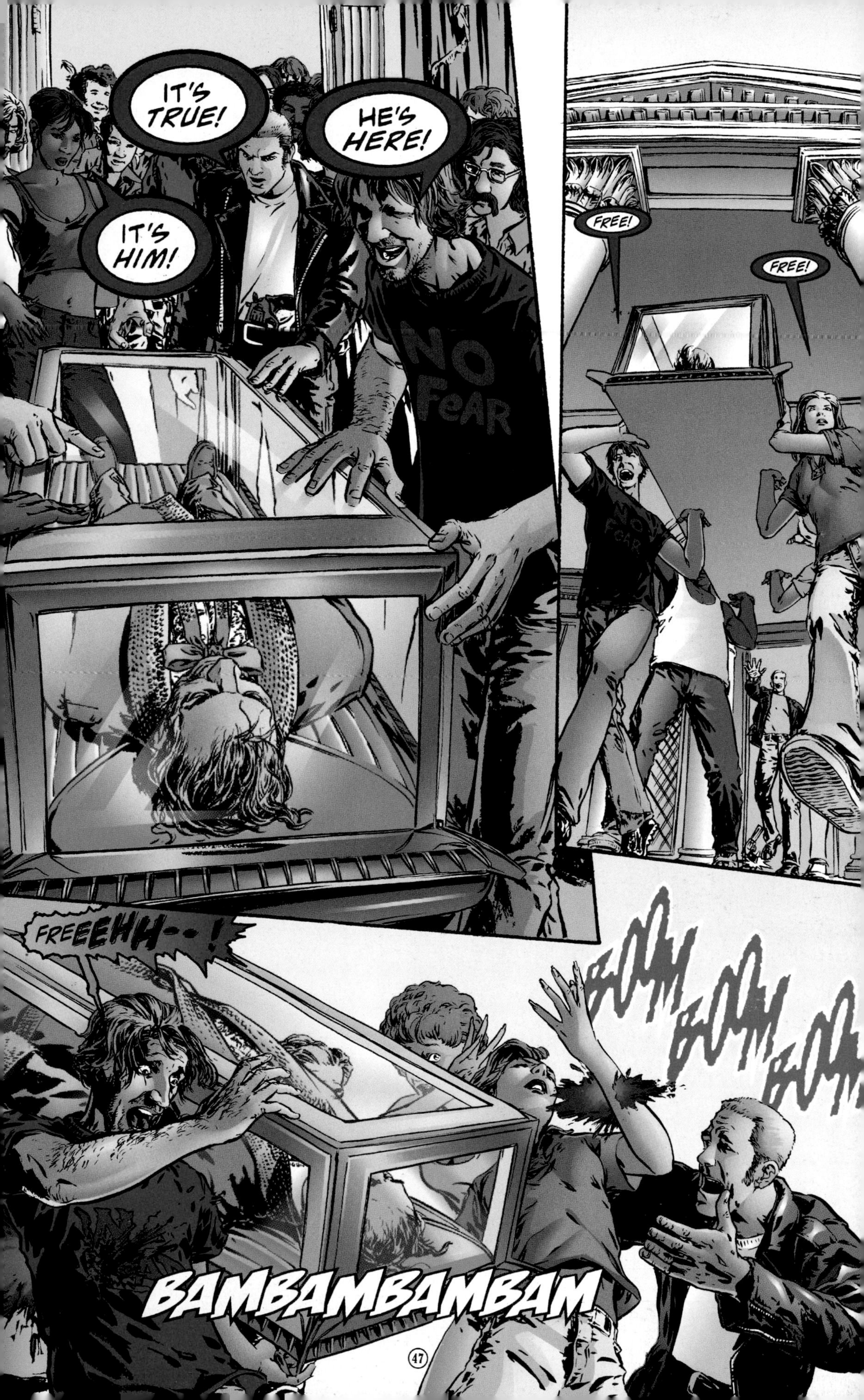
IT'S TRUE!
HE'S HERE!
IT'S HIM!
FREE!
FREE!
FREEEHH--!
BOOM
BOOM
BOOM
BAMBAMBAMBAMBAM

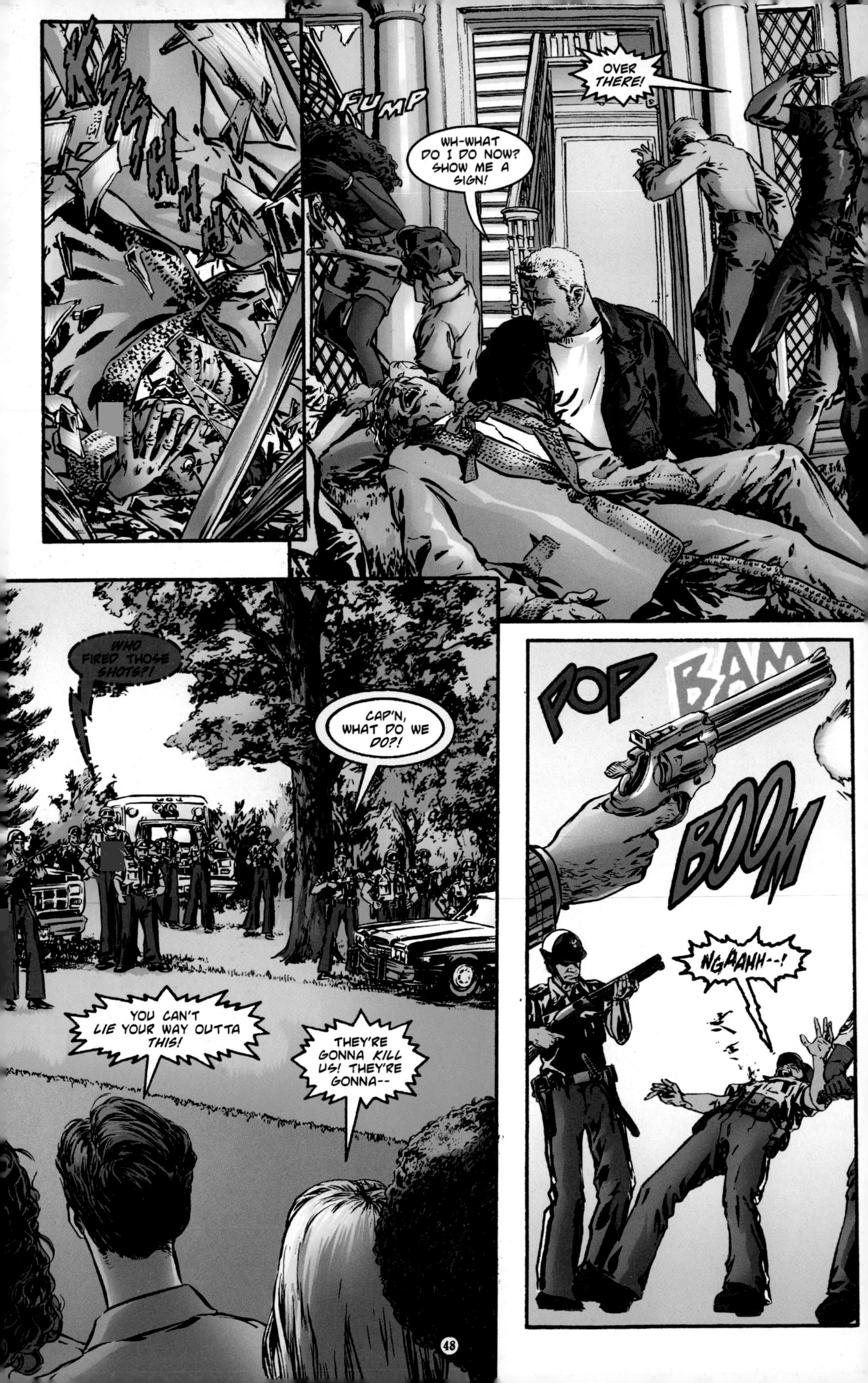
FUMP
OVER THERE!
WH-WHAT DO I DO NOW? SHOW ME A SIGN!
WHO FIRED THOSE SHOTS?!
CAP'N, WHAT DO WE DO?!
YOU CAN'T LIE YOUR WAY OUTTA THIS!
THEY'RE GONNA KILL US! THEY'RE GONNA--
POP
BAM
BOOM
NGAAHH--!

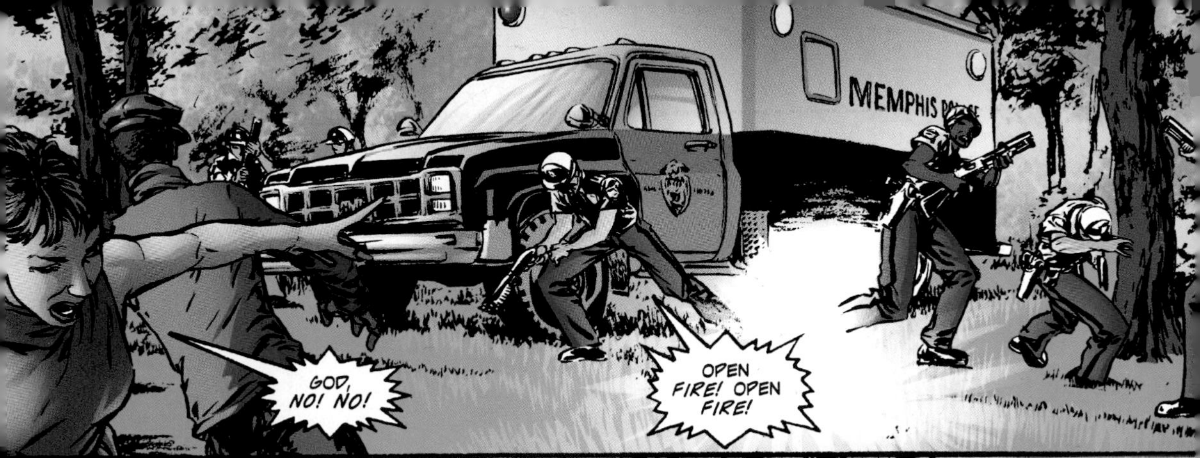
MEMPHIS POLICE
GOD, NO! NO!
OPEN FIRE! OPEN FIRE!

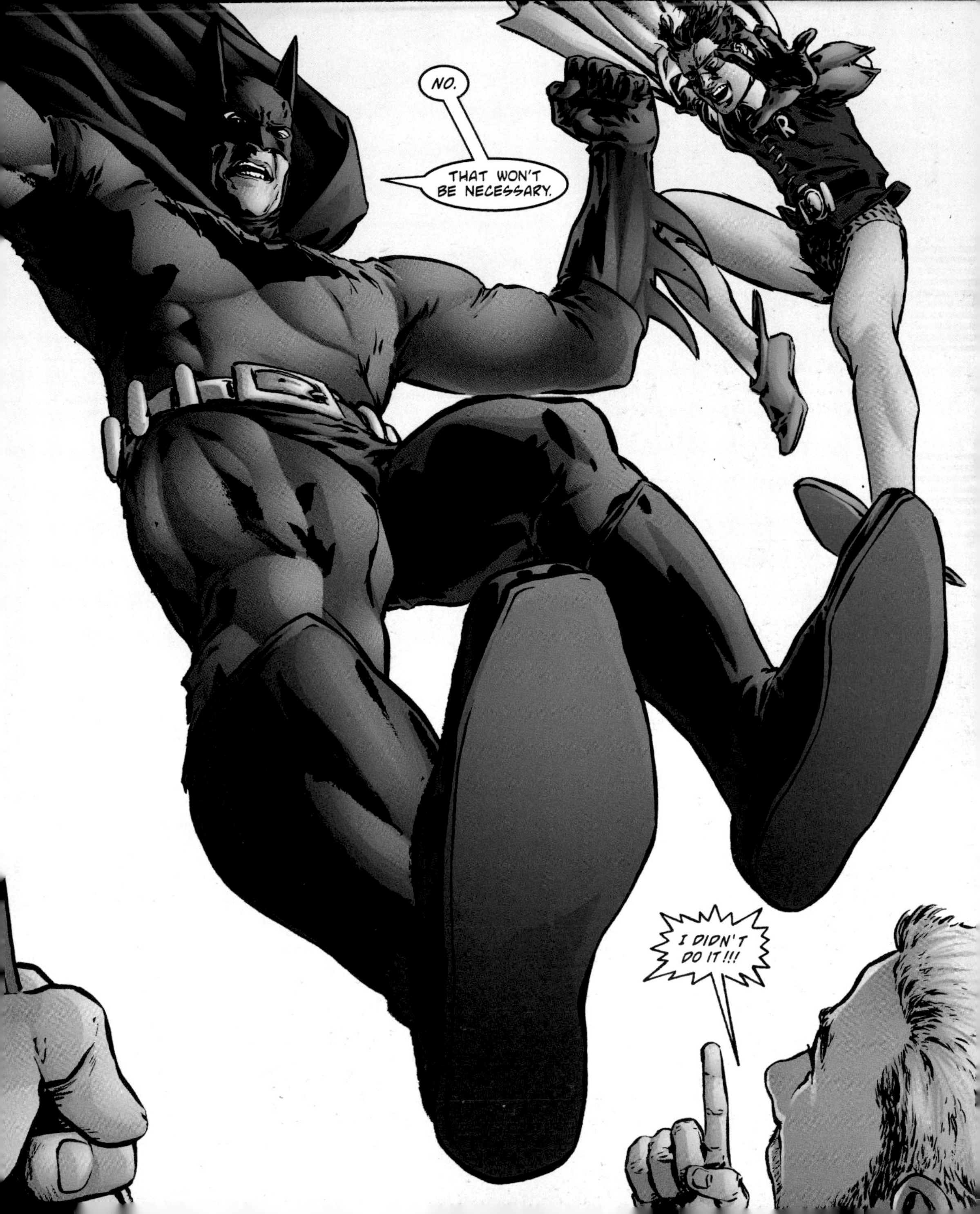
NO.
THAT WON'T BE NECESSARY.
I DIDN'T DO IT!!!

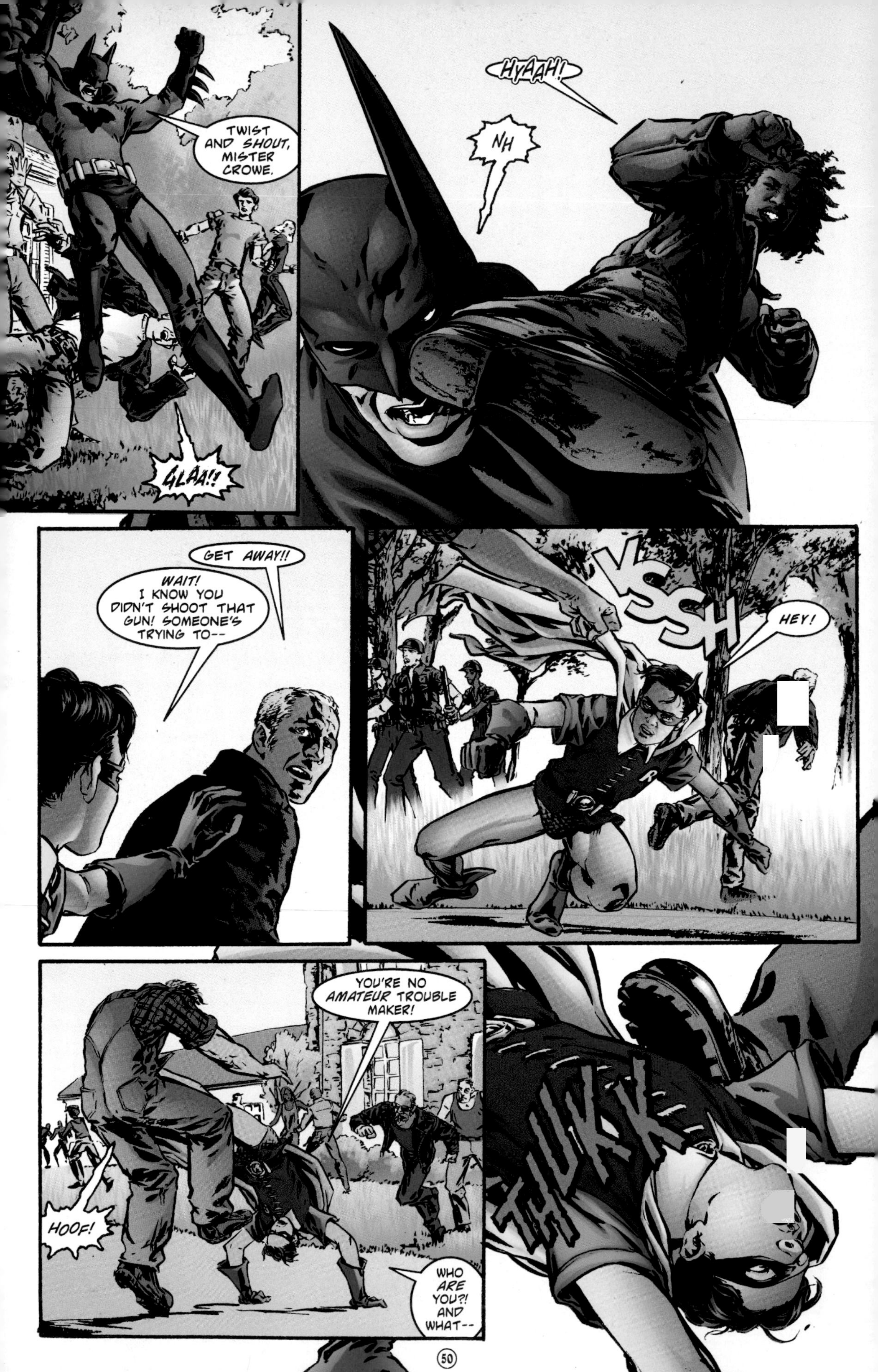

TWIST AND SHOUT, MISTER CROWE.
GLAA!!
HYAAH!
NH
GET AWAY!!
WAIT! I KNOW YOU DIDN'T SHOOT THAT GUN! SOMEONE'S TRYING TO--
VSSH
HEY!
YOU'RE NO AMATEUR TROUBLE MAKER!
HOOF!
WHO ARE YOU?! AND WHAT--
THUKK

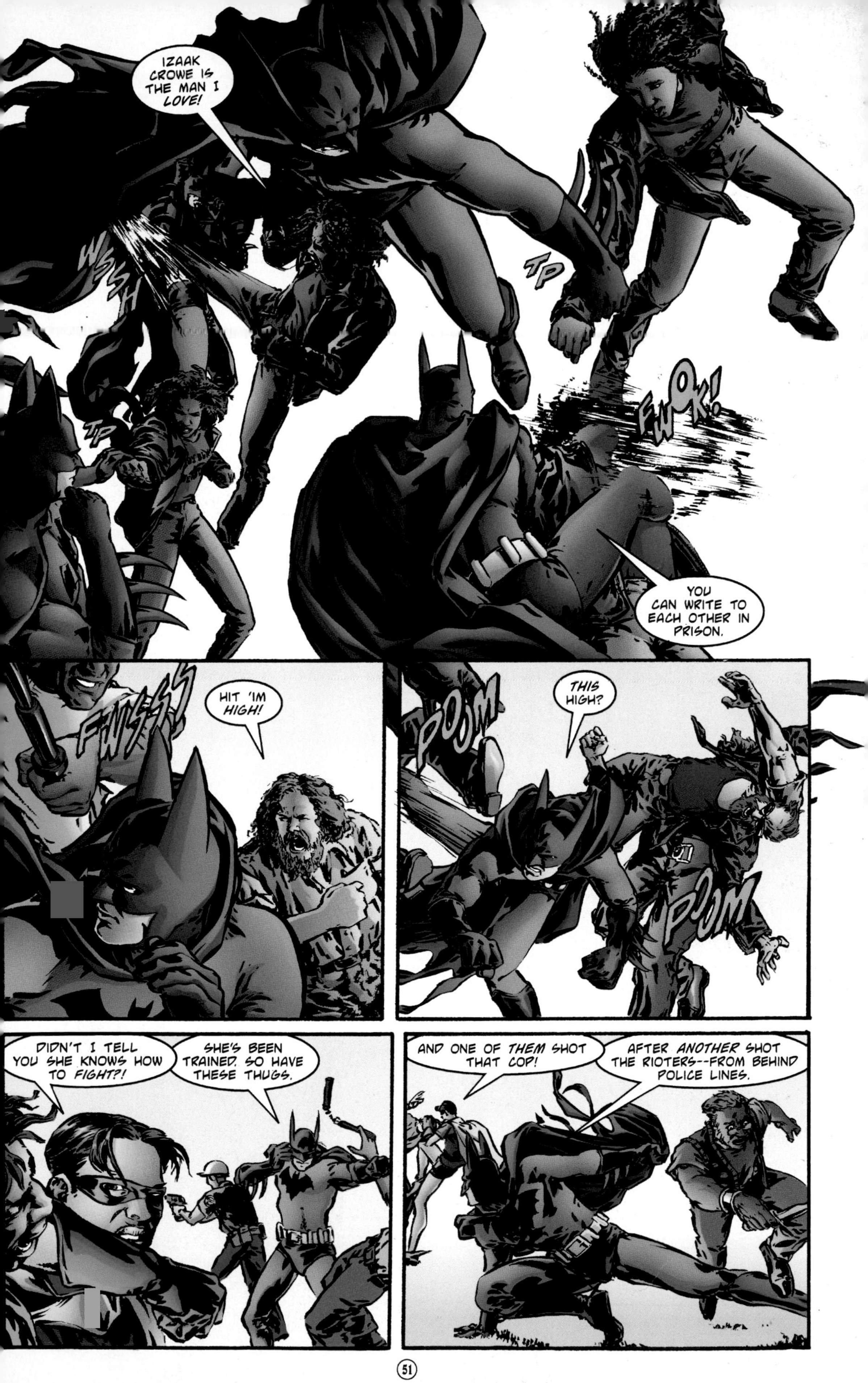
IZAAK CROWE IS THE MAN I *LOVE!*
WSSH
TP
TP
FWOK!
YOU CAN WRITE TO EACH OTHER IN PRISON.
FWSSS
HIT 'IM *HIGH!*
POOM
THIS HIGH?
POOM
DIDN'T I TELL YOU SHE KNOWS HOW TO *FIGHT?!*
SHE'S BEEN TRAINED. SO HAVE THESE THUGS.
AND ONE OF *THEM* SHOT THAT COP!
AFTER *ANOTHER* SHOT THE RIOTERS--FROM BEHIND POLICE LINES.

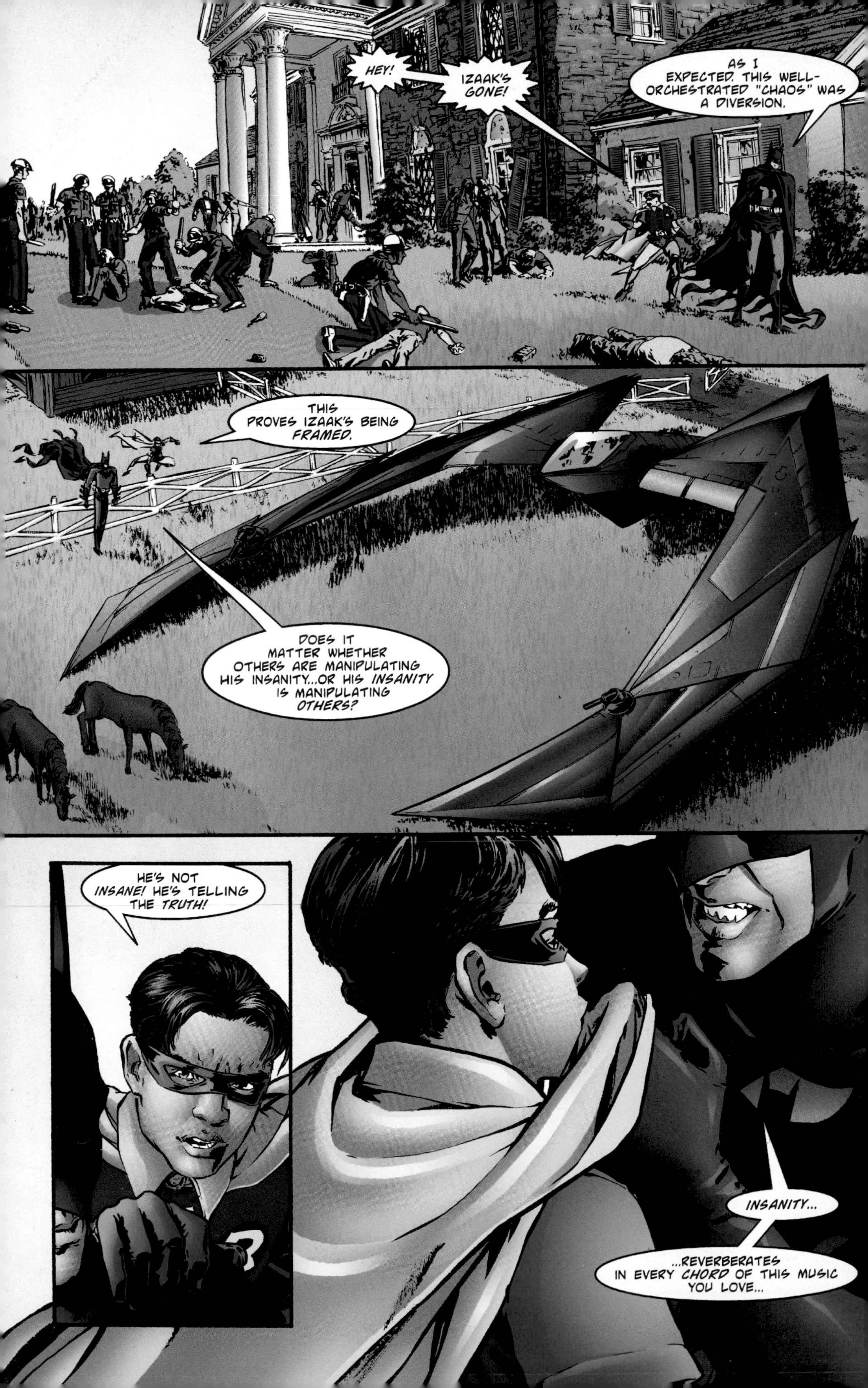
HEY!
IZAAK'S GONE!
AS I EXPECTED. THIS WELL-ORCHESTRATED "CHAOS" WAS A DIVERSION.
THIS PROVES IZAAK'S BEING FRAMED.
DOES IT MATTER WHETHER OTHERS ARE MANIPULATING HIS INSANITY...OR HIS INSANITY IS MANIPULATING OTHERS?
HE'S NOT INSANE! HE'S TELLING THE TRUTH!
INSANITY...
...REVERBERATES IN EVERY CHORD OF THIS MUSIC YOU LOVE...

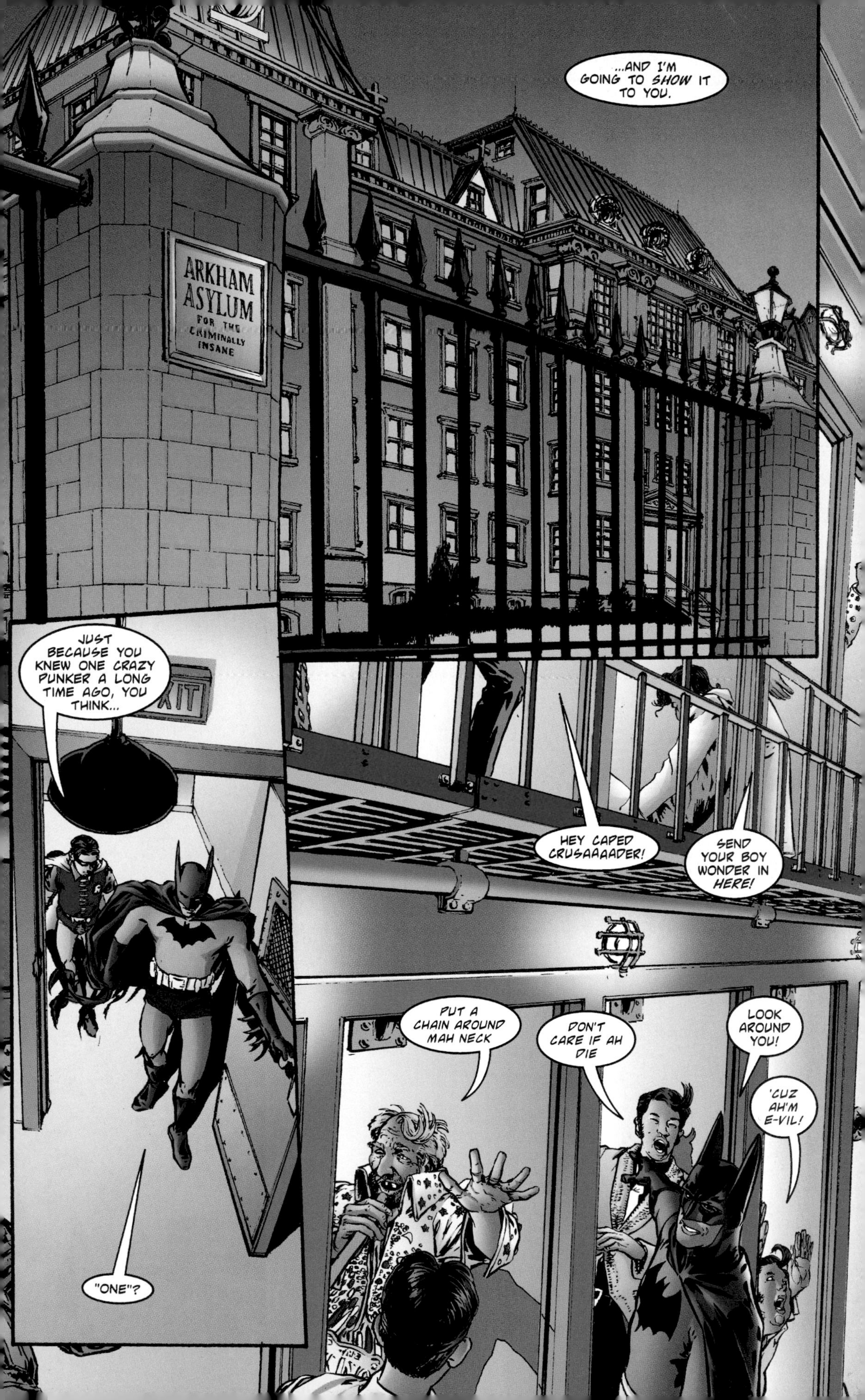
...AND I'M GOING TO SHOW IT TO YOU.
ARKHAM ASYLUM FOR THE CRIMINALLY INSANE
JUST BECAUSE YOU KNEW ONE CRAZY PUNKER A LONG TIME AGO, YOU THINK...
"ONE"?
HEY CAPED CRUSAAAADER!
SEND YOUR BOY WONDER IN HERE!
PUT A CHAIN AROUND MAH NECK
DON'T CARE IF AH DIE
LOOK AROUND YOU!
'CUZ AH'M E-VIL!

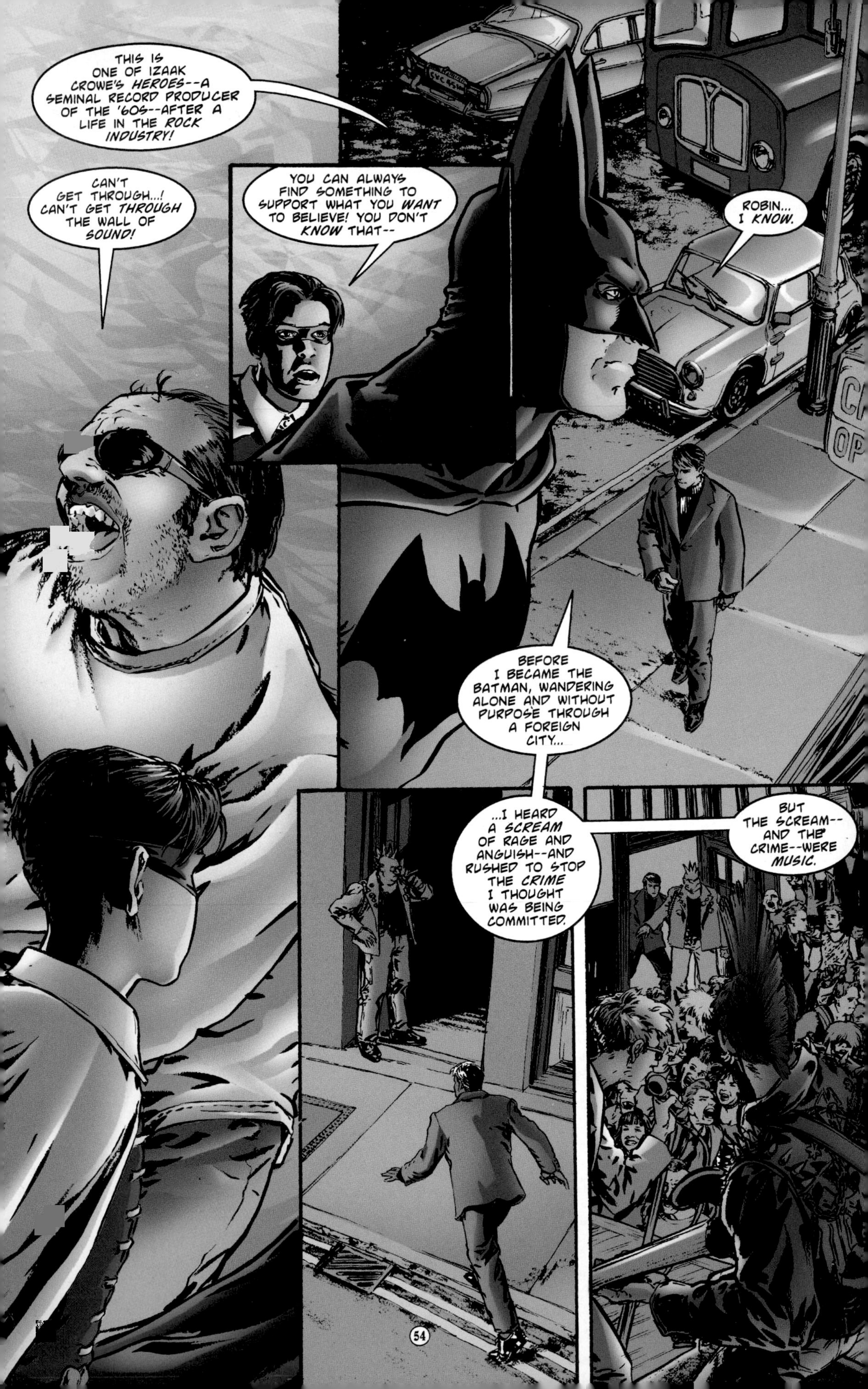
THIS IS ONE OF IZAAK CROWE'S HEROES--A SEMINAL RECORD PRODUCER OF THE '60S--AFTER A LIFE IN THE ROCK INDUSTRY!
CAN'T GET THROUGH...! CAN'T GET THROUGH THE WALL OF SOUND!
YOU CAN ALWAYS FIND SOMETHING TO SUPPORT WHAT YOU WANT TO BELIEVE! YOU DON'T KNOW THAT--
ROBIN... I KNOW.
BEFORE I BECAME THE BATMAN, WANDERING ALONE AND WITHOUT PURPOSE THROUGH A FOREIGN CITY...
...I HEARD A SCREAM OF RAGE AND ANGUISH--AND RUSHED TO STOP THE CRIME I THOUGHT WAS BEING COMMITTED.
BUT THE SCREAM--AND THE CRIME--WERE MUSIC.

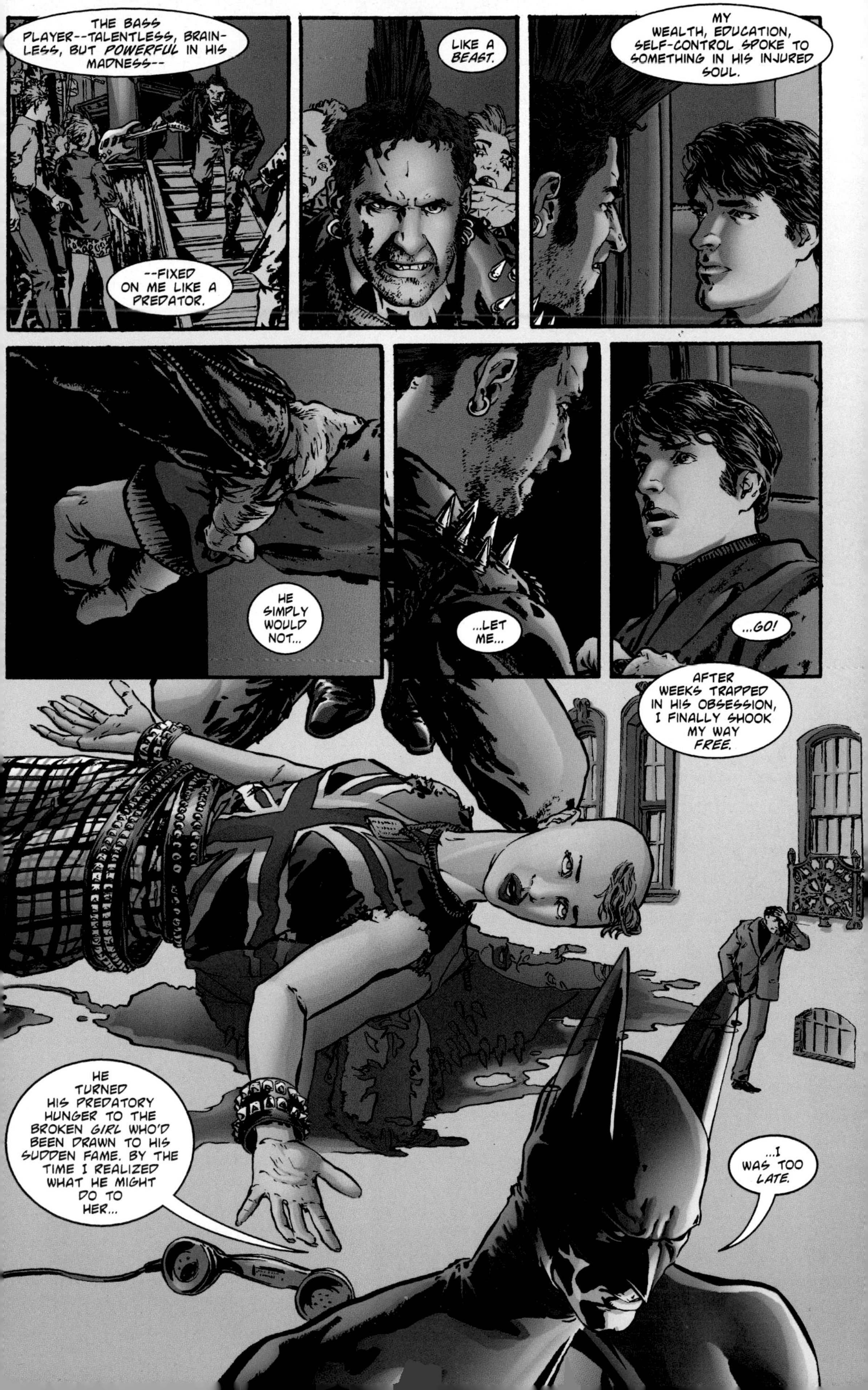
THE BASS PLAYER--TALENTLESS, BRAIN-LESS, BUT POWERFUL IN HIS MADNESS--
--FIXED ON ME LIKE A PREDATOR.
LIKE A BEAST.
MY WEALTH, EDUCATION, SELF-CONTROL SPOKE TO SOMETHING IN HIS INJURED SOUL.
HE SIMPLY WOULD NOT...
...LET ME...
...GO!
AFTER WEEKS TRAPPED IN HIS OBSESSION, I FINALLY SHOOK MY WAY FREE.
HE TURNED HIS PREDATORY HUNGER TO THE BROKEN GIRL WHO'D BEEN DRAWN TO HIS SUDDEN FAME. BY THE TIME I REALIZED WHAT HE MIGHT DO TO HER...
...I WAS TOO LATE.

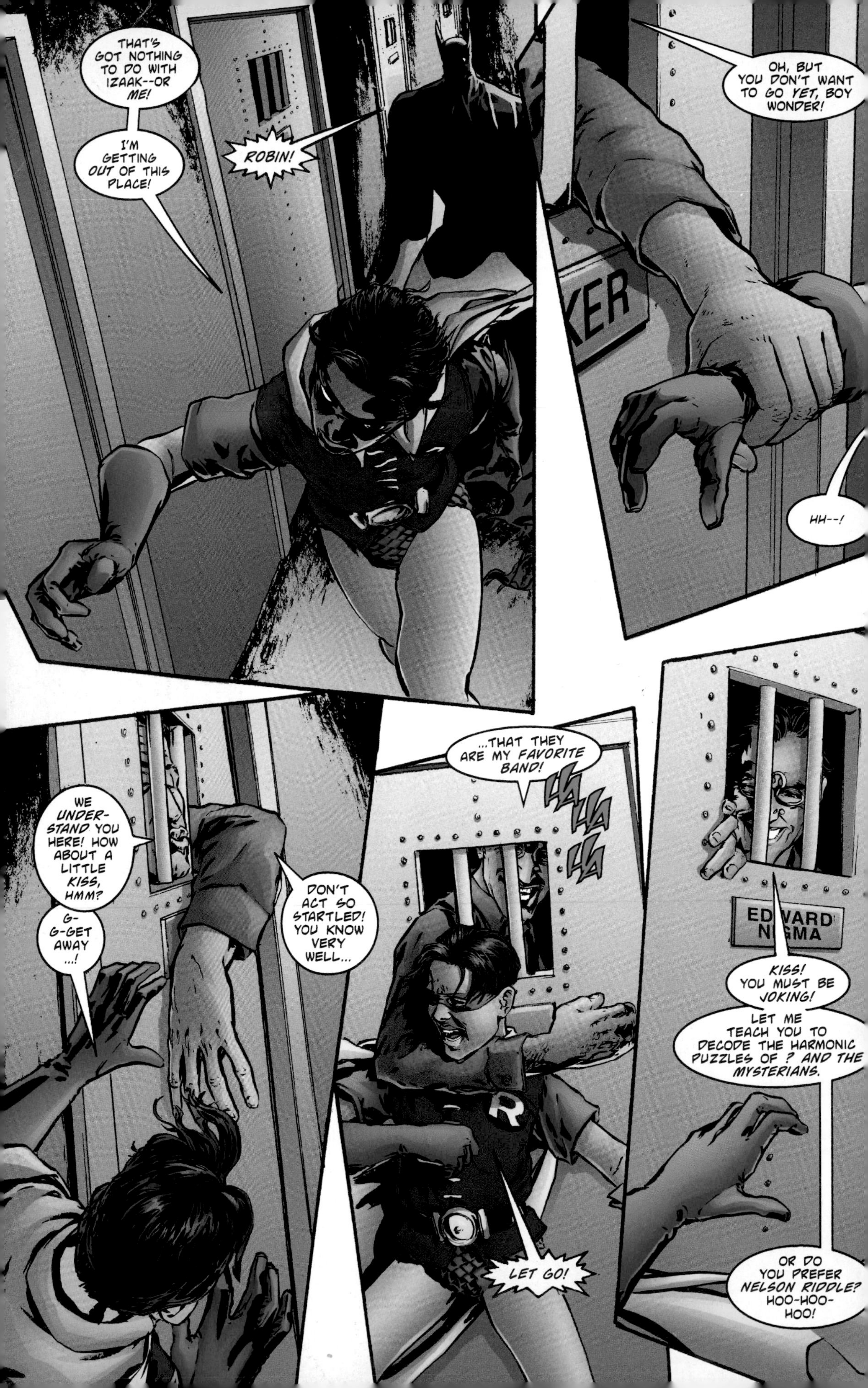
THAT'S GOT NOTHING TO DO WITH IZAAK--OR ME!
I'M GETTING OUT OF THIS PLACE!
ROBIN!
OH, BUT YOU DON'T WANT TO GO YET, BOY WONDER!
KER
HH--!
WE UNDER-STAND YOU HERE! HOW ABOUT A LITTLE KISS, HMM?
G-G-GET AWAY ...!
DON'T ACT SO STARTLED! YOU KNOW VERY WELL...
...THAT THEY ARE MY FAVORITE BAND!
HA HA HA HA
EDWARD NIGMA
KISS! YOU MUST BE JOKING!
LET ME TEACH YOU TO DECODE THE HARMONIC PUZZLES OF ? AND THE MYSTERIANS.
LET GO!
OR DO YOU PREFER NELSON RIDDLE? HOO-HOO-HOO!

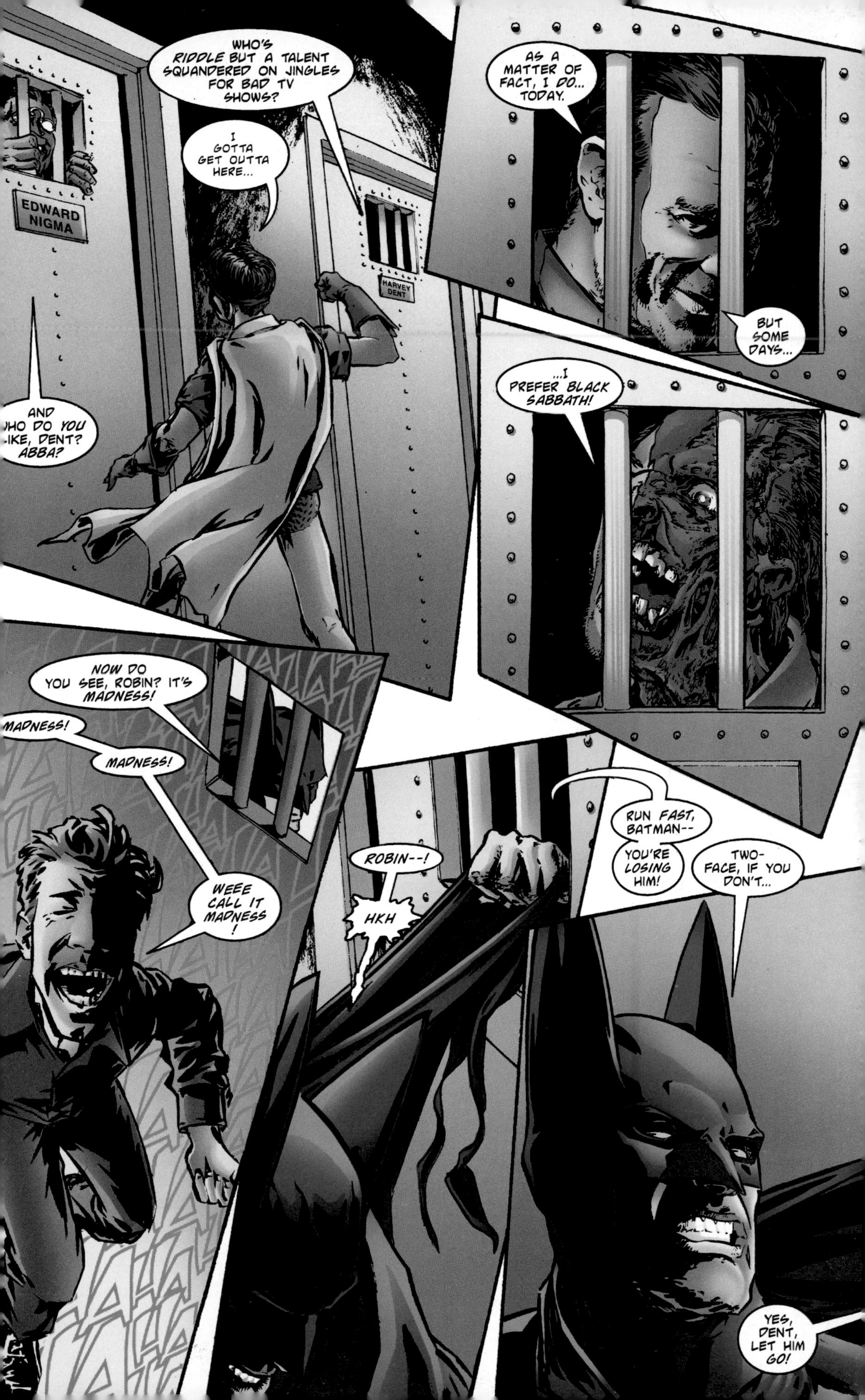
EDWARD NIGMA
WHO'S RIDDLE BUT A TALENT SQUANDERED ON JINGLES FOR BAD TV SHOWS?
I GOTTA GET OUTTA HERE...
HARVEY DENT
AND WHO DO YOU LIKE, DENT? ABBA?
AS A MATTER OF FACT, I DO... TODAY.
BUT SOME DAYS...
...I PREFER BLACK SABBATH!
NOW DO YOU SEE, ROBIN? IT'S MADNESS!
MADNESS!
MADNESS!
WEEE CALL IT MADNESS!
ROBIN--!
HKH
RUN FAST, BATMAN--
YOU'RE LOSING HIM!
TWO-FACE, IF YOU DON'T...
YES, DENT, LET HIM GO!

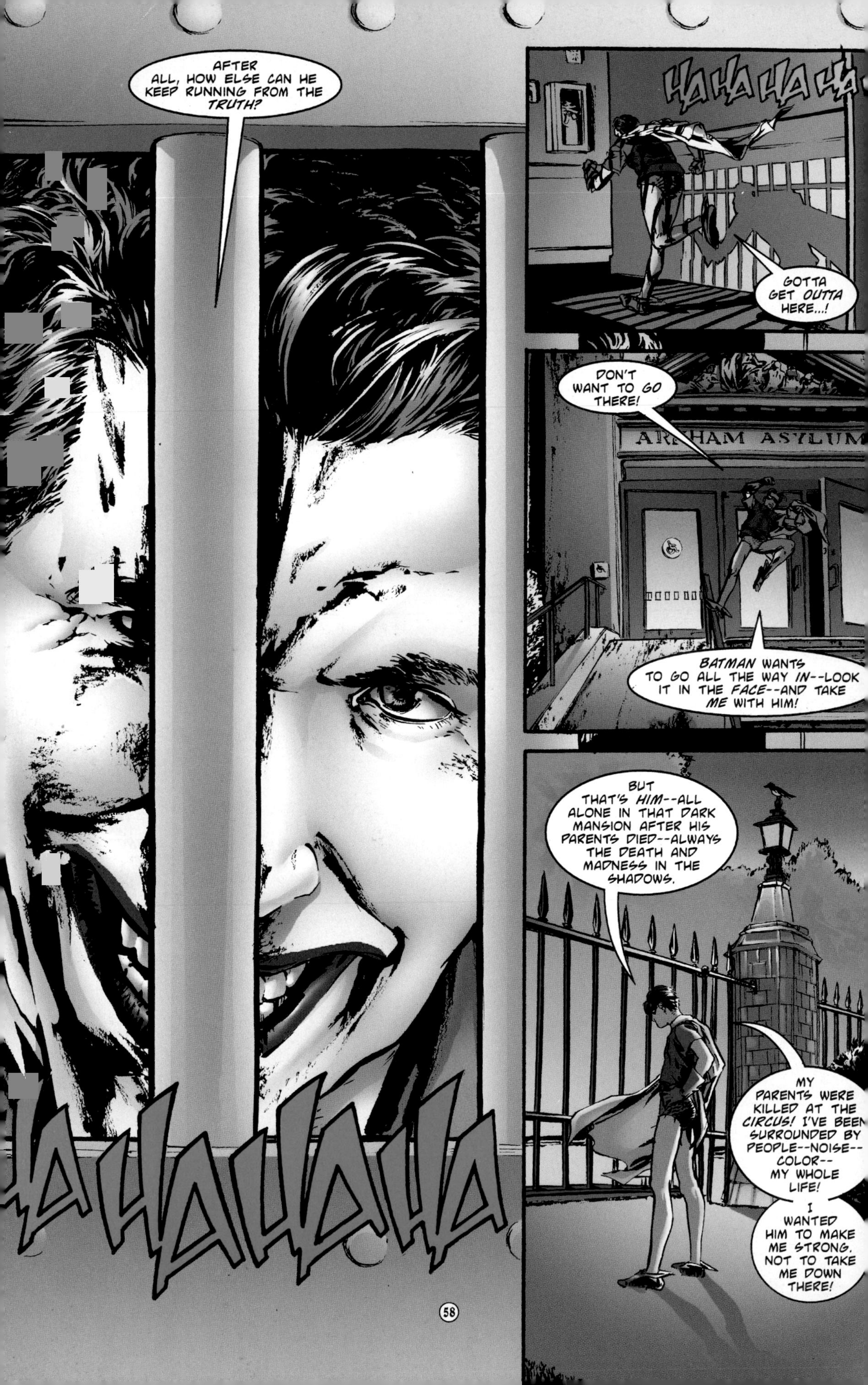

AFTER ALL, HOW ELSE CAN HE KEEP RUNNING FROM THE TRUTH?
HAHAHAHA
HAHAHAHA
GOTTA GET OUTTA HERE...!
DON'T WANT TO GO THERE!
ARKHAM ASYLUM
BATMAN WANTS TO GO ALL THE WAY IN--LOOK IT IN THE FACE--AND TAKE ME WITH HIM!
BUT THAT'S HIM--ALL ALONE IN THAT DARK MANSION AFTER HIS PARENTS DIED--ALWAYS THE DEATH AND MADNESS IN THE SHADOWS.
MY PARENTS WERE KILLED AT THE CIRCUS! I'VE BEEN SURROUNDED BY PEOPLE--NOISE--COLOR--MY WHOLE LIFE!
I WANTED HIM TO MAKE ME STRONG. NOT TO TAKE ME DOWN THERE!

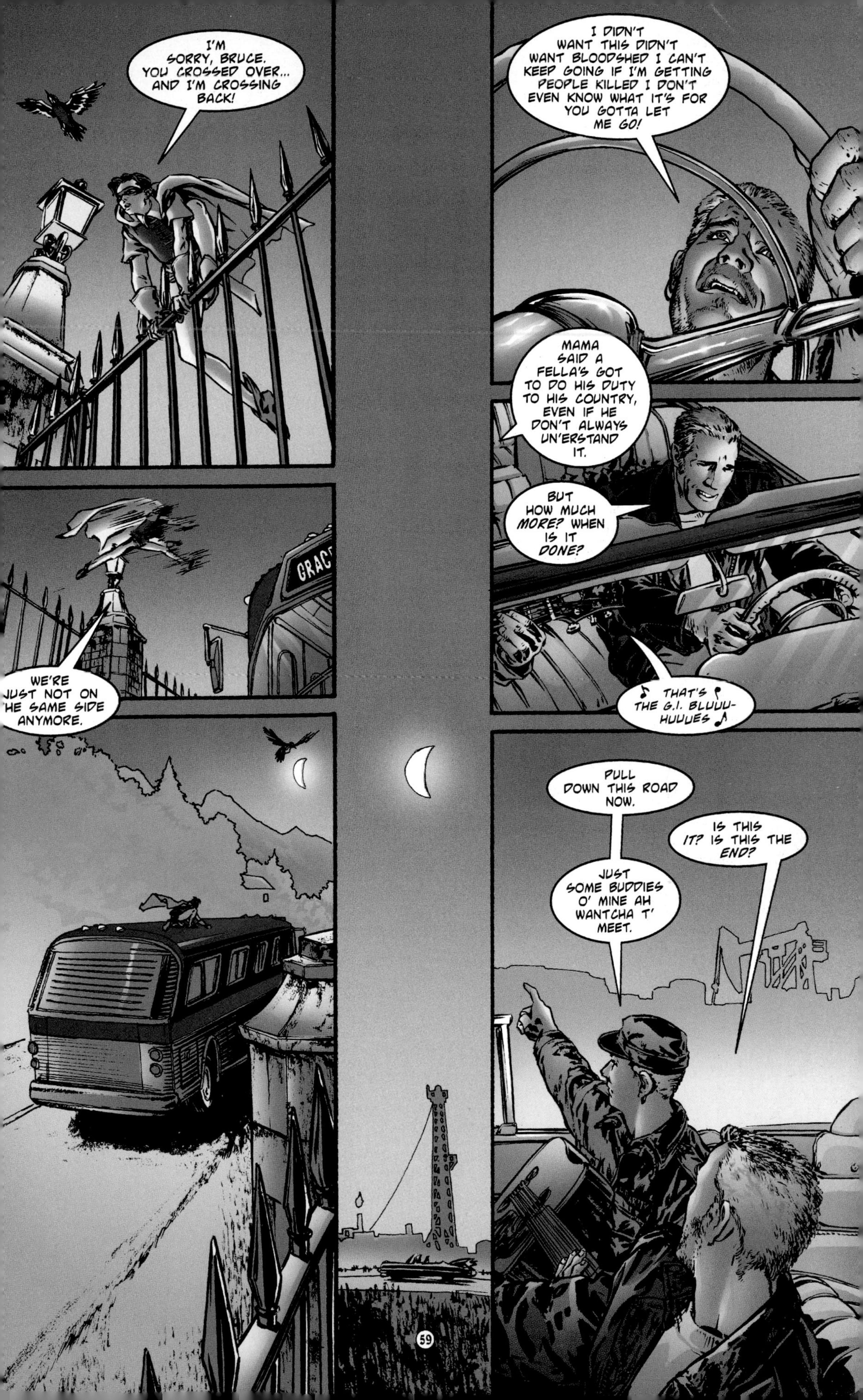

I'M SORRY, BRUCE. YOU CROSSED OVER... AND I'M CROSSING BACK!
I DIDN'T WANT THIS DIDN'T WANT BLOODSHED I CAN'T KEEP GOING IF I'M GETTING PEOPLE KILLED I DON'T EVEN KNOW WHAT IT'S FOR YOU GOTTA LET ME GO!
WE'RE JUST NOT ON HE SAME SIDE ANYMORE.
MAMA SAID A FELLA'S GOT TO DO HIS DUTY TO HIS COUNTRY, EVEN IF HE DON'T ALWAYS UN'ERSTAND IT.
BUT HOW MUCH MORE? WHEN IS IT DONE?
GRAC
♪ THAT'S THE G.I. BLUUU-HUUUES ♪
PULL DOWN THIS ROAD NOW.
JUST SOME BUDDIES O' MINE AH WANTCHA T' MEET.
IS THIS IT? IS THIS THE END?

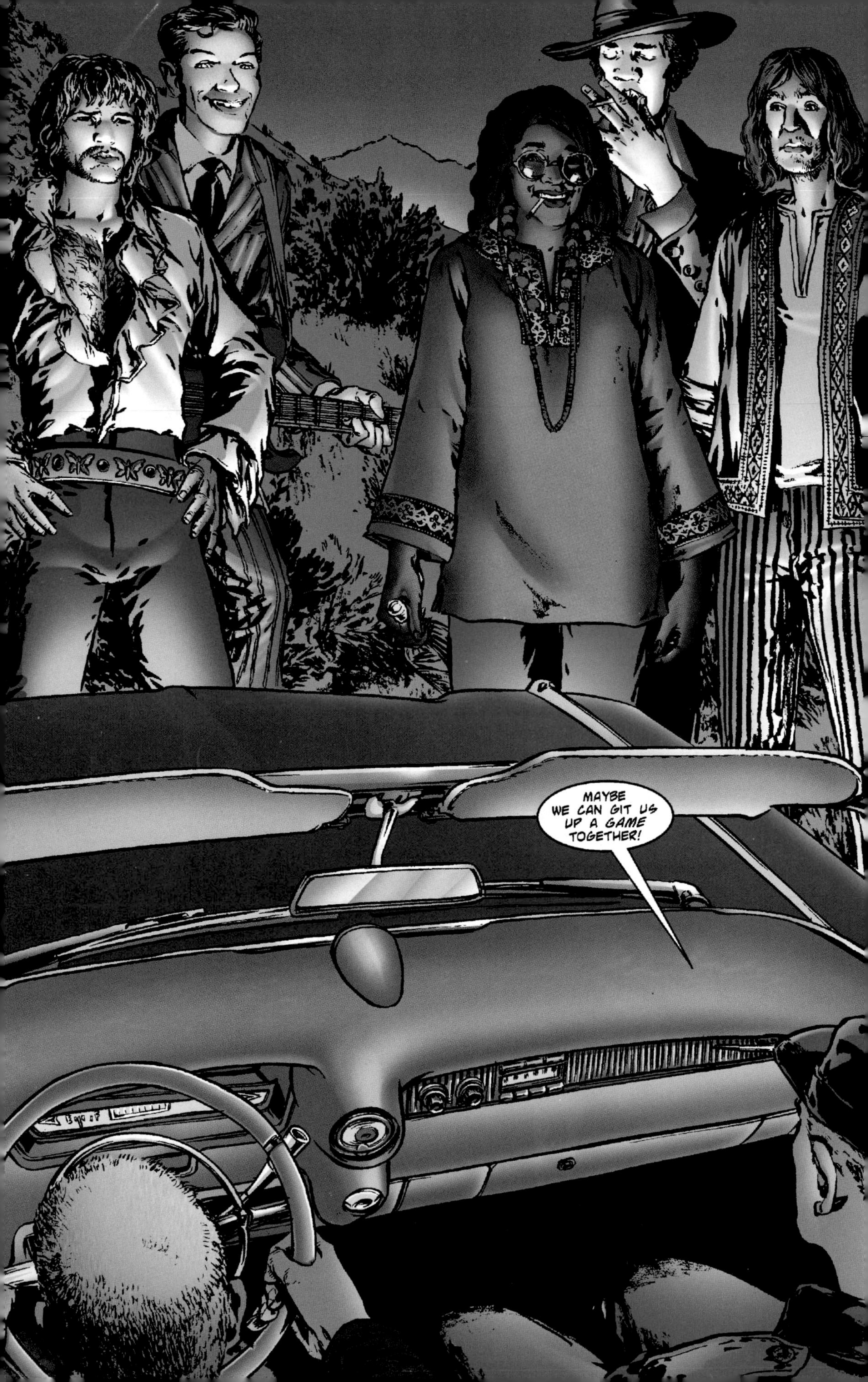
MAYBE WE CAN GIT US UP A GAME TOGETHER!

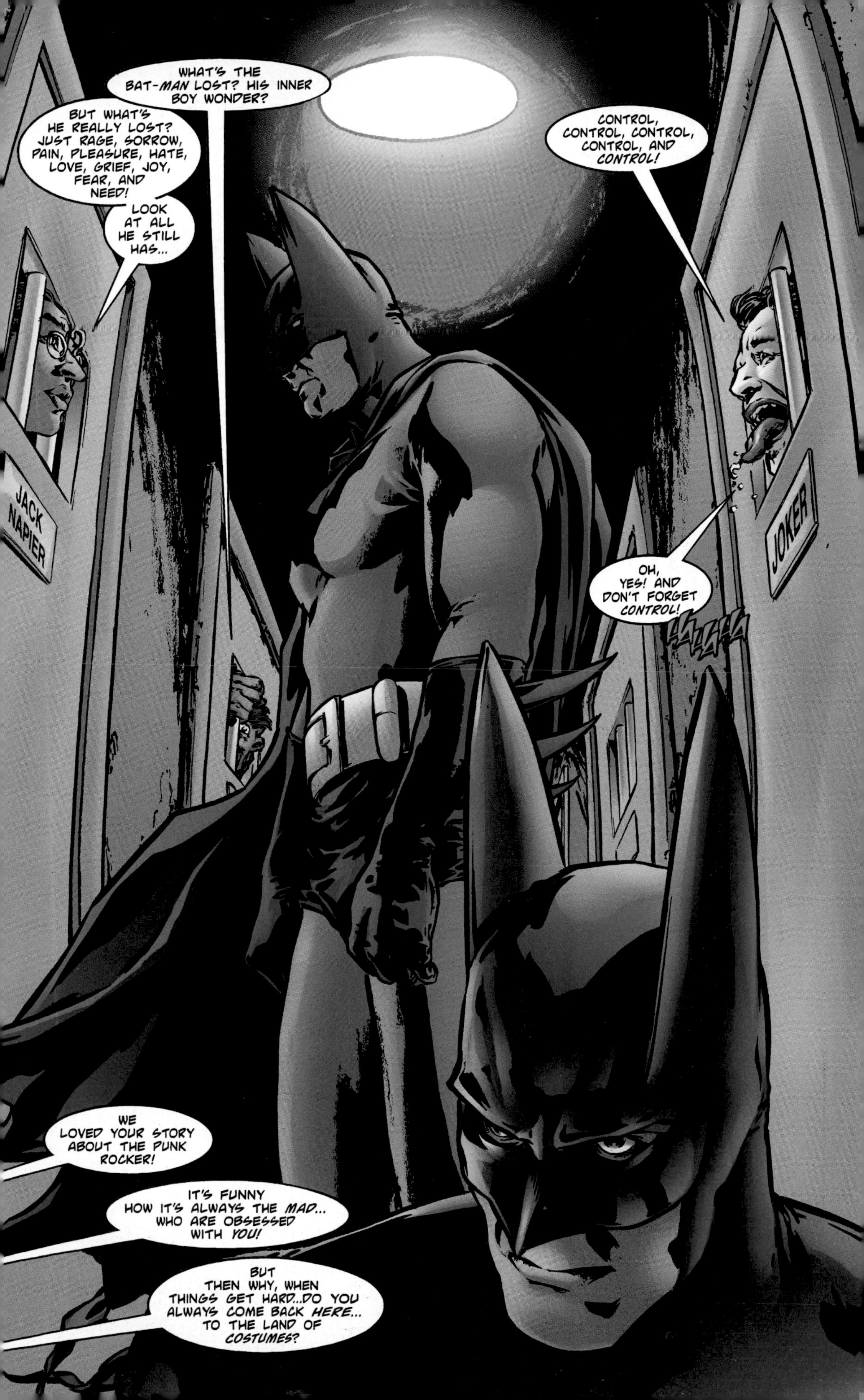
WHAT'S THE BAT-*MAN* LOST? HIS INNER BOY WONDER?
BUT WHAT'S HE REALLY LOST? JUST RAGE, SORROW, PAIN, PLEASURE, HATE, LOVE, GRIEF, JOY, FEAR, AND NEED!
LOOK AT ALL HE STILL HAS...
JACK NAPIER
CONTROL, CONTROL, CONTROL, CONTROL, AND *CONTROL!*
JOKER
OH, YES! AND DON'T FORGET *CONTROL!*
WE LOVED YOUR STORY ABOUT THE PUNK ROCKER!
IT'S FUNNY HOW IT'S ALWAYS THE *MAD*... WHO ARE OBSESSED WITH *YOU!*
BUT THEN WHY, WHEN THINGS GET HARD...DO YOU ALWAYS COME BACK *HERE*... TO THE LAND OF *COSTUMES?*

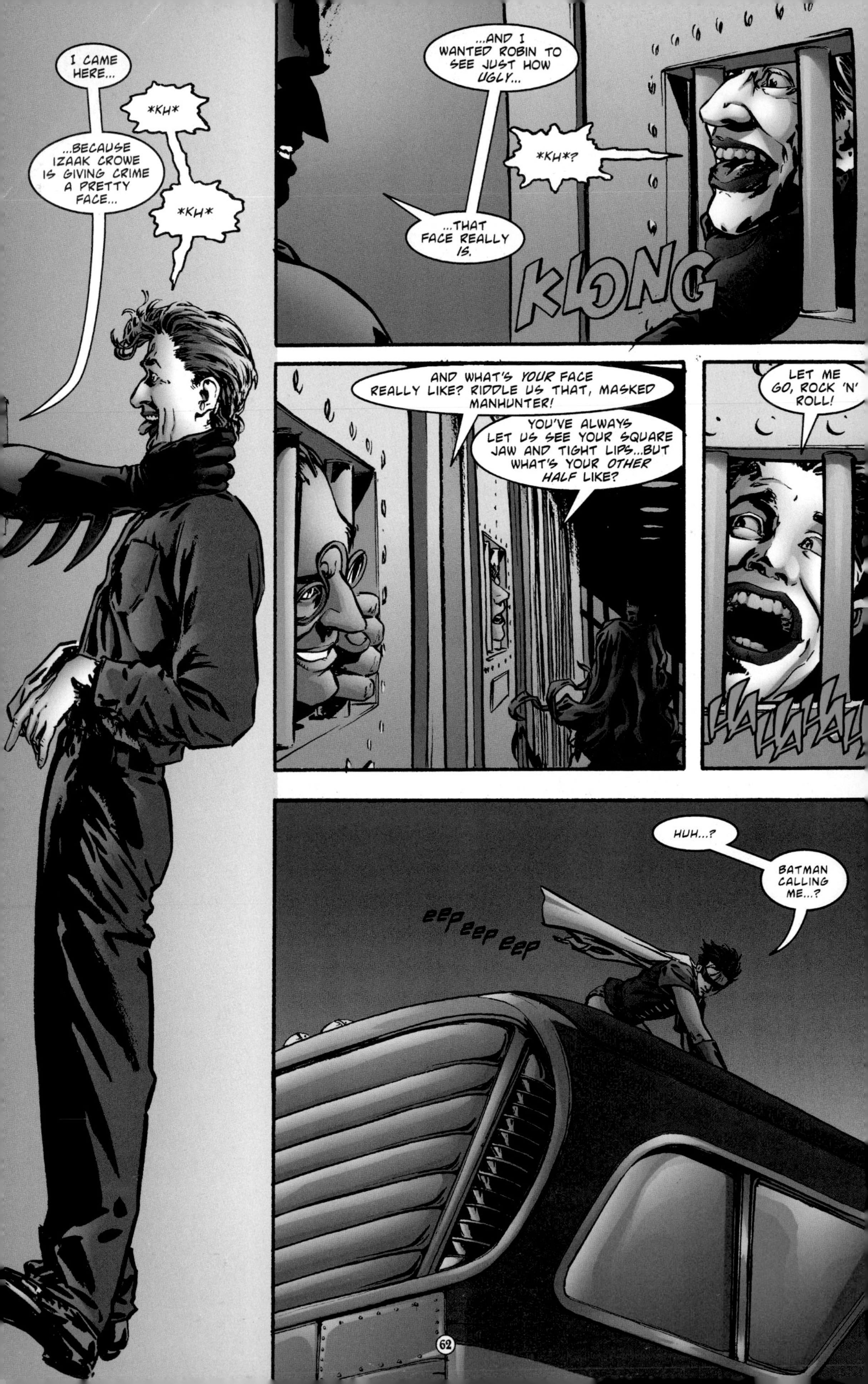
I CAME HERE...
KH
...BECAUSE IZAAK CROWE IS GIVING CRIME A PRETTY FACE...
KH
...AND I WANTED ROBIN TO SEE JUST HOW UGLY...
KH?
...THAT FACE REALLY IS.
KLONG
AND WHAT'S YOUR FACE REALLY LIKE? RIDDLE US THAT, MASKED MANHUNTER!
YOU'VE ALWAYS LET US SEE YOUR SQUARE JAW AND TIGHT LIPS...BUT WHAT'S YOUR OTHER HALF LIKE?
LET ME GO, ROCK 'N' ROLL!
HUH...?
BATMAN CALLING ME...?
eep eep eep

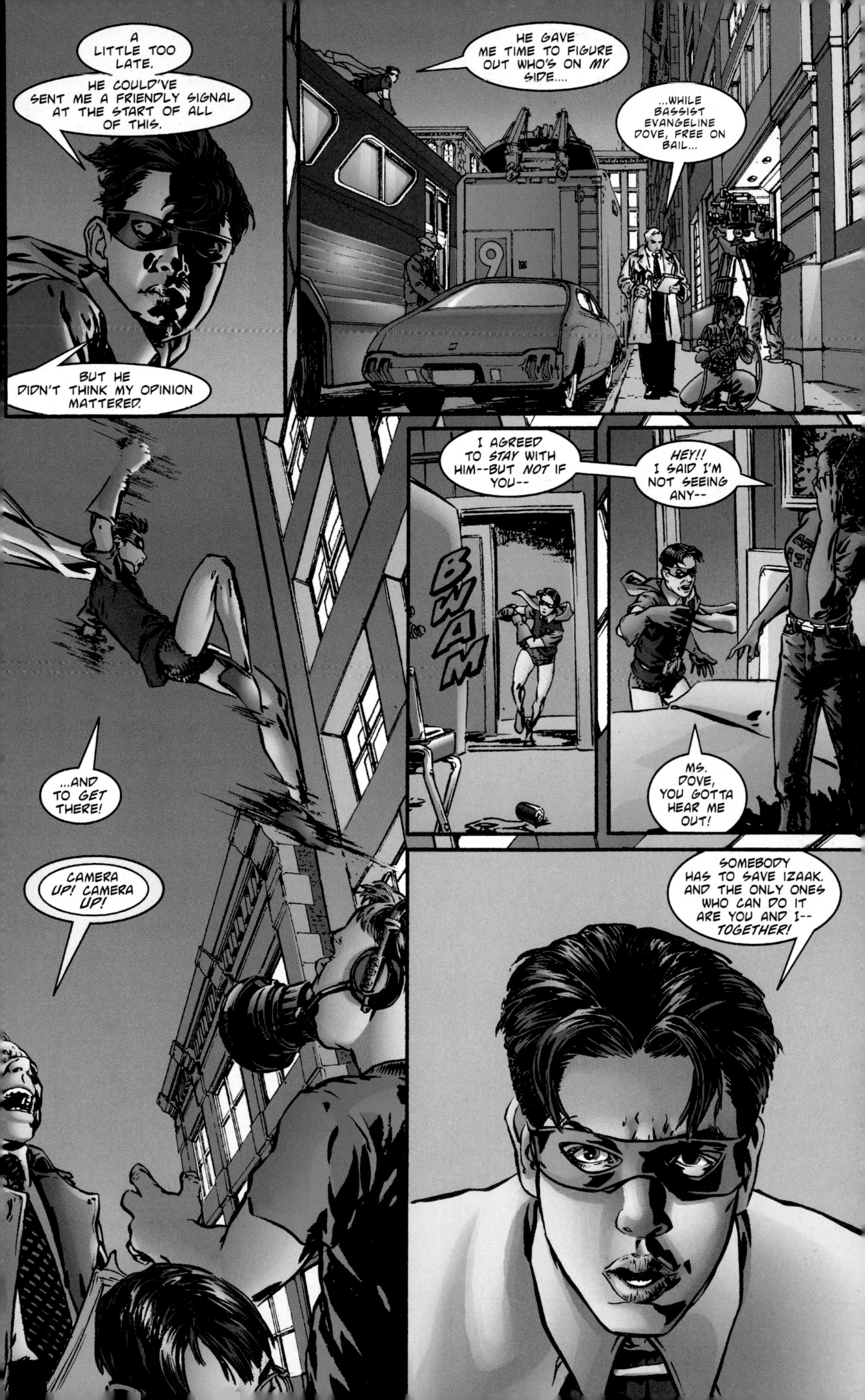
A LITTLE TOO LATE.
HE COULD'VE SENT ME A FRIENDLY SIGNAL AT THE START OF ALL OF THIS.
BUT HE DIDN'T THINK MY OPINION MATTERED.
HE GAVE ME TIME TO FIGURE OUT WHO'S ON *MY* SIDE....
...WHILE BASSIST EVANGELINE DOVE, FREE ON BAIL...
...AND TO GET THERE!
CAMERA *UP!* CAMERA *UP!*
I AGREED TO *STAY* WITH HIM--BUT *NOT* IF YOU--
BWAM
HEY!! I SAID I'M NOT SEEING ANY--
MS. DOVE, YOU GOTTA HEAR ME OUT!
SOMEBODY HAS TO SAVE IZAAK. AND THE ONLY ONES WHO CAN DO IT ARE YOU AND I-- *TOGETHER!*

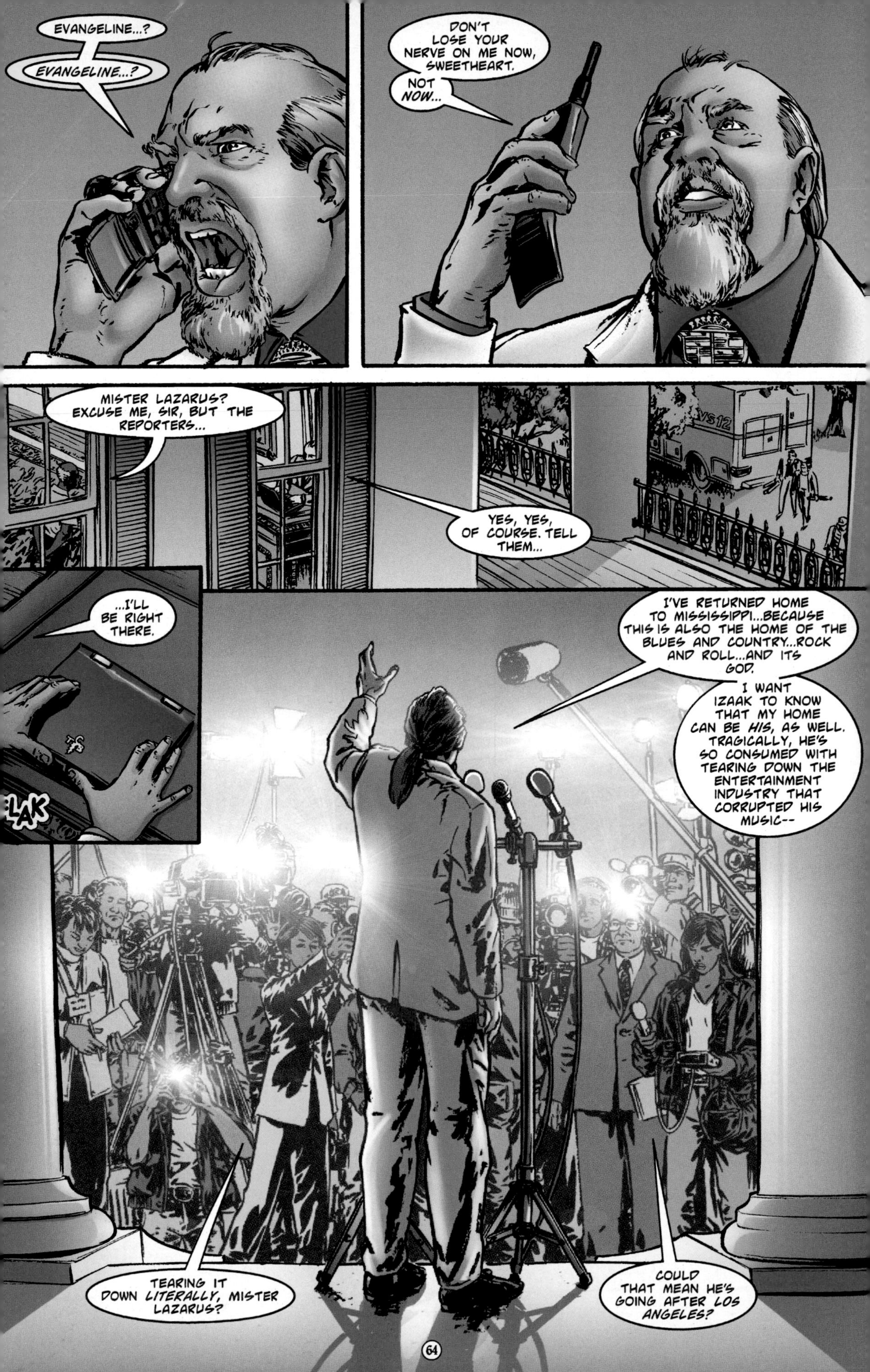
EVANGELINE...?
EVANGELINE...?
DON'T LOSE YOUR NERVE ON ME NOW, SWEETHEART.
NOT NOW...
MISTER LAZARUS? EXCUSE ME, SIR, BUT THE REPORTERS...
YES, YES, OF COURSE. TELL THEM...
...I'LL BE RIGHT THERE.
LAK
I'VE RETURNED HOME TO MISSISSIPPI...BECAUSE THIS IS ALSO THE HOME OF THE BLUES AND COUNTRY...ROCK AND ROLL...AND ITS GOD.
I WANT IZAAK TO KNOW THAT MY HOME CAN BE HIS, AS WELL. TRAGICALLY, HE'S SO CONSUMED WITH TEARING DOWN THE ENTERTAINMENT INDUSTRY THAT CORRUPTED HIS MUSIC--
TEARING IT DOWN LITERALLY, MISTER LAZARUS?
COULD THAT MEAN HE'S GOING AFTER LOS ANGELES?

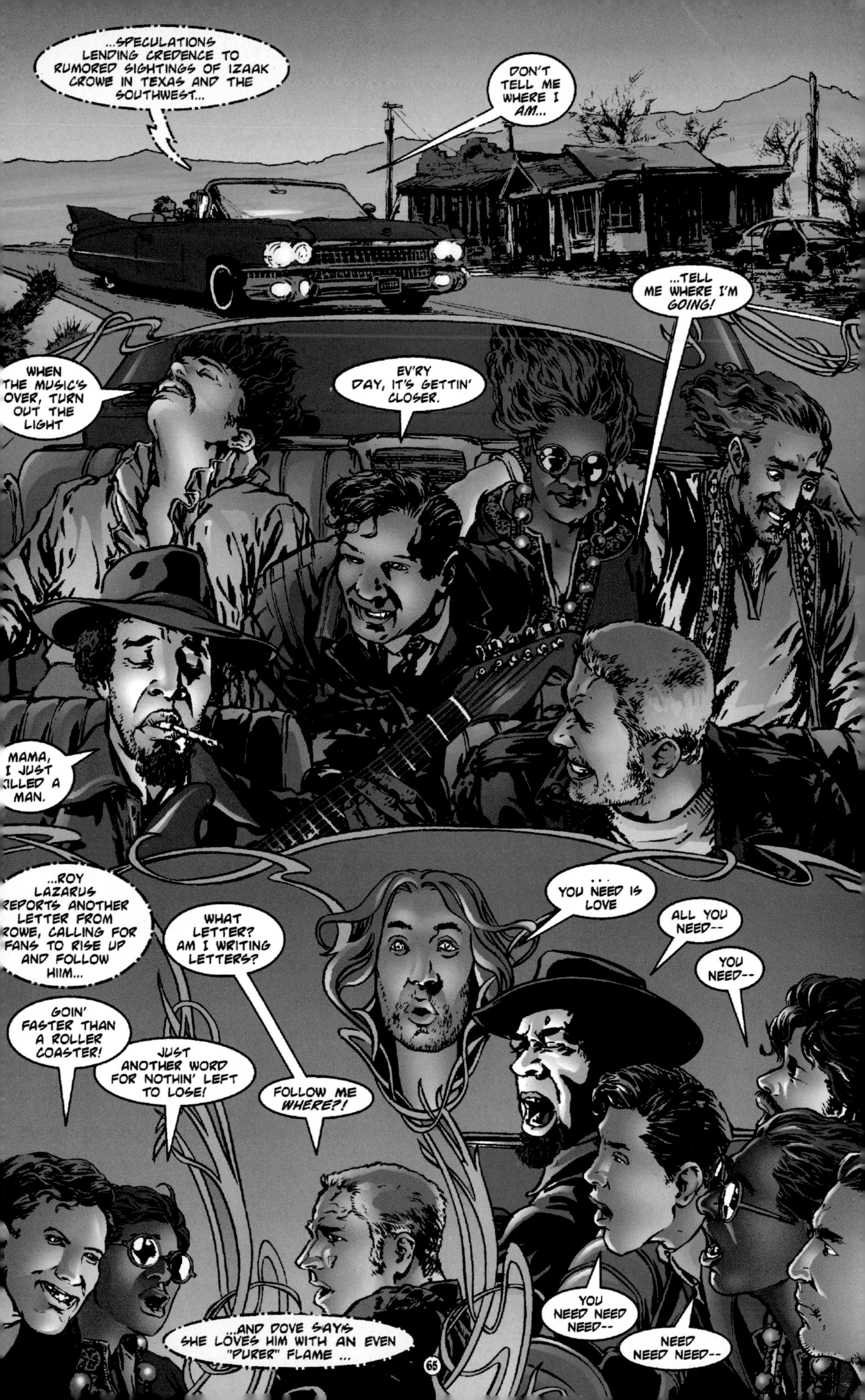
...SPECULATIONS LENDING CREDENCE TO RUMORED SIGHTINGS OF IZAAK CROWE IN TEXAS AND THE SOUTHWEST...
DON'T TELL ME WHERE I AM...
...TELL ME WHERE I'M GOING!
WHEN THE MUSIC'S OVER, TURN OUT THE LIGHT
EV'RY DAY, IT'S GETTIN' CLOSER.
MAMA, I JUST KILLED A MAN.
...ROY LAZARUS REPORTS ANOTHER LETTER FROM CROWE, CALLING FOR FANS TO RISE UP AND FOLLOW HIIM...
WHAT LETTER? AM I WRITING LETTERS?
...YOU NEED IS LOVE
ALL YOU NEED--
YOU NEED--
GOIN' FASTER THAN A ROLLER COASTER!
JUST ANOTHER WORD FOR NOTHIN' LEFT TO LOSE!
FOLLOW ME WHERE?!
YOU NEED NEED NEED--
...AND DOVE SAYS SHE LOVES HIM WITH AN EVEN "PURER" FLAME ...
NEED NEED NEED--

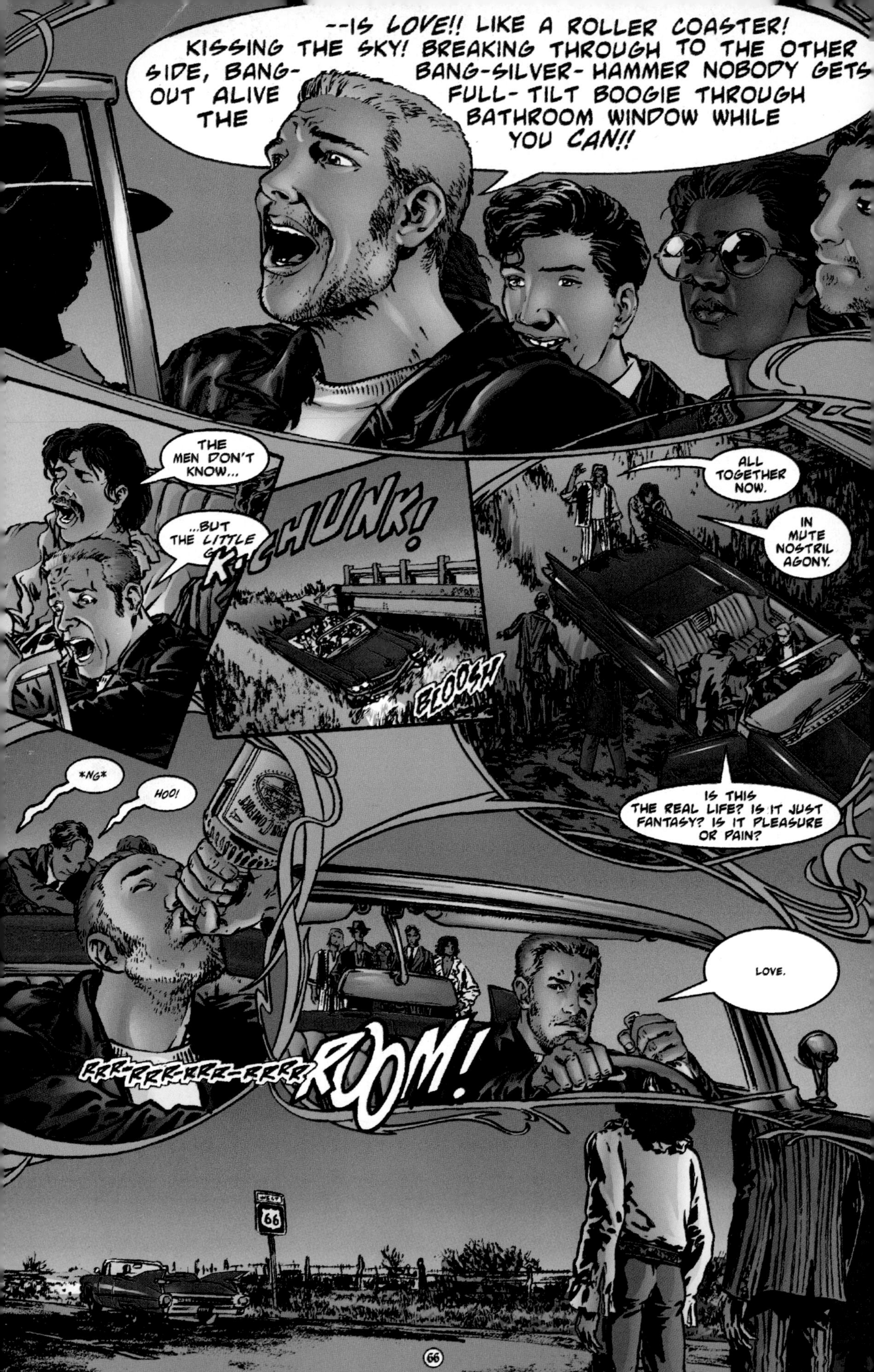
--IS LOVE!! LIKE A ROLLER COASTER! KISSING THE SKY! BREAKING THROUGH TO THE OTHER SIDE, BANG-BANG-SILVER-HAMMER NOBODY GETS OUT ALIVE FULL-TILT BOOGIE THROUGH THE BATHROOM WINDOW WHILE YOU CAN!!
THE MEN DON'T KNOW...
...BUT THE LITTLE G...
K-CHUNK!
BLOOSH
ALL TOGETHER NOW.
IN MUTE NOSTRIL AGONY.
IS THIS THE REAL LIFE? IS IT JUST FANTASY? IS IT PLEASURE OR PAIN?
NG
HOO!
LOVE.
RRR-RRR-RRR-RRRROOM!
66

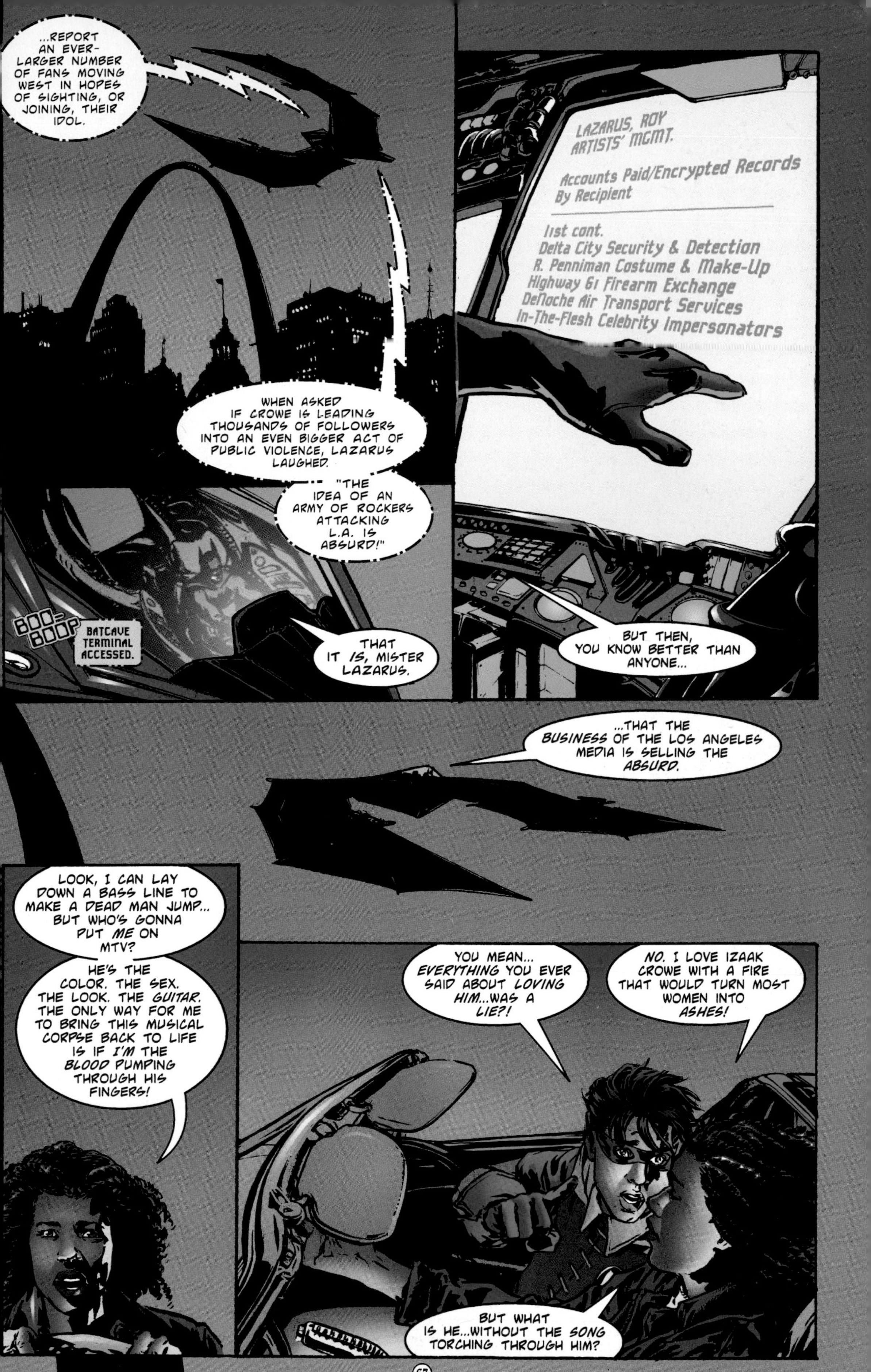

...REPORT AN EVER-LARGER NUMBER OF FANS MOVING WEST IN HOPES OF SIGHTING, OR JOINING, THEIR IDOL.
LAZARUS, ROY
ARTISTS' MGMT.
Accounts Paid/Encrypted Records
By Recipient
list cont.
Delta City Security & Detection
R. Penniman Costume & Make-Up
Highway 61 Firearm Exchange
DeNoche Air Transport Services
In-The-Flesh Celebrity Impersonators
WHEN ASKED IF CROWE IS LEADING THOUSANDS OF FOLLOWERS INTO AN EVEN BIGGER ACT OF PUBLIC VIOLENCE, LAZARUS LAUGHED.
"THE IDEA OF AN ARMY OF ROCKERS ATTACKING L.A. IS ABSURD!"
BOO-BOOP
BATCAVE TERMINAL ACCESSED.
THAT IT *IS*, MISTER LAZARUS.
BUT THEN, YOU KNOW BETTER THAN ANYONE...
...THAT THE *BUSINESS* OF THE LOS ANGELES MEDIA IS SELLING THE *ABSURD*.
LOOK, I CAN LAY DOWN A BASS LINE TO MAKE A DEAD MAN JUMP... BUT WHO'S GONNA PUT *ME* ON MTV?
HE'S THE COLOR. THE SEX. THE LOOK. THE *GUITAR*. THE ONLY WAY FOR ME TO BRING THIS MUSICAL CORPSE BACK TO LIFE IS IF *I'M* THE *BLOOD PUMPING* THROUGH HIS FINGERS!
YOU MEAN... *EVERYTHING* YOU EVER SAID ABOUT *LOVING* HIM...WAS A *LIE?!*
NO. I LOVE IZAAK CROWE WITH A FIRE THAT WOULD TURN MOST WOMEN INTO *ASHES!*
BUT WHAT IS HE...WITHOUT THE *SONG* TORCHING THROUGH HIM?

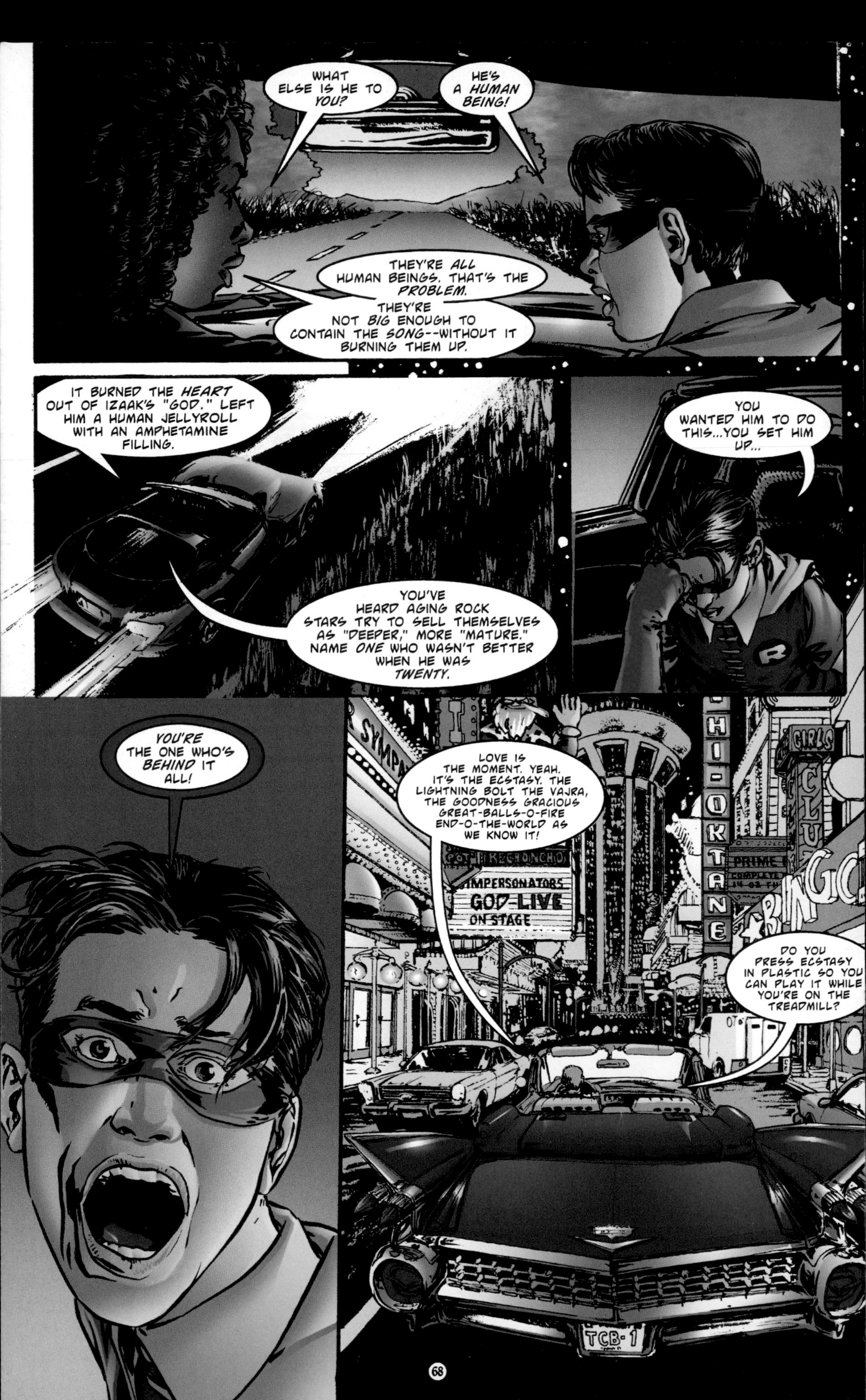
WHAT ELSE IS HE TO YOU?
HE'S A HUMAN BEING!
THEY'RE ALL HUMAN BEINGS. THAT'S THE PROBLEM.
THEY'RE NOT BIG ENOUGH TO CONTAIN THE SONG--WITHOUT IT BURNING THEM UP.
IT BURNED THE HEART OUT OF IZAAK'S "GOD." LEFT HIM A HUMAN JELLYROLL WITH AN AMPHETAMINE FILLING.
YOU'VE HEARD AGING ROCK STARS TRY TO SELL THEMSELVES AS "DEEPER," MORE "MATURE." NAME ONE WHO WASN'T BETTER WHEN HE WAS TWENTY.
YOU WANTED HIM TO DO THIS...YOU SET HIM UP...
YOU'RE THE ONE WHO'S BEHIND IT ALL!
LOVE IS THE MOMENT. YEAH. IT'S THE ECSTASY. THE LIGHTNING BOLT THE VAJRA, THE GOODNESS GRACIOUS GREAT-BALLS-O-FIRE END-O-THE-WORLD AS WE KNOW IT!
IMPERSONATORS
GOD-LIVE
ON STAGE
HI-OKTANE
GIRLS
CLU
PRIME
BINGO
DO YOU PRESS ECSTASY IN PLASTIC SO YOU CAN PLAY IT WHILE YOU'RE ON THE TREADMILL?
TCB-1

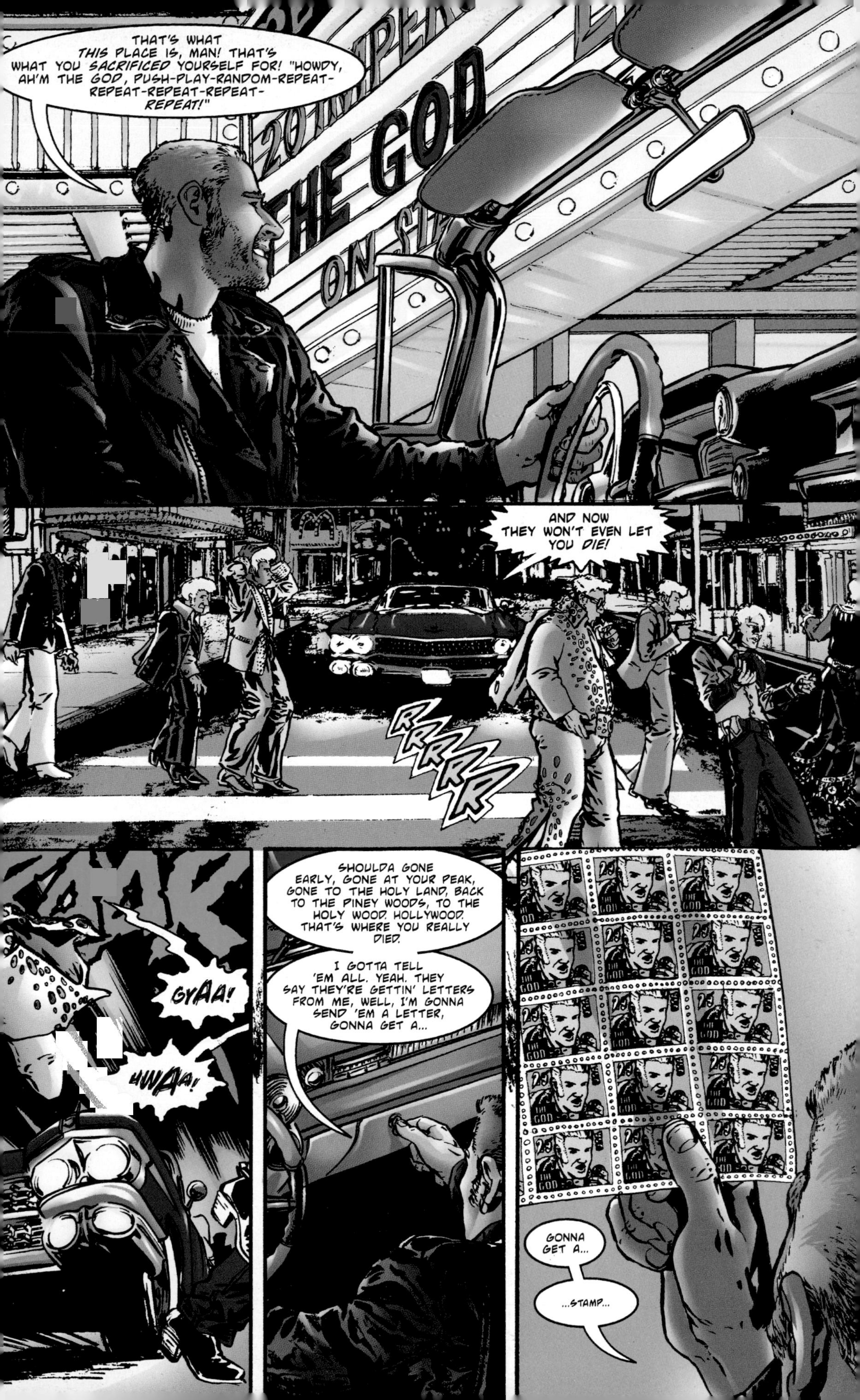
THAT'S WHAT THIS PLACE IS, MAN! THAT'S WHAT YOU SACRIFICED YOURSELF FOR! "HOWDY, AH'M THE GOD, PUSH-PLAY-RANDOM-REPEAT-REPEAT-REPEAT-REPEAT-REPEAT!"
THE GOD
ON ST
AND NOW THEY WON'T EVEN LET YOU DIE!
RRRRR
GYAA!
UWAA!
SHOULDA GONE EARLY, GONE AT YOUR PEAK, GONE TO THE HOLY LAND, BACK TO THE PINEY WOODS, TO THE HOLY WOOD. HOLLYWOOD. THAT'S WHERE YOU REALLY DIED.
I GOTTA TELL 'EM ALL. YEAH. THEY SAY THEY'RE GETTIN' LETTERS FROM ME, WELL, I'M GONNA SEND 'EM A LETTER, GONNA GET A...
GONNA GET A...
...STAMP...

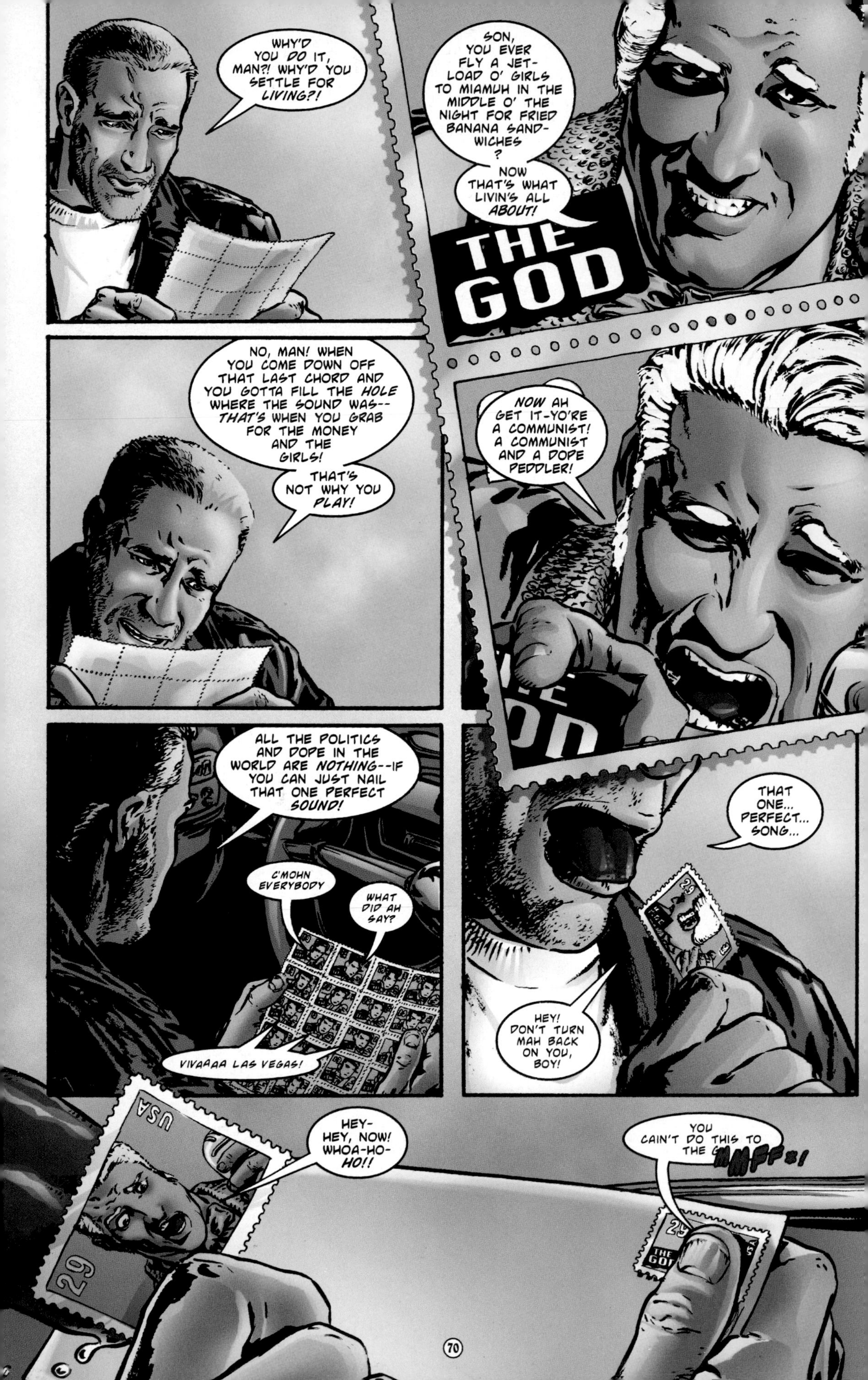
WHY'D YOU DO IT, MAN?! WHY'D YOU SETTLE FOR LIVING?!
SON, YOU EVER FLY A JET-LOAD O' GIRLS TO MIAMUH IN THE MIDDLE O' THE NIGHT FOR FRIED BANANA SANDWICHES ?
NOW THAT'S WHAT LIVIN'S ALL ABOUT!
THE GOD
NO, MAN! WHEN YOU COME DOWN OFF THAT LAST CHORD AND YOU GOTTA FILL THE HOLE WHERE THE SOUND WAS-- THAT'S WHEN YOU GRAB FOR THE MONEY AND THE GIRLS!
THAT'S NOT WHY YOU PLAY!
NOW AH GET IT-YO'RE A COMMUNIST! A COMMUNIST AND A DOPE PEDDLER!
ALL THE POLITICS AND DOPE IN THE WORLD ARE NOTHING--IF YOU CAN JUST NAIL THAT ONE PERFECT SOUND!
C'MOHN EVERYBODY
WHAT DID AH SAY?
VIVAAAA LAS VEGAS!
THAT ONE... PERFECT... SONG...
HEY! DON'T TURN MAH BACK ON YOU, BOY!
USA
29
HEY-HEY, NOW! WHOA-HO-HO!!
YOU CAIN'T DO THIS TO THE G
MMFF*!

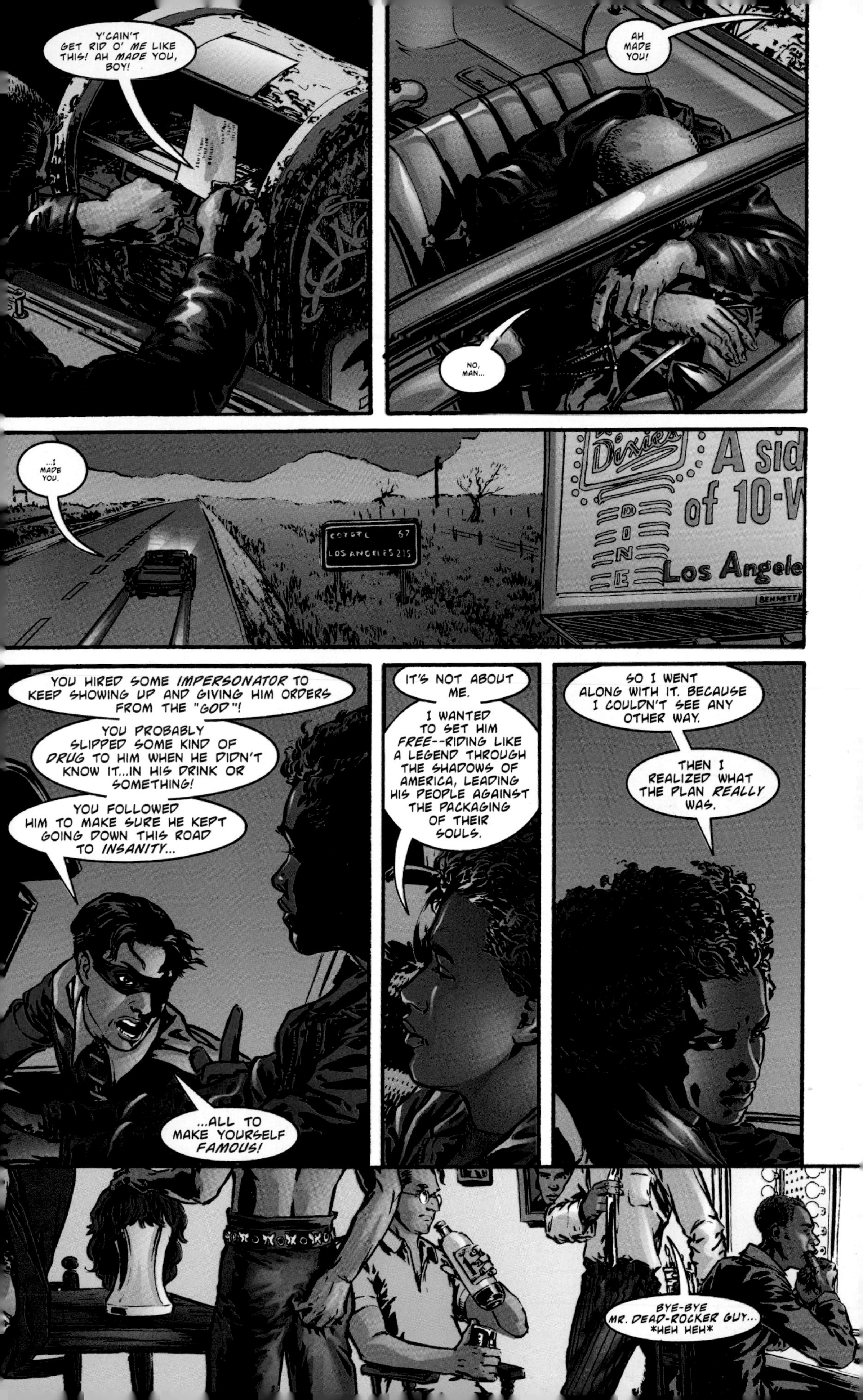
Y'CAIN'T GET RID O' ME LIKE THIS! AH MADE YOU, BOY!
AH MADE YOU!
NO, MAN...
...I MADE YOU.
COYOTL 67
LOS ANGELES 215
Dixie's
A sid
of 10-W
Los Angele
YOU HIRED SOME IMPERSONATOR TO KEEP SHOWING UP AND GIVING HIM ORDERS FROM THE "GOD"!
YOU PROBABLY SLIPPED SOME KIND OF DRUG TO HIM WHEN HE DIDN'T KNOW IT...IN HIS DRINK OR SOMETHING!
YOU FOLLOWED HIM TO MAKE SURE HE KEPT GOING DOWN THIS ROAD TO INSANITY...
...ALL TO MAKE YOURSELF FAMOUS!
IT'S NOT ABOUT ME.
I WANTED TO SET HIM FREE--RIDING LIKE A LEGEND THROUGH THE SHADOWS OF AMERICA, LEADING HIS PEOPLE AGAINST THE PACKAGING OF THEIR SOULS.
SO I WENT ALONG WITH IT. BECAUSE I COULDN'T SEE ANY OTHER WAY.
THEN I REALIZED WHAT THE PLAN REALLY WAS.
BYE-BYE MR. DEAD-ROCKER GUY... *HEH HEH*

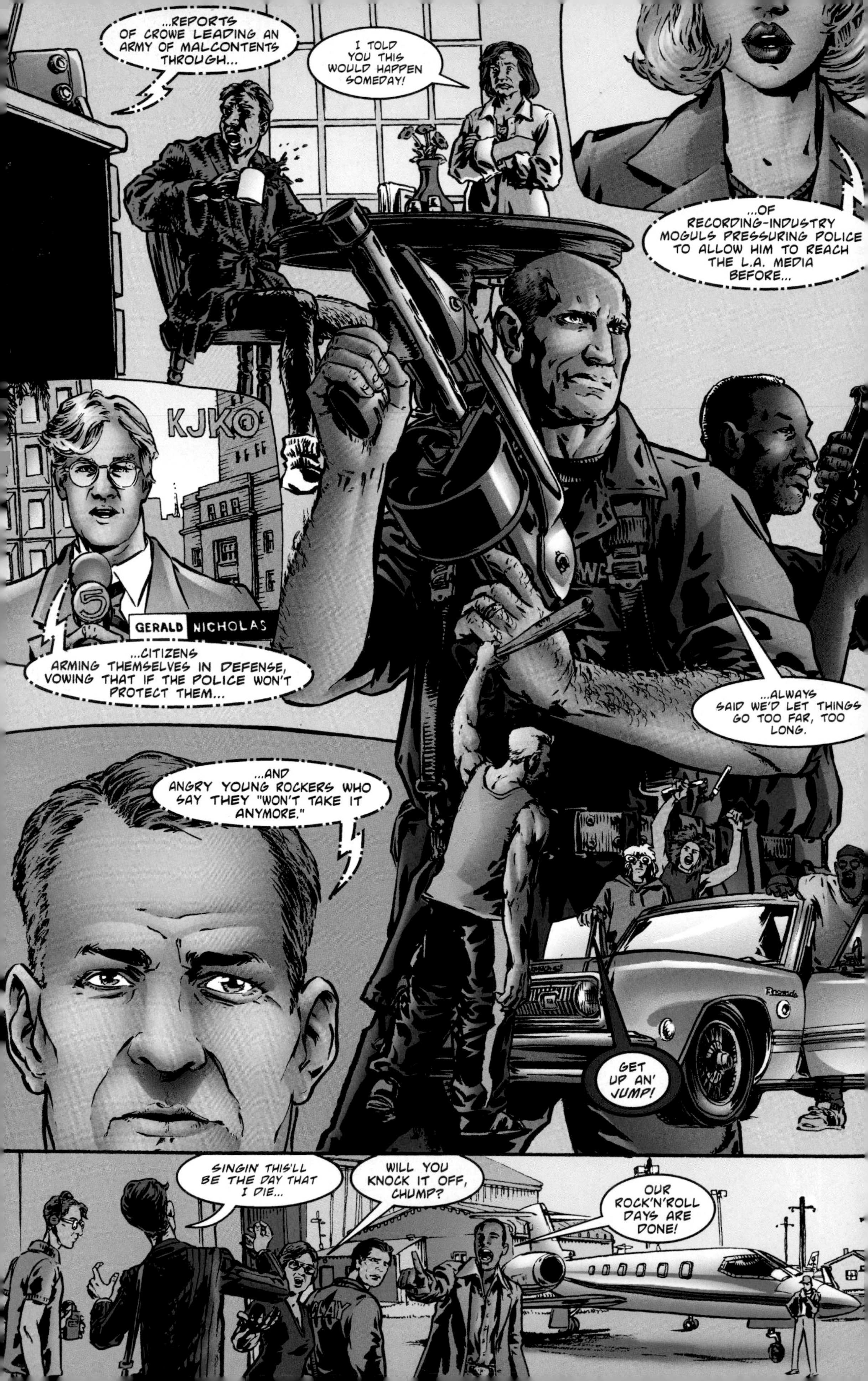
...REPORTS OF CROWE LEADING AN ARMY OF MALCONTENTS THROUGH...
I TOLD YOU THIS WOULD HAPPEN SOMEDAY!
...OF RECORDING-INDUSTRY MOGULS PRESSURING POLICE TO ALLOW HIM TO REACH THE L.A. MEDIA BEFORE...
KJKO
GERALD NICHOLAS
...CITIZENS ARMING THEMSELVES IN DEFENSE, VOWING THAT IF THE POLICE WON'T PROTECT THEM...
...ALWAYS SAID WE'D LET THINGS GO TOO FAR, TOO LONG.
...AND ANGRY YOUNG ROCKERS WHO SAY THEY "WON'T TAKE IT ANYMORE."
GET UP AN' JUMP!
SINGIN' THIS'LL BE THE DAY THAT I DIE...
WILL YOU KNOCK IT OFF, CHUMP?
OUR ROCK'N'ROLL DAYS ARE DONE!

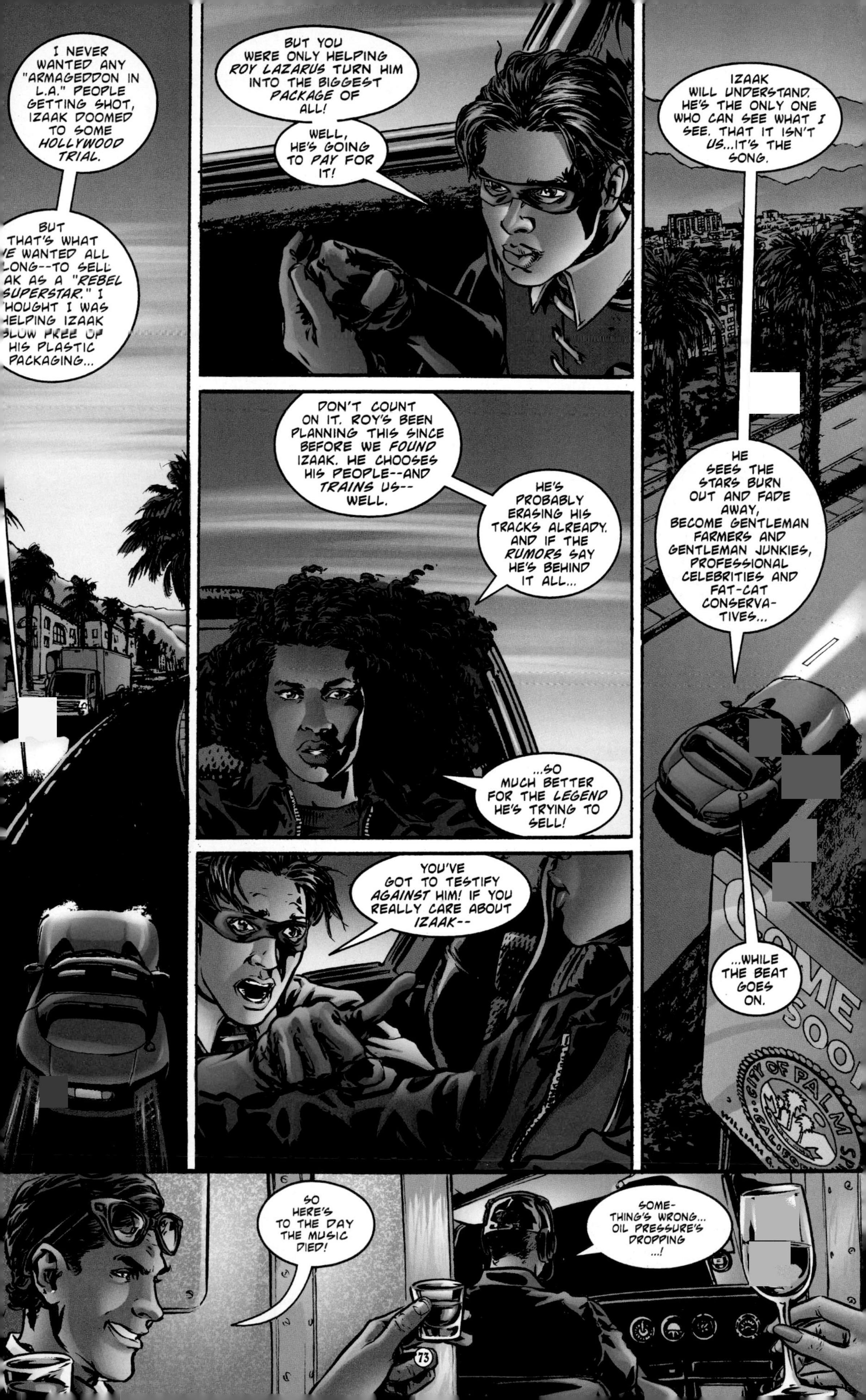

I NEVER WANTED ANY "ARMAGEDDON IN L.A." PEOPLE GETTING SHOT, IZAAK DOOMED TO SOME HOLLYWOOD TRIAL.
BUT THAT'S WHAT E WANTED ALL ONG--TO SELL AK AS A "REBEL SUPERSTAR." I HOUGHT I WAS HELPING IZAAK BLOW FREE OF HIS PLASTIC PACKAGING...
BUT YOU WERE ONLY HELPING ROY LAZARUS TURN HIM INTO THE BIGGEST PACKAGE OF ALL!
WELL, HE'S GOING TO PAY FOR IT!
DON'T COUNT ON IT. ROY'S BEEN PLANNING THIS SINCE BEFORE WE FOUND IZAAK. HE CHOOSES HIS PEOPLE--AND TRAINS US--WELL.
HE'S PROBABLY ERASING HIS TRACKS ALREADY. AND IF THE RUMORS SAY HE'S BEHIND IT ALL...
...SO MUCH BETTER FOR THE LEGEND HE'S TRYING TO SELL!
YOU'VE GOT TO TESTIFY AGAINST HIM! IF YOU REALLY CARE ABOUT IZAAK--
IZAAK WILL UNDERSTAND. HE'S THE ONLY ONE WHO CAN SEE WHAT I SEE. THAT IT ISN'T US...IT'S THE SONG.
HE SEES THE STARS BURN OUT AND FADE AWAY, BECOME GENTLEMAN FARMERS AND GENTLEMAN JUNKIES, PROFESSIONAL CELEBRITIES AND FAT-CAT CONSERVA-TIVES...
...WHILE THE BEAT GOES ON.
SO HERE'S TO THE DAY THE MUSIC DIED!
SOME-THING'S WRONG... OIL PRESSURE'S DROPPING ...!

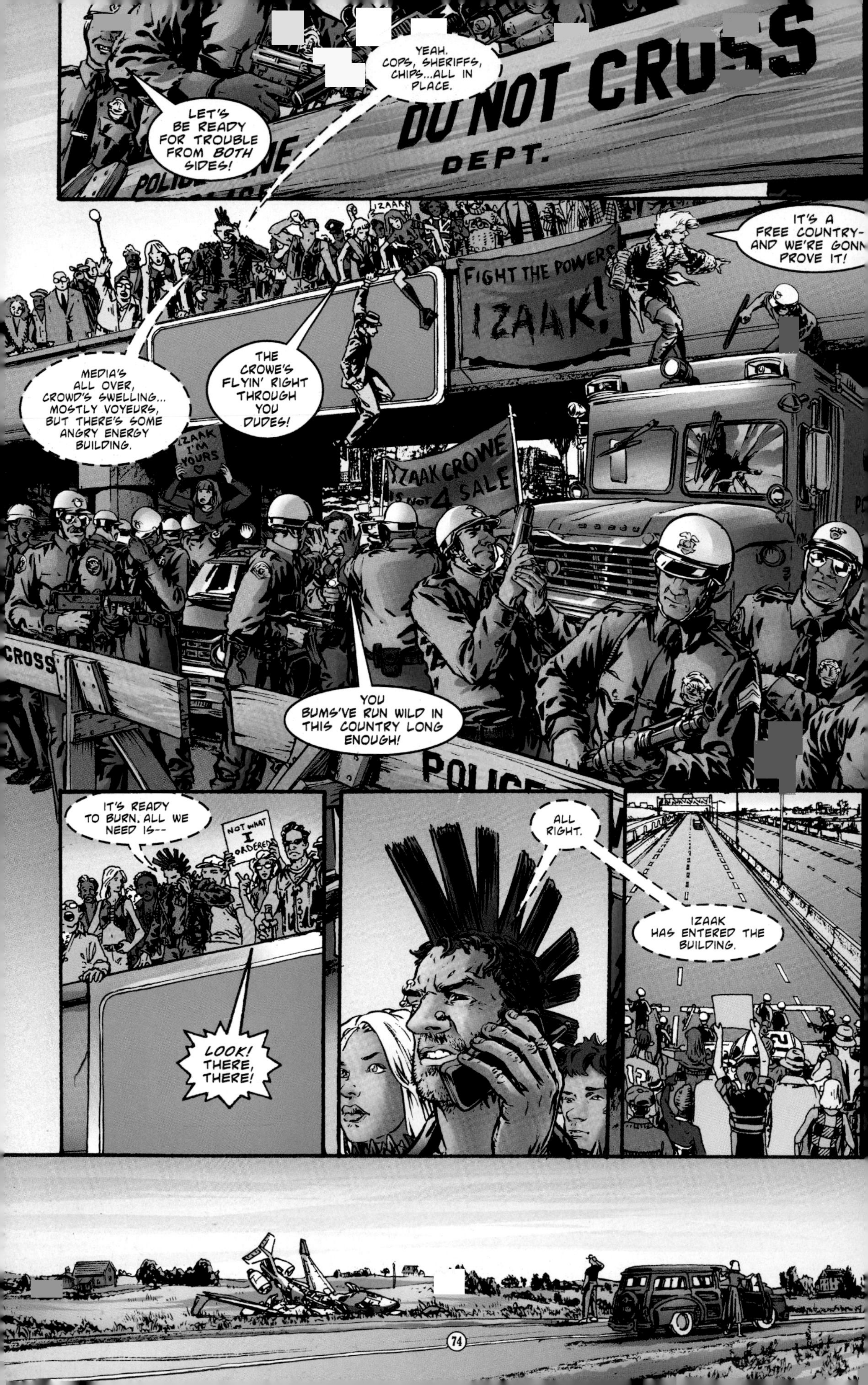

LET'S BE READY FOR TROUBLE FROM BOTH SIDES!
YEAH. COPS, SHERIFFS, CHIPS...ALL IN PLACE.
DO NOT CROSS
DEPT.
MEDIA'S ALL OVER, CROWD'S SWELLING... MOSTLY VOYEURS, BUT THERE'S SOME ANGRY ENERGY BUILDING.
THE CROWE'S FLYIN' RIGHT THROUGH YOU DUDES!
FIGHT THE POWERS IZAAK!
IT'S A FREE COUNTRY- AND WE'RE GONN PROVE IT!
IZAAK I'M YOURS
IZAAK CROWE IS NOT 4 SALE
CROSS
YOU BUMS'VE RUN WILD IN THIS COUNTRY LONG ENOUGH!
POLICE
IT'S READY TO BURN. ALL WE NEED IS--
NOT WHAT I ORDERED
LOOK! THERE, THERE!
ALL RIGHT.
IZAAK HAS ENTERED THE BUILDING.

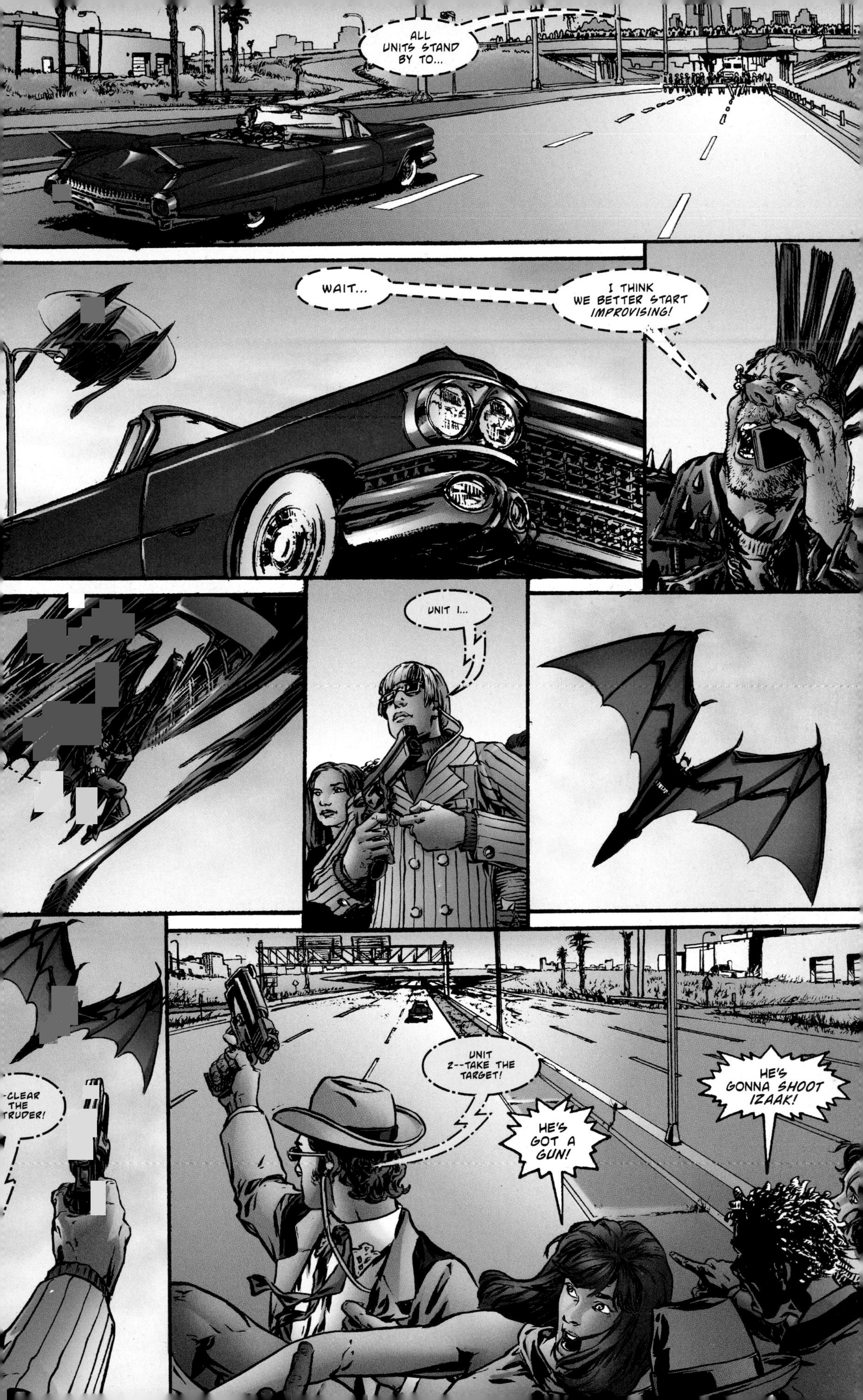
ALL UNITS STAND BY TO...
WAIT...
I THINK WE BETTER START IMPROVISING!
UNIT 1...
-CLEAR THE TRUDER!
UNIT 2--TAKE THE TARGET!
HE'S GOT A GUN!
HE'S GONNA SHOOT IZAAK!

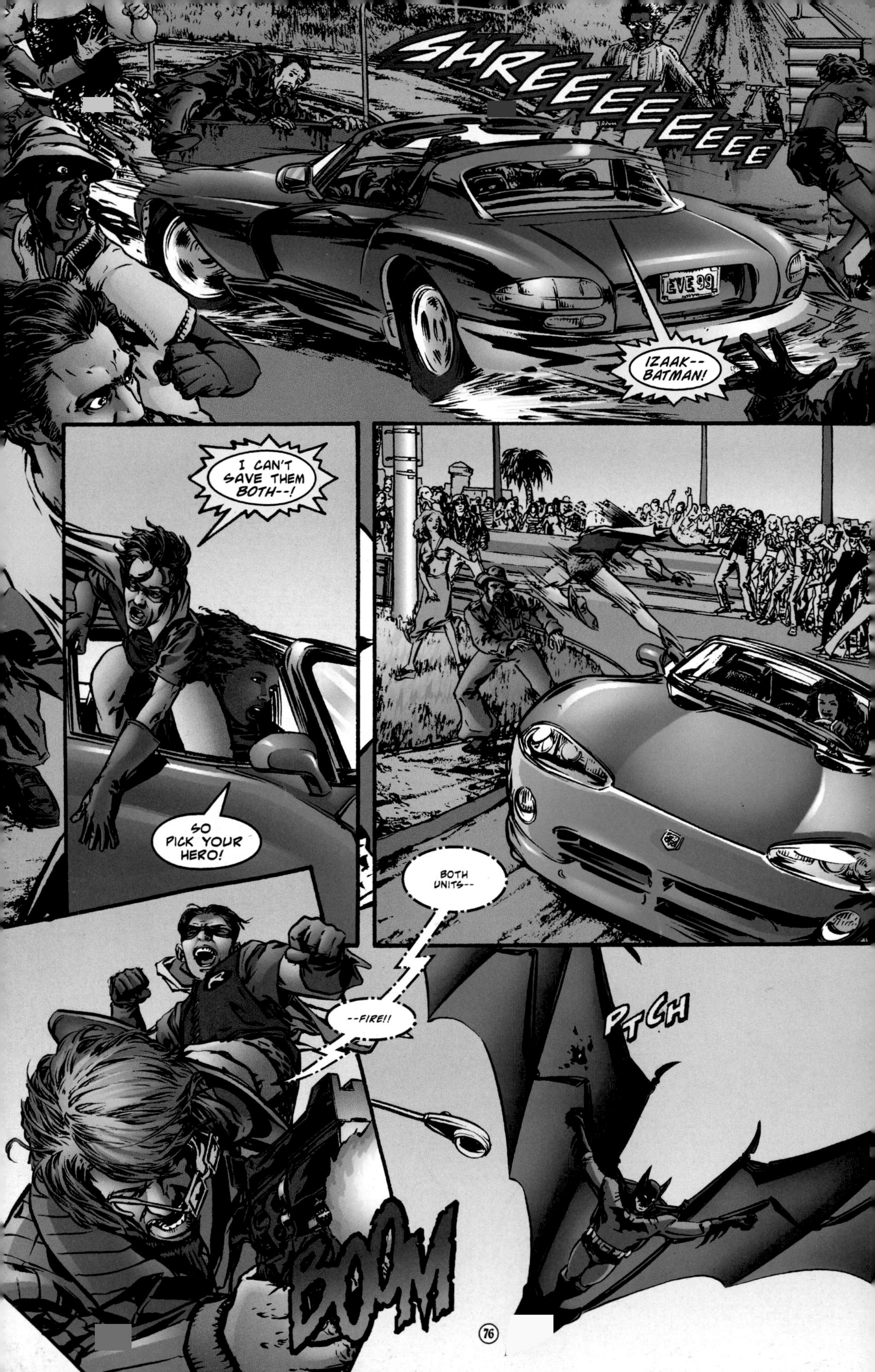
SHREEEEEEEE
EVE 99
IZAAK--
BATMAN!
I CAN'T SAVE THEM BOTH--!
SO PICK YOUR HERO!
BOTH UNITS--
--FIRE!!
PTCH
BOOM

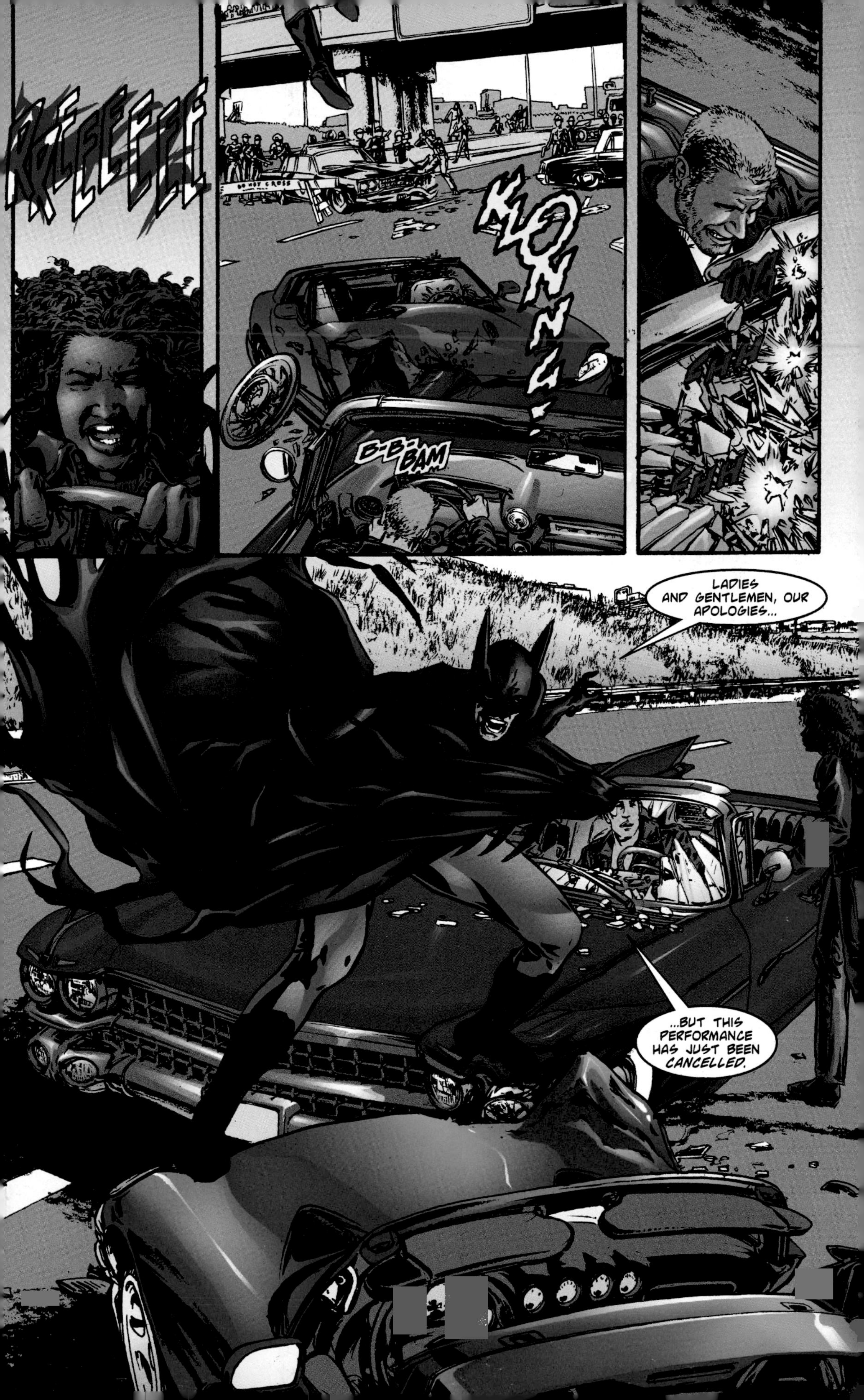
B-B-BAM
LADIES AND GENTLEMEN, OUR APOLOGIES...
...BUT THIS PERFORMANCE HAS JUST BEEN CANCELLED.

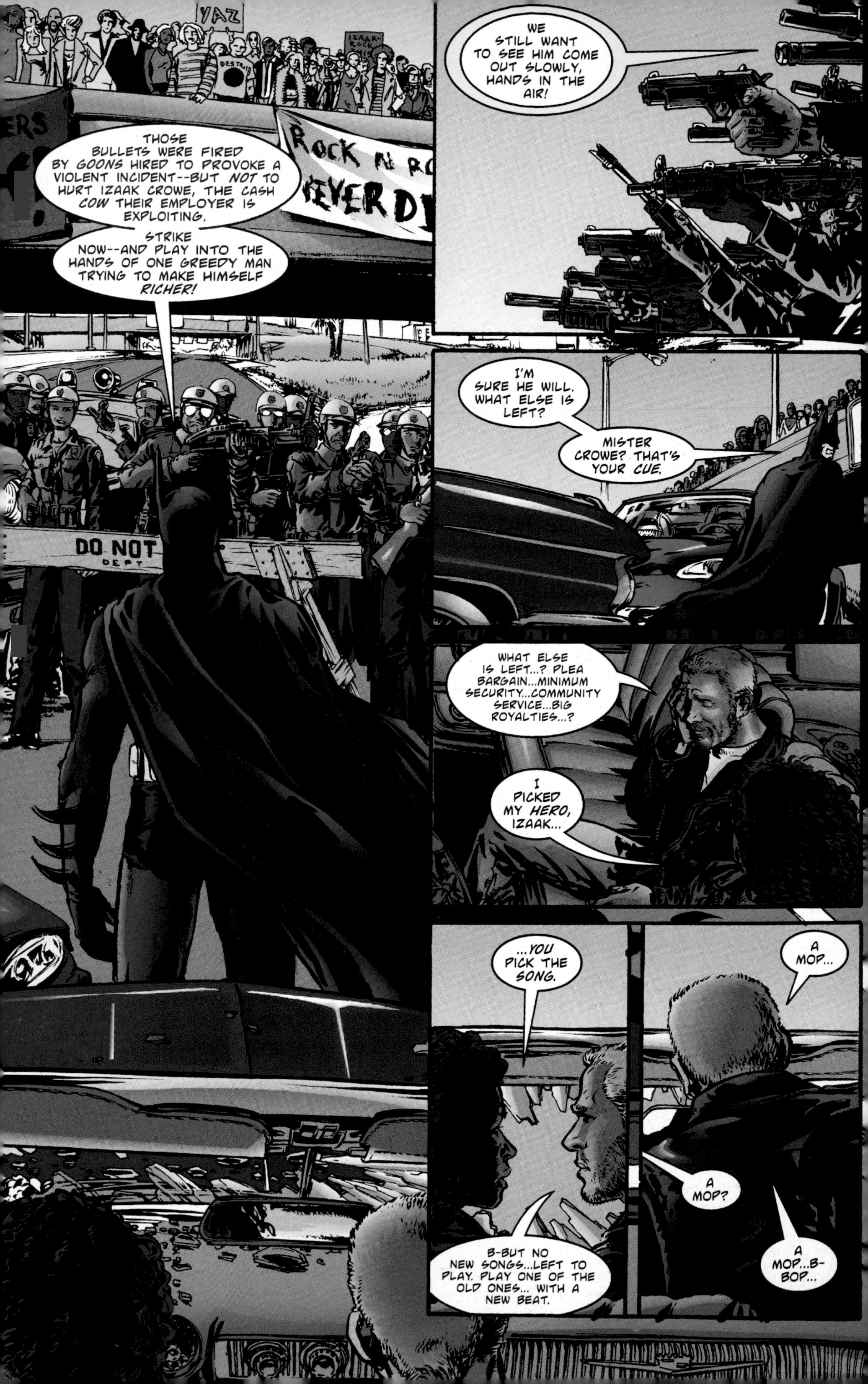
YAZ
IZAAK ROCKS
ROCK N ROLL NEVER DIES
THOSE BULLETS WERE FIRED BY GOONS HIRED TO PROVOKE A VIOLENT INCIDENT--BUT NOT TO HURT IZAAK CROWE, THE CASH COW THEIR EMPLOYER IS EXPLOITING.
STRIKE NOW--AND PLAY INTO THE HANDS OF ONE GREEDY MAN TRYING TO MAKE HIMSELF RICHER!
WE STILL WANT TO SEE HIM COME OUT SLOWLY, HANDS IN THE AIR!
DO NOT
I'M SURE HE WILL. WHAT ELSE IS LEFT?
MISTER CROWE? THAT'S YOUR CUE.
WHAT ELSE IS LEFT...? PLEA BARGAIN...MINIMUM SECURITY...COMMUNITY SERVICE...BIG ROYALTIES...?
I PICKED MY HERO, IZAAK...
...YOU PICK THE SONG.
B-BUT NO NEW SONGS...LEFT TO PLAY. PLAY ONE OF THE OLD ONES... WITH A NEW BEAT.
A MOP...
A MOP?
A MOP...B-BOP...

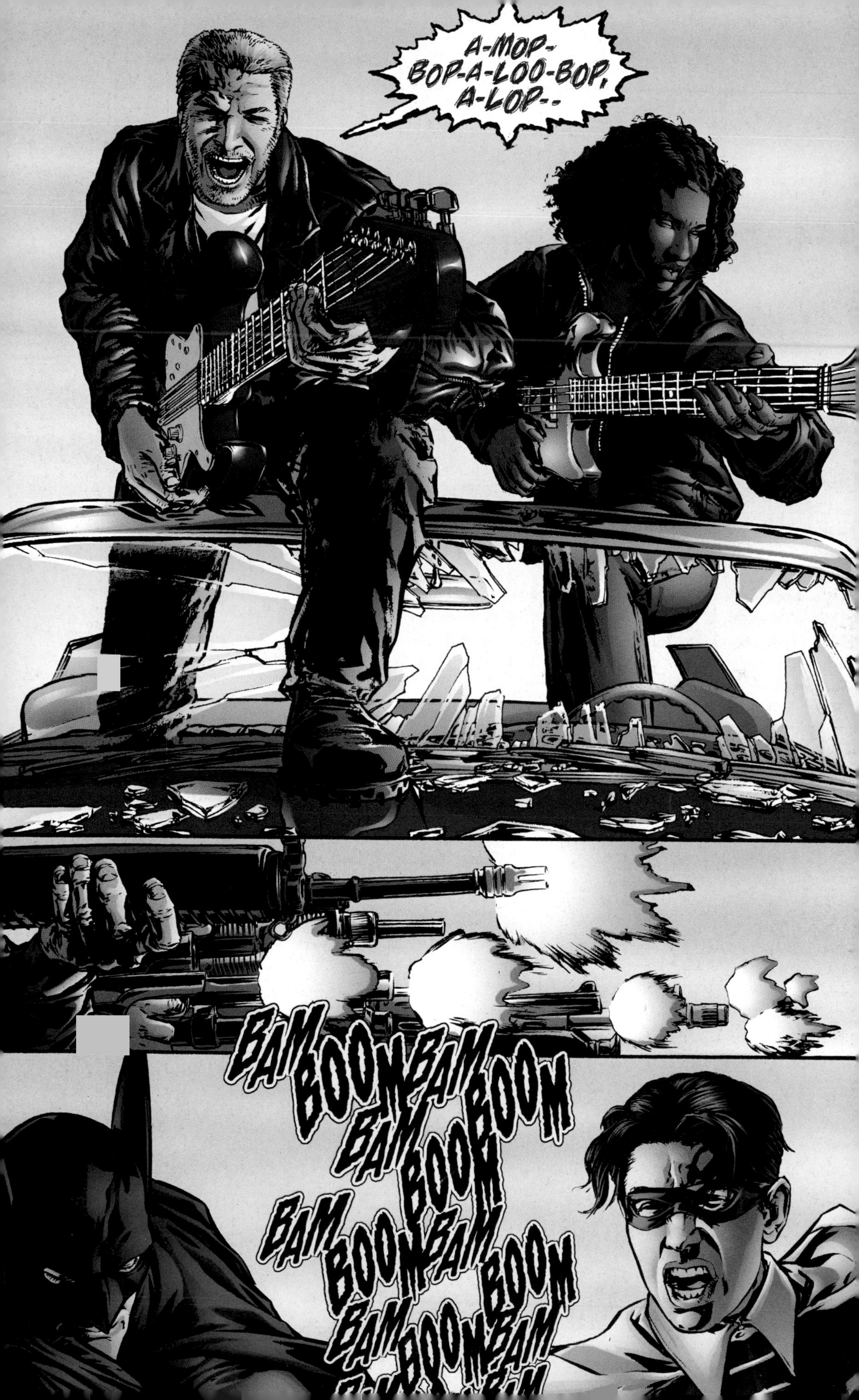
A-MOP-BOP-A-LOO-BOP, A-LOP--
BAM BOOM BAM BOOM
BAM BOOM
BAM BOOM BAM BOOM
BAM BOOM BAM

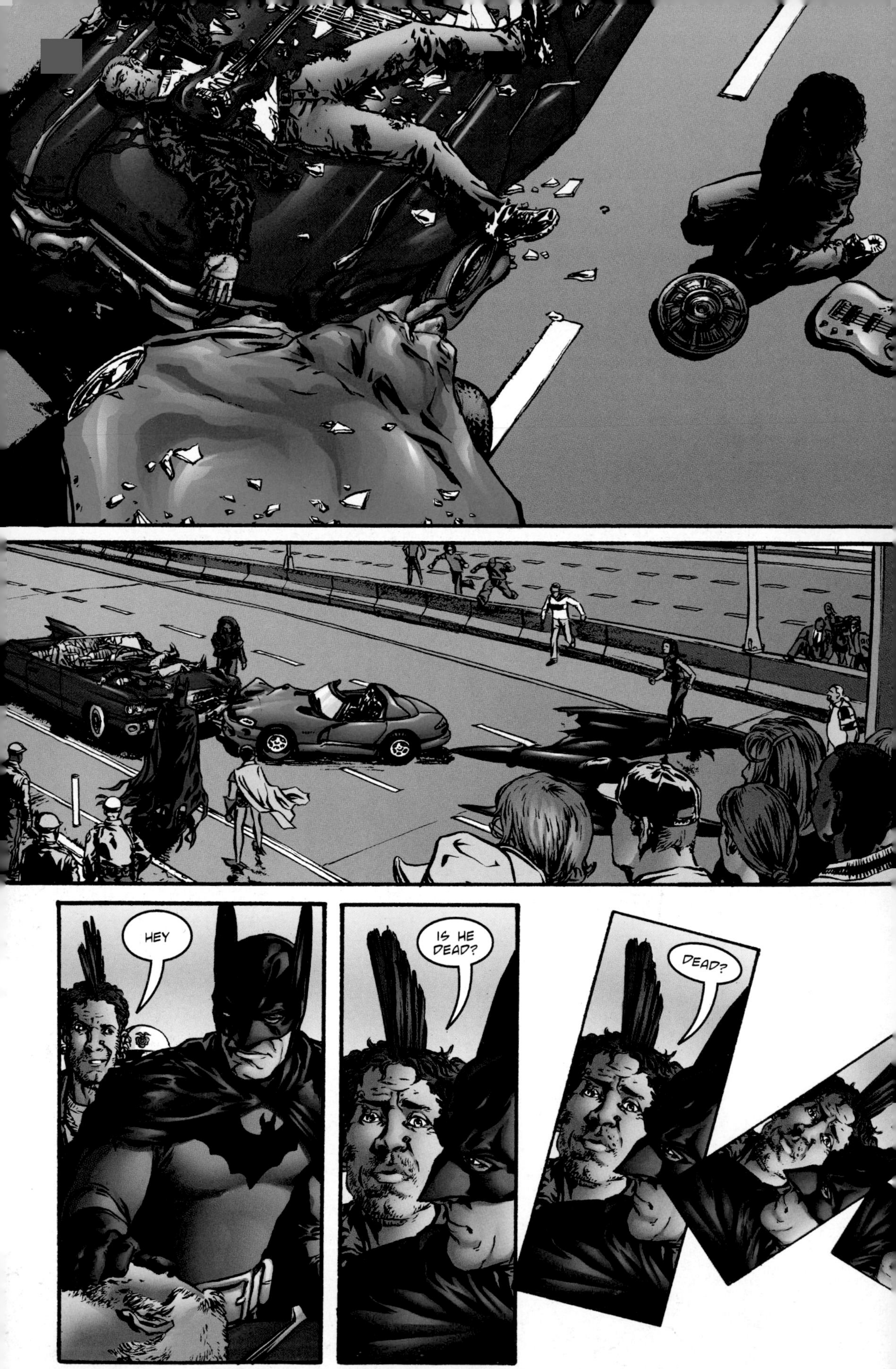
HEY
IS HE DEAD?
DEAD?

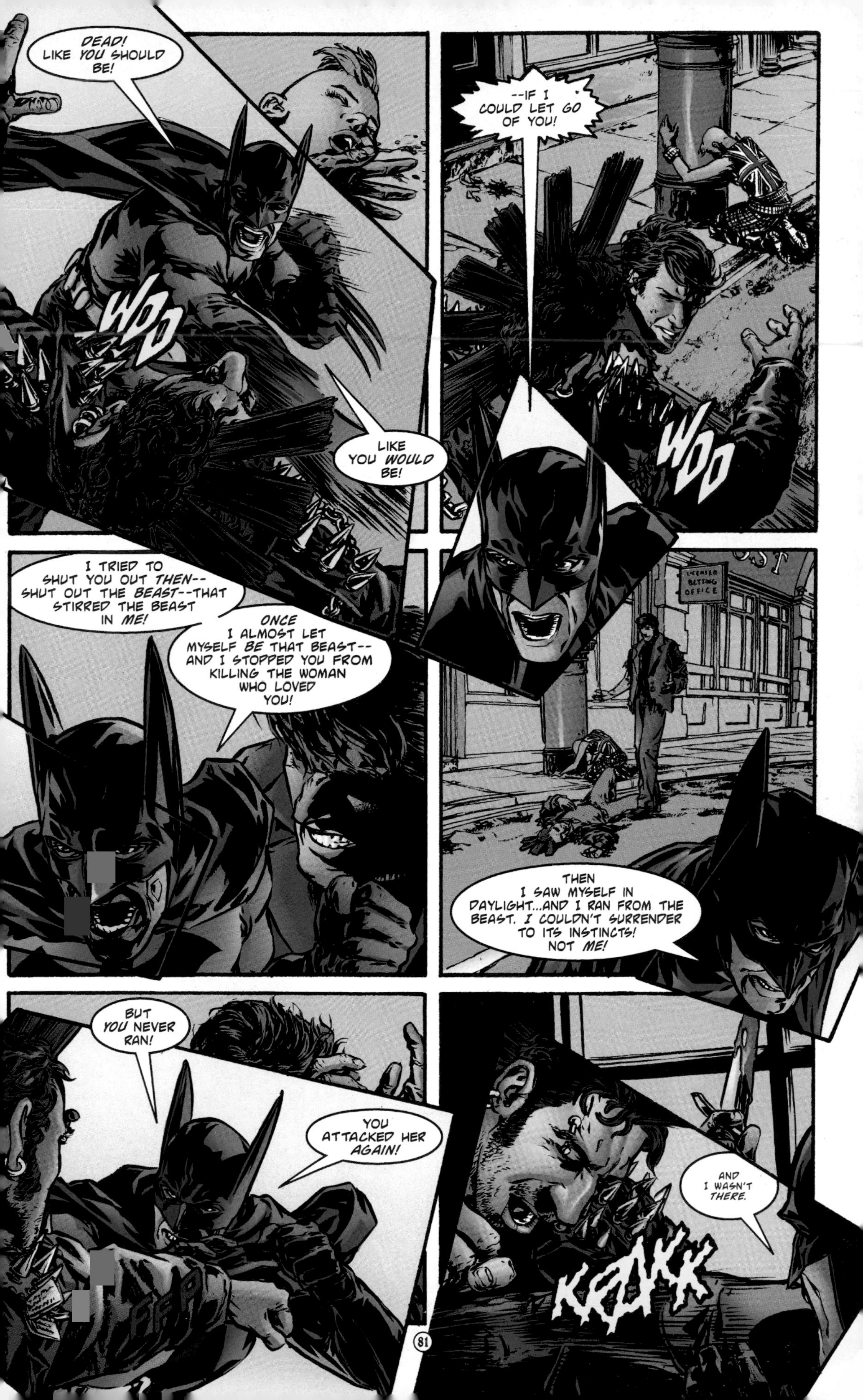
DEAD! LIKE YOU SHOULD BE!
LIKE YOU WOULD BE!
WOO
--IF I COULD LET GO OF YOU!
WOO
I TRIED TO SHUT YOU OUT THEN--SHUT OUT THE BEAST--THAT STIRRED THE BEAST IN ME!
ONCE I ALMOST LET MYSELF BE THAT BEAST--AND I STOPPED YOU FROM KILLING THE WOMAN WHO LOVED YOU!
LICENSED BETTING OFFICE
THEN I SAW MYSELF IN DAYLIGHT...AND I RAN FROM THE BEAST. I COULDN'T SURRENDER TO ITS INSTINCTS! NOT ME!
BUT YOU NEVER RAN!
YOU ATTACKED HER AGAIN!
AND I WASN'T THERE.
KRAKK

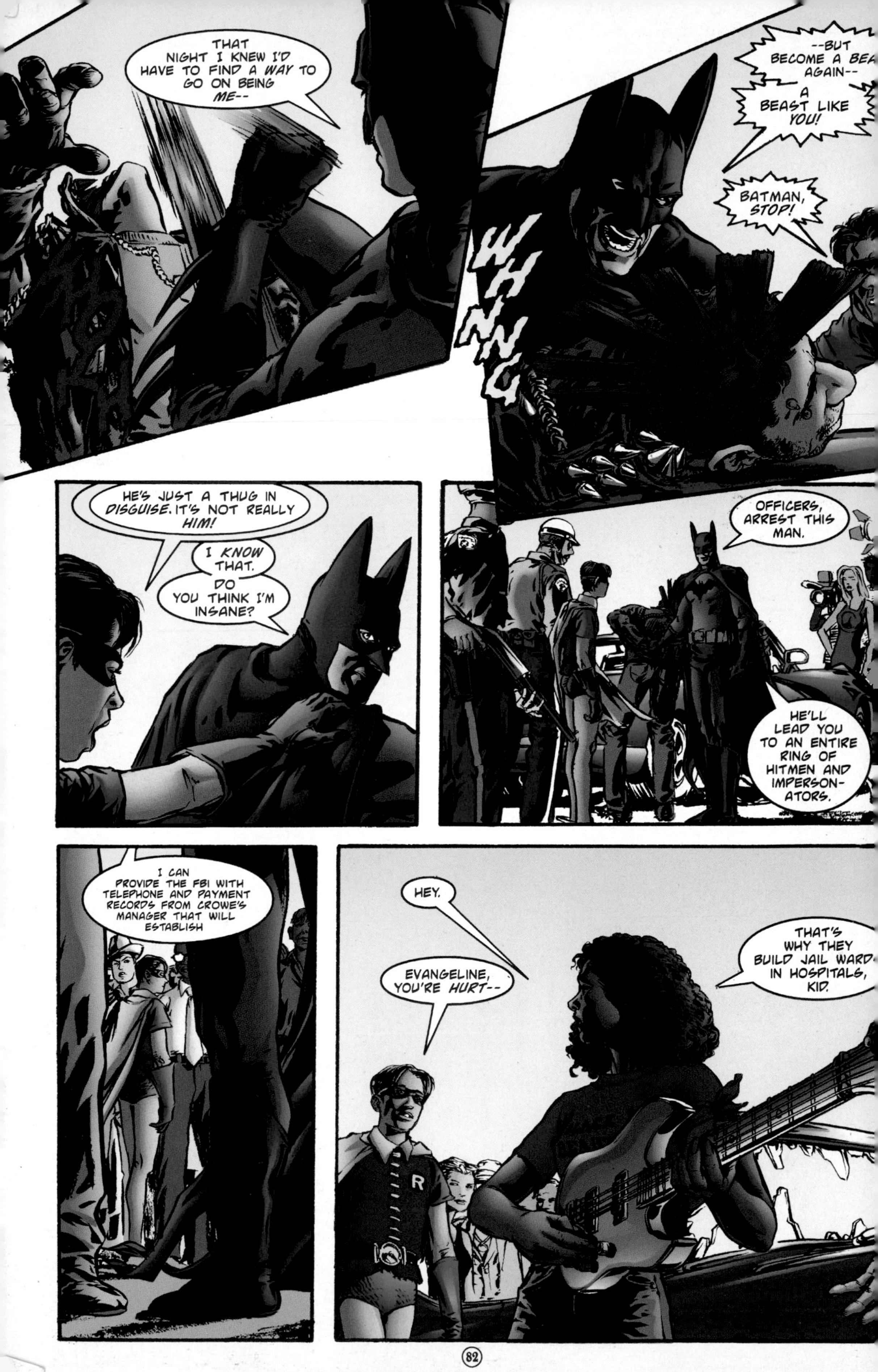
THAT NIGHT I KNEW I'D HAVE TO FIND A WAY TO GO ON BEING ME--
--BUT BECOME A BEA AGAIN--
A BEAST LIKE YOU!
BATMAN, STOP!
WHNG
HE'S JUST A THUG IN DISGUISE. IT'S NOT REALLY HIM!
I KNOW THAT.
DO YOU THINK I'M INSANE?
OFFICERS, ARREST THIS MAN.
HE'LL LEAD YOU TO AN ENTIRE RING OF HITMEN AND IMPERSON-ATORS.
I CAN PROVIDE THE FBI WITH TELEPHONE AND PAYMENT RECORDS FROM CROWE'S MANAGER THAT WILL ESTABLISH
HEY.
EVANGELINE, YOU'RE HURT--
THAT'S WHY THEY BUILD JAIL WARD IN HOSPITALS, KID.

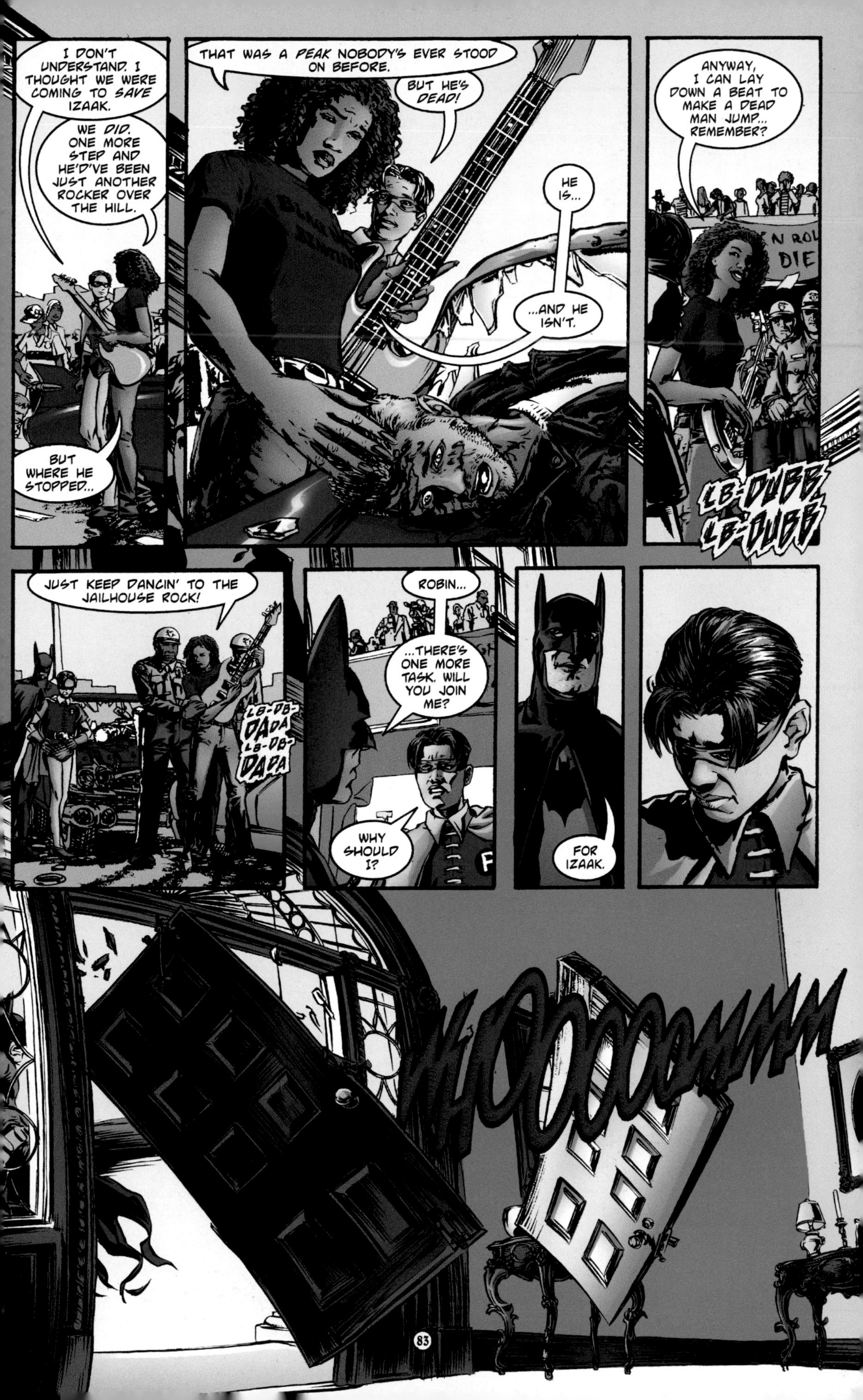
I DON'T UNDERSTAND. I THOUGHT WE WERE COMING TO SAVE IZAAK.
WE DID. ONE MORE STEP AND HE'D'VE BEEN JUST ANOTHER ROCKER OVER THE HILL.
BUT WHERE HE STOPPED...
THAT WAS A PEAK NOBODY'S EVER STOOD ON BEFORE.
BUT HE'S DEAD!
HE IS...
...AND HE ISN'T.
ANYWAY, I CAN LAY DOWN A BEAT TO MAKE A DEAD MAN JUMP... REMEMBER?
DIE
LB-DUBB LB-DUBB
JUST KEEP DANCIN' TO THE JAILHOUSE ROCK!
LB-DB-DADA LB-DB-DADA
ROBIN...
...THERE'S ONE MORE TASK. WILL YOU JOIN ME?
WHY SHOULD I?
FOR IZAAK.
WHOOOOMMM

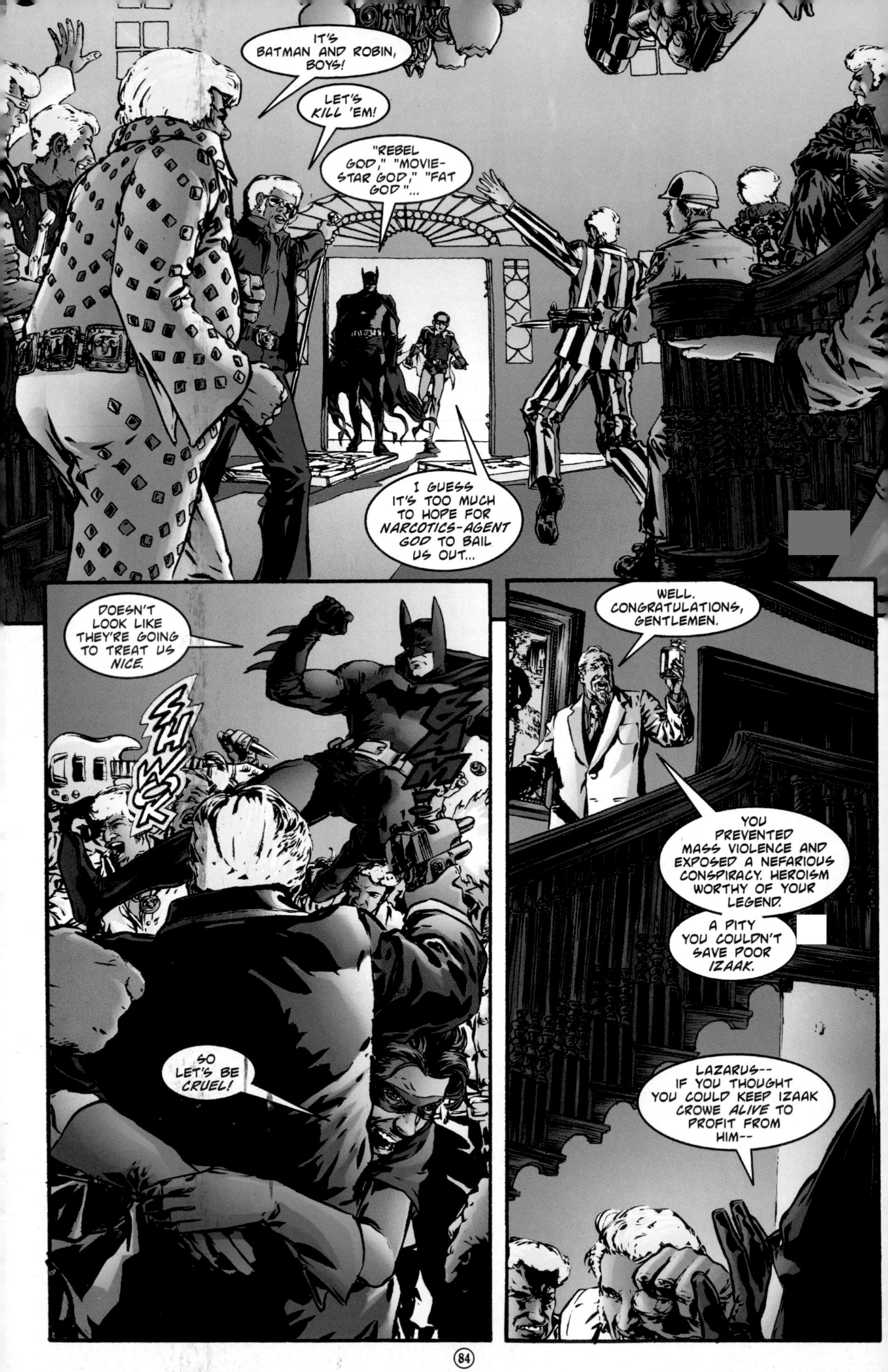
IT'S BATMAN AND ROBIN, BOYS!
LET'S KILL 'EM!
"REBEL GOD," "MOVIE-STAR GOD," "FAT GOD"...
I GUESS IT'S TOO MUCH TO HOPE FOR NARCOTICS-AGENT GOD TO BAIL US OUT...
DOESN'T LOOK LIKE THEY'RE GOING TO TREAT US NICE.
SHWOCK
BAM
SO LET'S BE CRUEL!
WELL. CONGRATULATIONS, GENTLEMEN.
YOU PREVENTED MASS VIOLENCE AND EXPOSED A NEFARIOUS CONSPIRACY. HEROISM WORTHY OF YOUR LEGEND.
A PITY YOU COULDN'T SAVE POOR IZAAK.
LAZARUS-- IF YOU THOUGHT YOU COULD KEEP IZAAK CROWE ALIVE TO PROFIT FROM HIM--

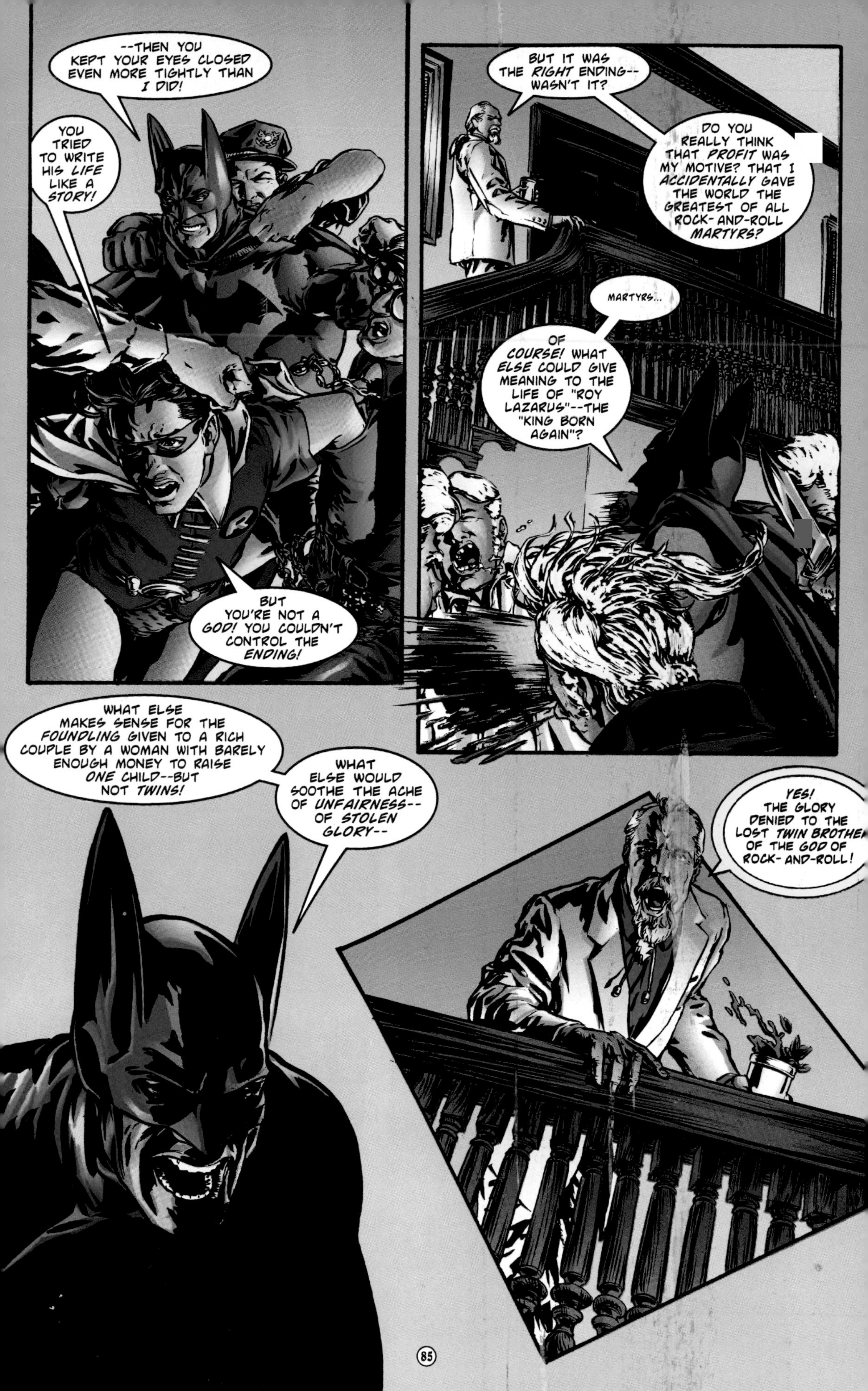
--THEN YOU KEPT YOUR EYES CLOSED EVEN MORE TIGHTLY THAN I DID!
YOU TRIED TO WRITE HIS LIFE LIKE A STORY!
BUT YOU'RE NOT A GOD! YOU COULDN'T CONTROL THE ENDING!
BUT IT WAS THE RIGHT ENDING--WASN'T IT?
DO YOU REALLY THINK THAT PROFIT WAS MY MOTIVE? THAT I ACCIDENTALLY GAVE THE WORLD THE GREATEST OF ALL ROCK-AND-ROLL MARTYRS?
MARTYRS...
OF COURSE! WHAT ELSE COULD GIVE MEANING TO THE LIFE OF "ROY LAZARUS"--THE "KING BORN AGAIN"?
WHAT ELSE MAKES SENSE FOR THE FOUNDLING GIVEN TO A RICH COUPLE BY A WOMAN WITH BARELY ENOUGH MONEY TO RAISE ONE CHILD--BUT NOT TWINS!
WHAT ELSE WOULD SOOTHE THE ACHE OF UNFAIRNESS--OF STOLEN GLORY--
YES! THE GLORY DENIED TO THE LOST TWIN BROTHE OF THE GOD OF ROCK-AND-ROLL!

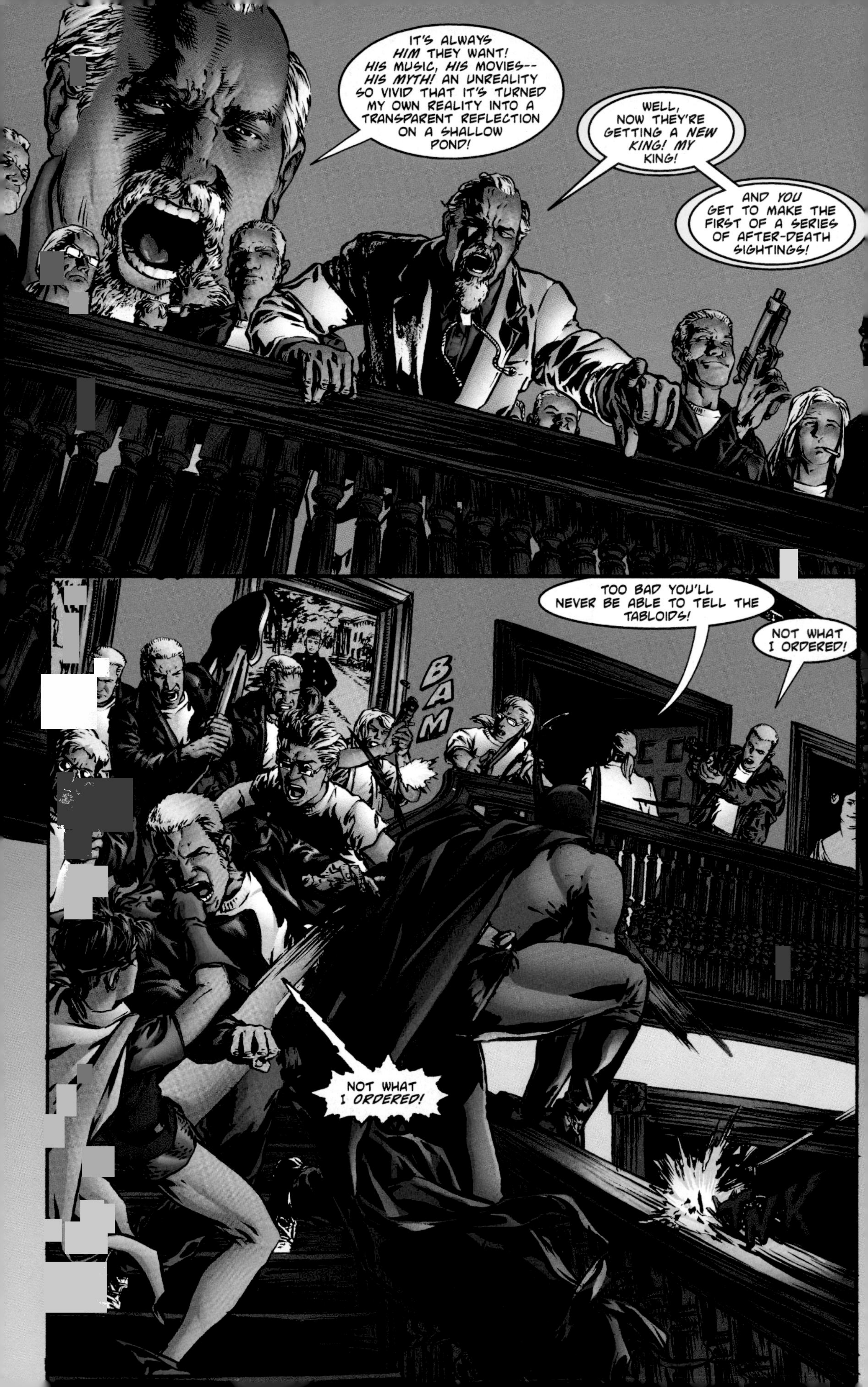
IT'S ALWAYS *HIM* THEY WANT! *HIS* MUSIC, *HIS* MOVIES-- *HIS MYTH!* AN UNREALITY SO VIVID THAT IT'S TURNED MY OWN REALITY INTO A TRANSPARENT REFLECTION ON A SHALLOW POND!
WELL, NOW THEY'RE GETTING A *NEW KING! MY* KING!
AND *YOU* GET TO MAKE THE FIRST OF A SERIES OF AFTER-DEATH SIGHTINGS!
BAM
TOO BAD YOU'LL NEVER BE ABLE TO TELL THE TABLOIDS!
NOT WHAT I ORDERED!
NOT WHAT I *ORDERED!*

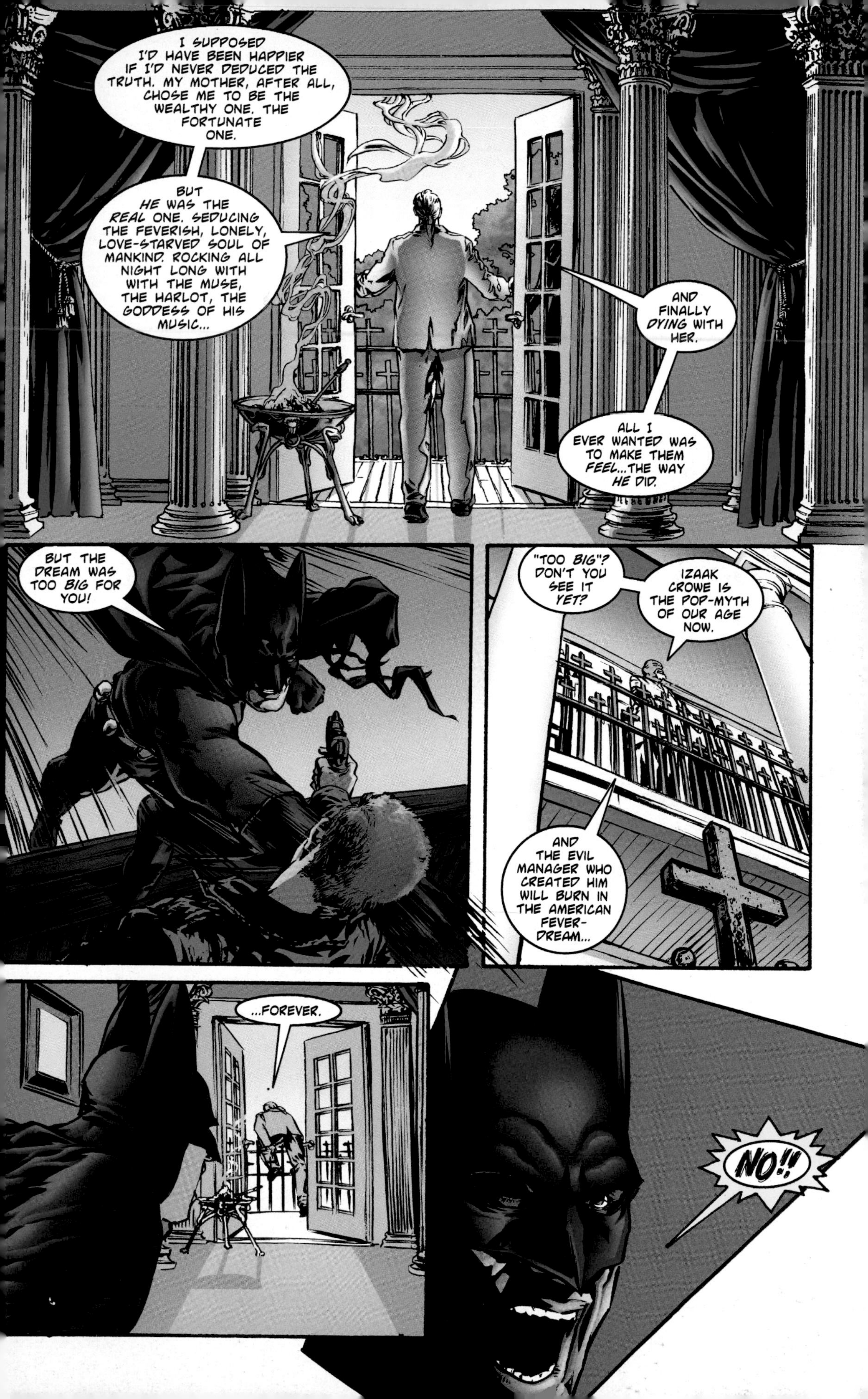
I SUPPOSED I'D HAVE BEEN HAPPIER IF I'D NEVER DEDUCED THE TRUTH. MY MOTHER, AFTER ALL, CHOSE ME TO BE THE WEALTHY ONE. THE FORTUNATE ONE.
BUT *HE* WAS THE *REAL* ONE. SEDUCING THE FEVERISH, LONELY, LOVE-STARVED SOUL OF MANKIND. ROCKING ALL NIGHT LONG WITH WITH THE MUSE, THE HARLOT, THE GODDESS OF HIS MUSIC...
AND FINALLY *DYING* WITH HER.
ALL I EVER WANTED WAS TO MAKE THEM *FEEL*...THE WAY *HE* DID.
BUT THE DREAM WAS TOO *BIG* FOR YOU!
"TOO *BIG*"? DON'T YOU SEE IT *YET*?
IZAAK CROWE IS THE POP-MYTH OF OUR AGE NOW.
AND THE EVIL MANAGER WHO CREATED HIM WILL BURN IN THE AMERICAN FEVER-DREAM...
...FOREVER.
NO!!

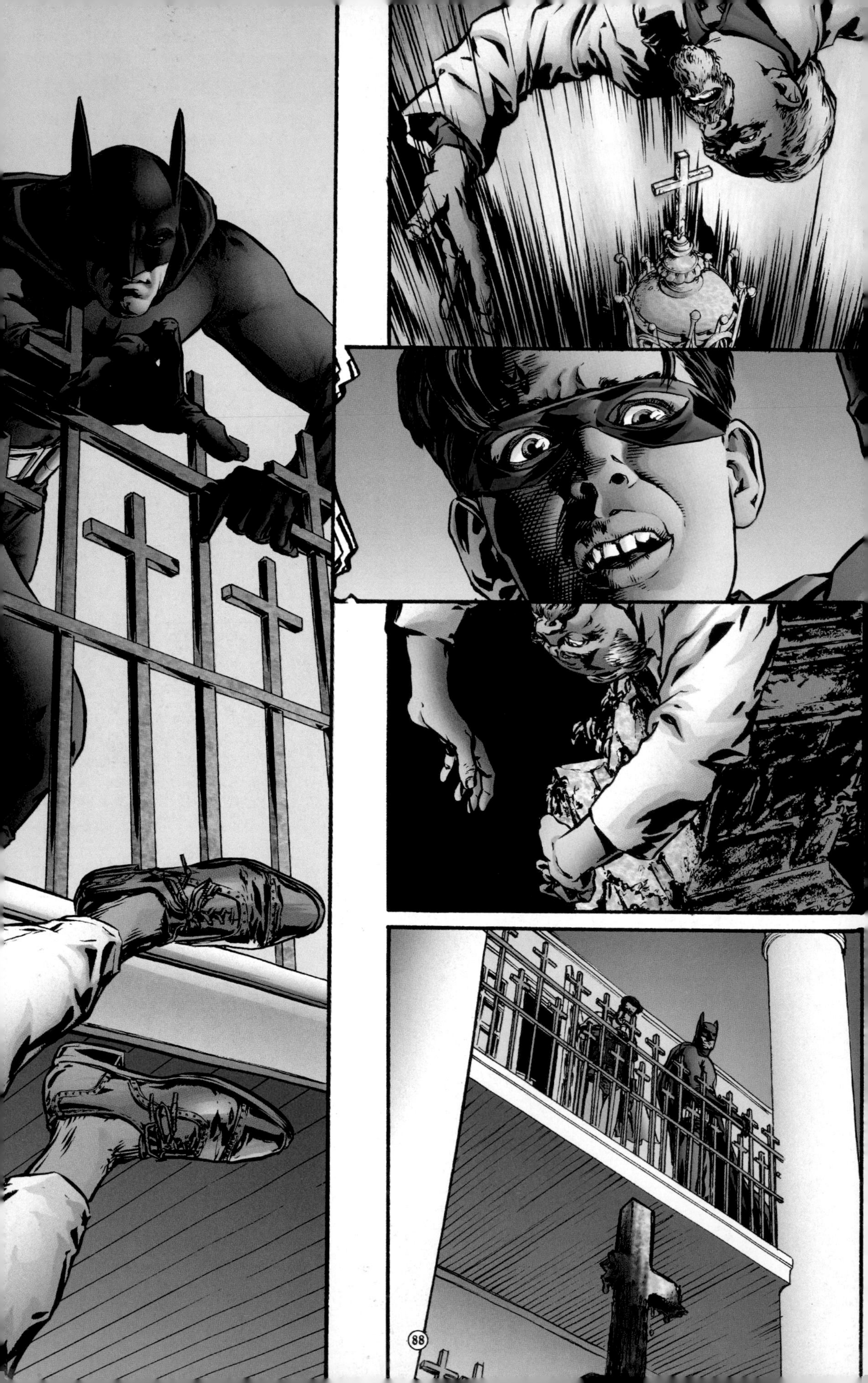

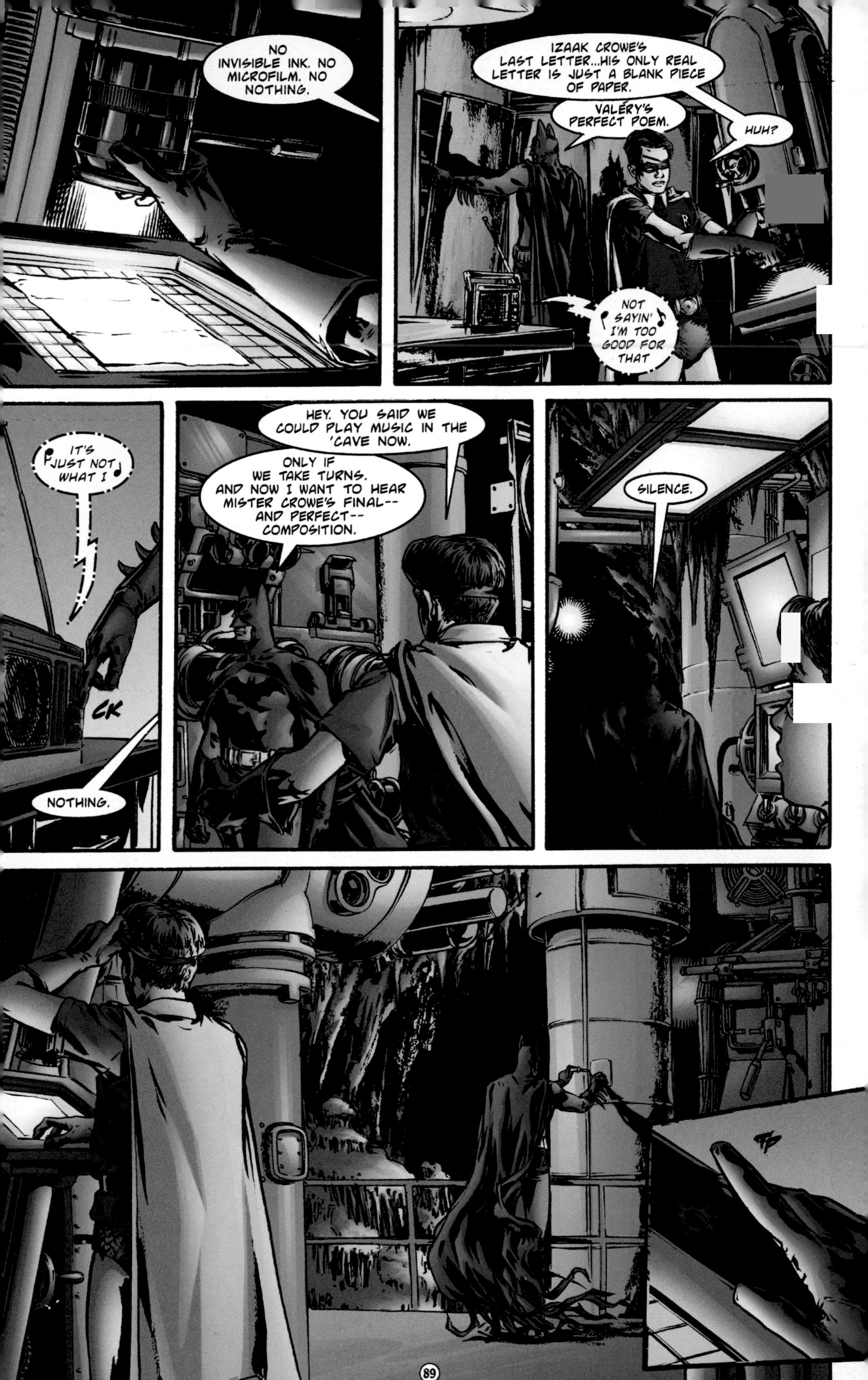

NO INVISIBLE INK. NO MICROFILM. NO NOTHING.
IZAAK CROWE'S LAST LETTER...HIS ONLY REAL LETTER IS JUST A BLANK PIECE OF PAPER.
VALÉRY'S PERFECT POEM.
HUH?
NOT SAYIN' I'M TOO GOOD FOR THAT
IT'S JUST NOT WHAT I
CK
NOTHING.
HEY, YOU SAID WE COULD PLAY MUSIC IN THE 'CAVE NOW.
ONLY IF WE TAKE TURNS. AND NOW I WANT TO HEAR MISTER CROWE'S FINAL-- AND PERFECT-- COMPOSITION.
SILENCE.

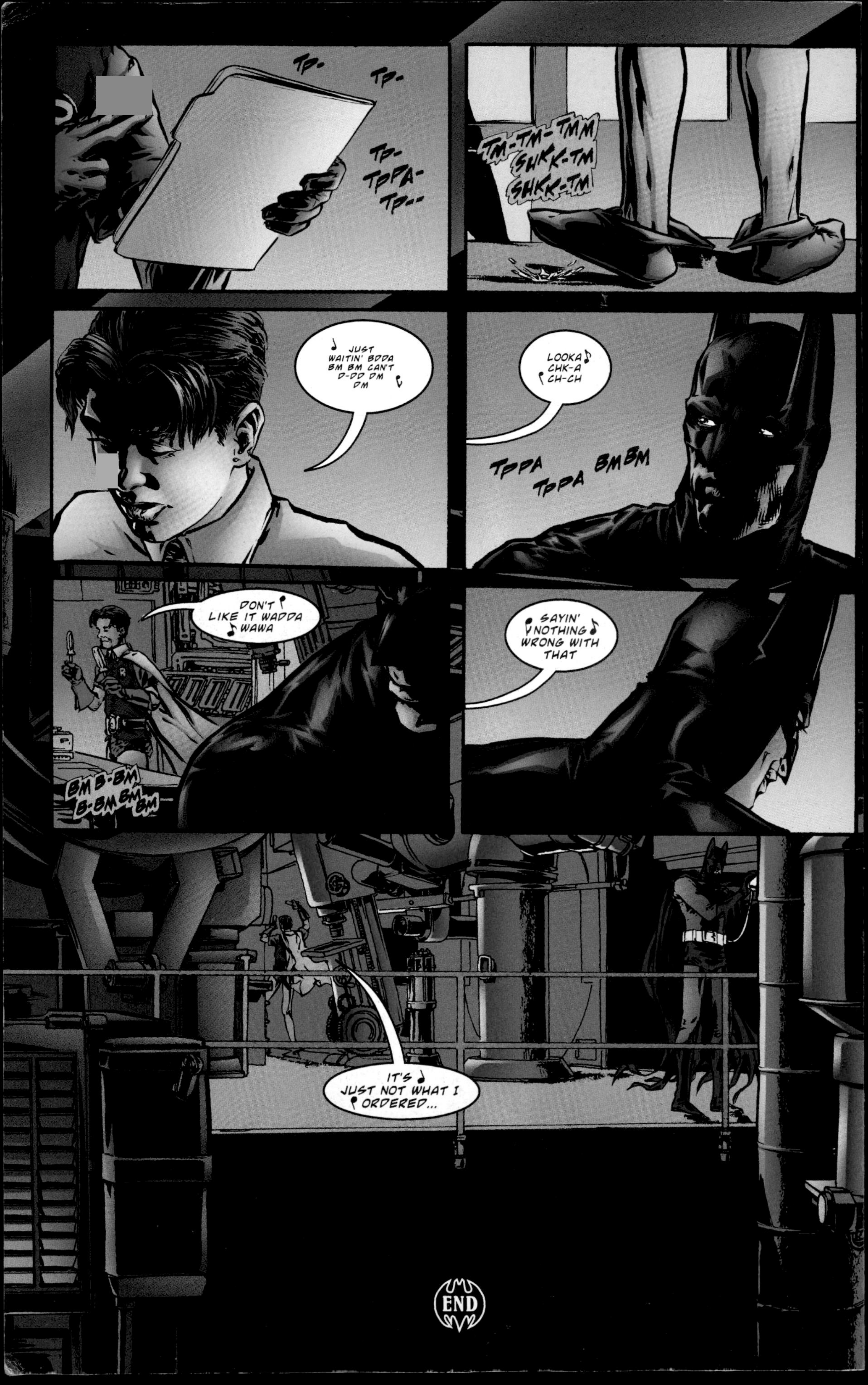
Tp- Tp- Tp- TpPA- Tp--
TM-TM-TMM SHKK-TM SHKK-TM
JUST WAITIN' BDDA BM BM CAN'T D-DD DM DM
LOOKA CHK-A CH-CH
TPPA TPPA BMBM
DON'T LIKE IT WADDA WAWA
BMB-BM B-BMBMBM
SAYIN' NOTHING WRONG WITH THAT
IT'S JUST NOT WHAT I ORDERED...
END

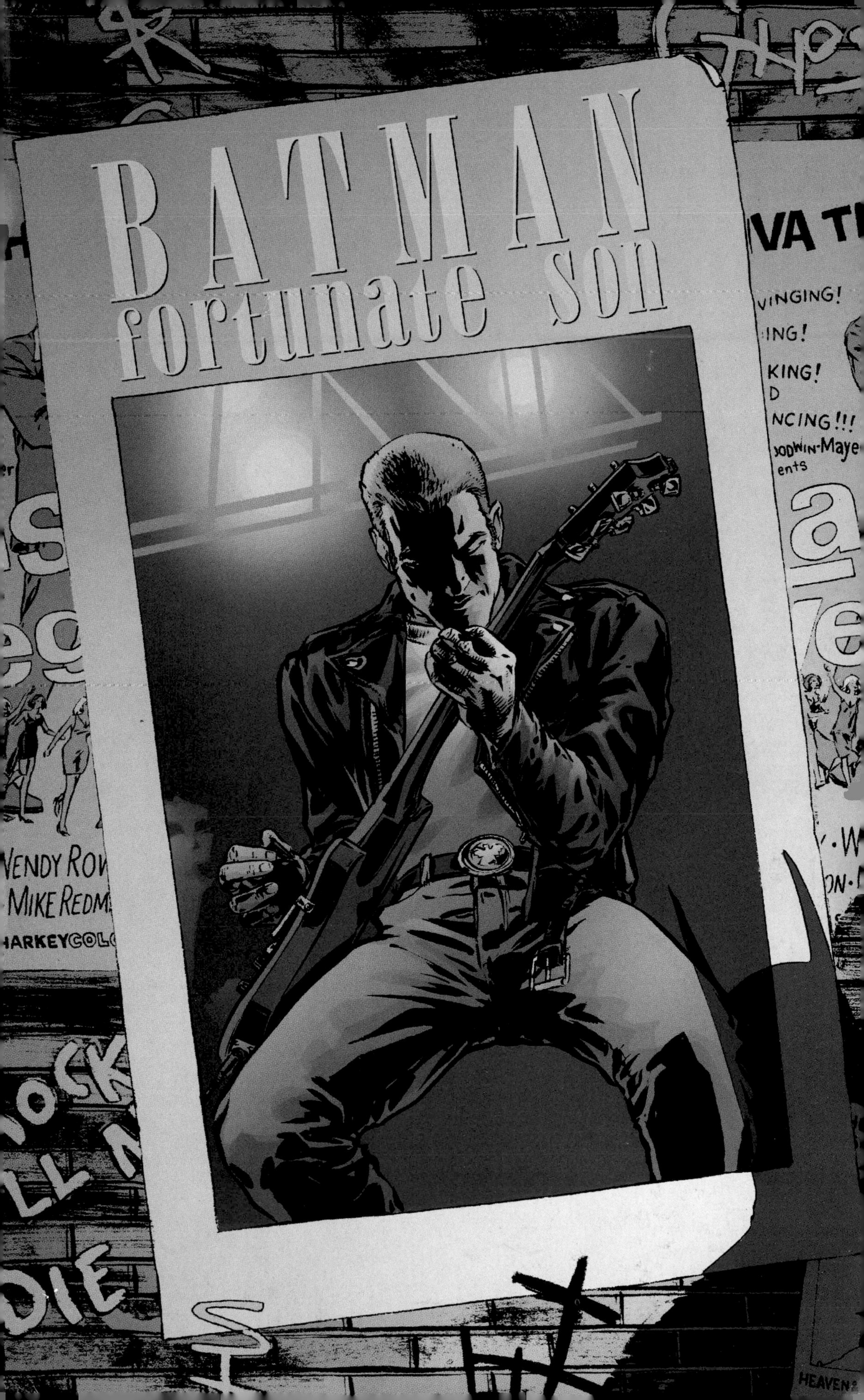
BATMAN
fortunate son
VINGING!
ING!
KING!
NCING!!!
VENDY ROW
MIKE REDM
HARKEY
HEAVEN

When Archie Goodwin first suggested a rock-and-roll Batman story, we responded with a ton of ideas but no central thread. Archie said, "Maybe there was a particular rock song or musician who meant something to Bruce Wayne when he was young. Maybe a song connected to a girl who meant something to him and he never saw again, or just a moment when Bruce could have changed things, could have been someone different." It was a simple idea, but it was exactly the piece we needed. With Batman's connection to the music established, his conflict with Robin was established, and then Robin's connection with Evangeline, Evangeline's true purpose, the emotional content of Izaak's mission and Roy's plans. A bunch of pop-culture conceits became a story.

Every time we worked with Archie it was the same: he wasted no time on superfluities and trivia, wasted no energy on power-tripping or second-guessing. He saw what was needed in the story and the art and gave us just enough to find it ourselves. Not surprisingly, neither of us has ever met anyone who understood how to tell a comics story as well as he did. For the last nine years of his life and career, Archie knew that he was dying of cancer. Happily for us, he chose to remain an editor until the end. As his strength failed and his hospital visits grew longer, he was forced to use his time more and more wisely. He was able to do so with complete grace, because his use of time was already wise. He allowed time for plot discussions, and for clear and specific notes; for talk about life and health and kids, and for jokes. Never for anything that he could trust to a writer or artist, or comfortably leave to fate.

Archie died after seeing only the first draft of this comic book's script. But we will always think of this as Archie's project as much as our own.

Gerard Jones

Gene Ha